Contents

The Online Copywriter's Handbook

Everything You Need to Know to Write
Electronic Copy That Sells

Robert W. Bly

McGraw·Hill

New York   Chicago   San Francisco   Lisbon   London   Madrid   Mexico City
Milan   New Delhi   San Juan   Seoul   Singapore   Sydney   Toronto

Library of Congress Cataloging-in-Publication Data

Bly, Robert W.
  The online copywriter's handbook / Robert W. Bly.
      p.   cm.
  Includes index.
  ISBN 0-658-02114-1 (hardcover)
      0-658-02099-4 (paperback)
      1. Internet marketing.   2. Advertising copy.   3. Electronic commerce.
  I. Title.

  HF5415.1265 B59   2002
  659.1'0285'4678—dc21   2001044467

14   DOH/DOH   13

ISBN 0-658-02114-1 (hardcover)
    0-658-02099-4 (paperback)

Interior design by Scott Rattray

McGraw-Hill books are available at special quantity discounts to use as premiums and sales promotions, or for use in corporate training programs. For more information, please write to the Director of Special Sales, Professional Publishing, McGraw-Hill, Two Penn Plaza, New York, NY 10121-2298. Or contact your local bookstore.

This book is printed on acid-free paper.

To Ben and Kay Buffett—in memory

Acknowledgments

THANKS ONCE AGAIN to my agent, Bonita Nelson, and my editors, Danielle Egan-Miller and Nancy Hall, for making this book possible.

Thanks also to the marketers who allowed me to reprint their campaigns, documents, and ideas throughout this manuscript.

Special thanks to Roger C. Parker for allowing me to reprint some of his work in Chapter 4.

Introduction

"Revolutions are both exciting and terrifying. The thrill of the new competes with the angst of the unknown."

George M. Taber, *Business News*, September 5, 2000

UNLESS YOU LIVE in a cave or on a deserted island, you've heard a lot about the Internet and how it is revolutionizing the way computer users communicate—and how businesses market their products and services. This book is written to help you make your Internet communications—particularly those used for marketing or customer service—correct, clear, compelling, and effective.

More than one hundred million people worldwide use the Internet, and more than half of the people surfing the Web have annual incomes of $55,000 or more. Web surfing by business prospects is projected to double over the next eighteen months. In a recent online survey, more than 50 percent of direct marketers polled by Edith Roman Associates said they now use the Internet as a marketing tool.

CIO Web Business magazine reports that, while it took thirty-eight years for fifty million American users to get radio, it only took four years for fifty million American users to get on the Web. According to an article in *Business 2.0* (June 13, 2000, p. 350), today's average online American will spend 17,500 hours of his or her life on the Internet.

Peter Eder, president of IM&C, an Internet consulting firm, reports that one out of three corporations uses the Internet to generate new revenue streams, and six out of ten use the Internet to communicate with their customers (as cited in *Proof*, April 1997). Forrester Research estimates e-commerce (sales of products and services over the Internet) will exceed $187.9 billion annually by 2004.

The Online Copywriter's Handbook is designed to be a clear, practical, and authoritative guide to writing copy for this new medium. It will help the novice take the first steps for getting started with Internet marketing, including e-mail marketing, e-zines, ads, websites, and e-commerce. Those already doing marketing on the Internet will be able to take their Web promotions to the next level of sophistication, effectiveness, and results.

Most seminars, books, and articles on Web marketing focus—mistakenly so, in my opinion—on technology or graphics. But on the Internet, as in print, it is the words—on the screen or on the page—that communicate your offer and persuade (or fail to persuade) people to buy.

While the principles of persuasion are well-established and do not change when you move from print to the Web, the Internet is a uniquely interactive and visual environment that has created new challenges for copywriters and other marketers. By reading this book, you will learn how to write effectively for this new medium using the time-tested principles of persuasion.

Part I deals with the fundamentals of writing effective copy for the Web. It covers how to write persuasively, the key differences between writing for the Internet versus writing for print, and how to adapt existing print documents for the Web.

Part II covers specific Web copywriting tasks. These include websites, home pages, landing pages, Internet direct mail, e-zines, e-zine ads, banner ads, and Web-based documents. The Resource section lists resources for marketers who use the Web as a communications tool.

This Book Will Never Go out of Date!

This book is kept up to date through three websites.

The first, bly.com, periodically posts new samples of websites, e-mail marketing campaigns, Web ads, and articles on Internet marketing.

The second, espeakonline.com, is a community of interest for people who like to think about Internet communication and how the Internet is changing the way we write, speak, and publish.

The third, evendorsonline.com, updates the e-vendors directory presented in the Resource section, so you can more easily find vendors who have solutions to help you implement your e-business initiatives.

I do have a favor to ask. If you have a resource, tip, strategy, or successful online communication, why not send it to me so I can share it with readers of the next edition? You will receive full credit, of course. Contact:

Bob Bly
22 E. Quackenbush Avenue
Dumont, NJ 07628
Phone: 201-385-1220
Fax: 201-385-1138
E-mail: rwbly@bly.com

PART I

FUNDAMENTALS OF WRITING COPY FOR THE WEB

IT'S IRONIC. The Internet is considered to be the medium of the programmer and designer, not the copywriter. Yet words carry content, convey marketing messages, draw individuals to Web pages, and persuade people to buy your product or service.

Chapter 1, Writing for the Internet, explores the Internet as a medium, focusing on online versus offline writing, and whether the Internet and print are similar or different. Chapter 2, Fundamentals of Persuasive Online Copy, shows how to apply proven principles of in-print persuasion to the Internet. Chapter 3, Adapting Existing Print Copy to the Web, outlines the steps required to take existing print documents and "Webize" them for posting on your site. Chapter 4, Illustrating Your Web Copy, covers both static and dynamic visuals for illustrating your online documents.

Writing for the Internet

IN THE WORLD of offline direct marketing—the world I come from—copywriters are high on the totem poll. The old saying among direct marketers is "copy is king." Words make the sale and get the order. Layout and graphics serve primarily to make the copy more readable and are not the key drivers. But in the online world, the attitude toward copy is completely different. Copy and copywriters rank—mistakenly so, in my opinion—low on the totem poll.

The reason? The Internet is technology driven, not content driven, although content is an essential element. The dot-com billionaires are never writers who created great copy for a website. They are either technical experts or clever entrepreneurs. Their innovation can be for a consumer e-commerce site (most of these eventually flounder; more than two hundred dot-coms failed in 2000) or a useful application to enable e-business (and these are the ones more likely to endure).

On the Internet, programmers, designers, and entrepreneurs rule. Venture capitalists and investors throw money behind new technology or new business models. *Time* magazine picks Jeff Bezos, founder of Amazon.com, as its Man of the Year, even though his company loses a small fortune every year.

In the online world, technical proficiency and entrepreneurship are valued, but words are not. The view is that anyone can write words. Writers, along with html coders, are considered by many to be the wage slaves of the new economy—a dime a dozen, and they work cheap.

This attitude is neatly summed up in Partners & Simon's ad that ran in the March 26, 2001, issue of *Adweek* magazine. "When you hire an interactive-only shop [an advertising agency specializing in the Internet], you'll get html coding, Shockwave, Domino, and Frame programming." The ad goes on to say, "What you *won't* get is good copy."

In my opinion, the lowly status accorded to online copy is a mistake, and my colleague Nick Usborne does a good job of articulating why. "Go to your favorite website, strip away the glamour of the design and technology, and you're left with words. This is unfortunate, because words are your last, best way to differentiate yourself online."

Right now, we are in a phase where Internet marketers are using technology to differentiate themselves and reach customers more effectively. But as the environment rapidly matures, the cost of e-business solutions falls. The technologies are rapidly adapted by everyone and become a commodity rather than a distinguishing factor.

Once a particular application is used universally, it is no longer a competitive advantage. We have seen this time and time again in the offline world. Whenever a new marketing technique is introduced, there is a window of opportunity where those who use it stand out from the crowd and grab market share. (Video brochures are a good example.) Then everyone jumps on the bandwagon, the method becomes commonplace or even overused, its effectiveness drops off, and it loses its power to grab customers away from your competitors.

In the offline world, most elements of marketing eventually achieve parity from marketer to marketer. The only element that continually provides opportunity to outsell the competition is copy: words.

The same is true online. Once the bells and whistles—like personalization, rich media, and Flash presentations—become commonplace, they no longer differentiate you and your message. Only one thing can consistently do that: powerful, attention-getting, and compelling online copy. Words that grab you by the lapel and don't let go. Words that speak to the prospect as a human being; tap into core feelings, beliefs, and desires; and position your product as the answer to her prayers.

Nick's recommendation—that you pay more attention to your Web copy and treat it as an essential element of your Web marketing— is slowly being taken seriously by Web marketers worldwide. This book is written to help you maximize the effectiveness of your Web marketing efforts through more effective Internet copywriting.

On- or Offline, People Are People

While the Internet is certainly a unique medium with some highly specialized features, the important thing to remember is that it does not alter human nature. Certainly the Internet has changed (read: upgraded) customer expectations in terms of information accessibility, responsiveness, convenience, and service levels. But it has not altered the basic motivations that people respond to when being sold or in any other human situation.

People are not fundamentally different beings when they go online; people remain people. They have the same fears, needs, and desires online as they have offline.

Don't think that the online world has a language all its own. It doesn't. Computer programmers may talk in html or Java Beans. But your prospects speak and read English (or their native language if they live outside of the United States), whether they're on- or offline.

My finding is that the basic rules of clear, persuasive communication do not change when we move from the print to the online worlds. As Peter Senge and Goran Carstedt observe in their article in *MIT Sloan Management Review* (Winter 2001, p. 24), "Much of what is said about the New Economy is not all that new."

Specifically, here are ten ways Internet copywriting and print copywriting are alike:

1. **People want to know, "What's in it for me?"** The bells and whistles of your website are secondary. Your company's background,

corporate image, branding, and other messaging—the stuff you think is so vital—are important mostly to you and your senior management, not to your visitors.

The prospect visiting your site wants to know, "What's in it for me if I spend time here?" If there is no benefit to be gained from perusing the site or ordering the product or service advertised, he'll leave.

2. **Write for the "important reader."** In Web marketing, concentrate all your efforts on the people you really want to talk to. For most of us, they're our prospects—the people who have the money, need, desire, and authority to buy our products and services. Yet most websites seem designed for the casual Web surfer, going to almost desperate measures to attract and retain the maximum number of visitors rather than qualified customers.

But Web hits and click-throughs are meaningless if you are not using the Web to bring prime prospects further along in the sales cycle. Websites should be focused squarely on the prospect—her needs, fears, problems, concerns, and desires. For a marketer, building a website whose primary function is to provide online amusement and entertainment for the masses is usually a massive waste of time and money.

3. **Break out of the clutter.** Some marketers tell me, "Search engines and links drive people to my website, so there's no need for me to make the site itself attention-grabbing." They are wrong.

According to an article in *CIO Web Business* (January 15, 2001, p. 32), there are 550 billion documents posted on the Web, and more than half a trillion e-mails sent annually. So there is enormous competition for your website or e-mail to get and hold the reader's attention, just like in the offline world, where the prospect is bombarded by direct-mail packages, newspaper ads, billboards, and radio and TV commercials. Online marketers who do not strive to engage and keep the customer's attention just as hard as their offline counterparts do, are sure to lose visitors and sales.

4. **Be relevant.** Everyone is suffering from information overload, and this is especially true on the Internet where information seems to be plentiful, free, and yours for the asking. According to a study

from the University of California at Berkeley, each year the human race produces about 1.5 exabytes of unique information in print, film, optical, and magnetic content worldwide. (An exabyte is a billion gigabytes.)

A common mistake in Internet copywriting is to load websites with tons of documents and links on interesting but largely irrelevant topics. The website creator thinks he is adding value by increasing the information content of his site, but in reality he is *reducing* value—by forcing prospects to search through a mountain of extraneous verbiage to find the real nuggets of gold.

"Customers visiting your site are on business," writes Kathy Henning in an article in *The Marketing Report* (January 15, 2001, p. 3). "They aren't looking for hype, they're looking for answers. The best info speaks directly to their needs."

Focus your Internet documents with laserlike intensity on your topic, on the subject your prospects want and need to know about. Make it easy to find—and jettison the rest. In a world of information overload, online writers who practice the art of selectivity provide the greatest level of service for their readers.

5. **Stress benefits.** While the Internet was created as a free medium for the dissemination and exchange of noncommercial information, it has evolved into a powerful tool for marketing products and services. The marketer's job is not to present a thesis or give away page after page of content for the joy of having people download from your site. The marketer's job is to sell.

Selling is accomplished by highlighting the benefits your products and services provide to your buyers. Leave websites that present every point of view equally to scholars and Web junkies. Your site should convince your prospect that your product is the one they should buy, now.

6. **Provide product information and application knowledge.** Present in a clear, concise, yet compelling fashion, the information your customer needs in order to make a decision about whether to buy. Give the product's key features and benefits, and respond to the buyer's questions and objections. Illustrate the breadth of applications in which your product can be used. Give prices including shipping

and handling, or if your prices are not standard and you need to prepare a quotation, provide an online request for quotation (RFQ) form that the prospect can fill out and submit to get a price from you.

7. **Prove your superiority.** Once the consumer is convinced that your product can handle his application, the question then becomes, "Why should I buy from you instead of your competitors?"

Your website and other Internet marketing efforts should help him decide in your favor by presenting the ways in which you, as a vendor, are the better choice. Chapter 2 explores in detail the kinds of proof you can present to win the prospect over.

One simple technique, used by many of the high-tech manufacturers including IBM and Lucent Technologies, is to post case histories on the website. These quick-reading stories show how a specific customer successfully solved a particular problem using an IBM or Lucent product. The message is straightforward: if our product worked for this customer, it can work for you too.

8. **Have clear offers.** When you visit Amazon.com, it's clear that the way to use the site is to fill up your shopping cart, provide your shipping and payment information, and order books or other items.

But on many other sites—especially those that are not business-to-consumer (B2C) e-commerce sites—the desired action or response is not so clear. Or if there is a clear response desired, such as filling out a registration page, there is no incentive for the online shopper to take action.

Print direct marketers have long known that having an "offer"—something you get in exchange for responding to a promotion—is vital to generating leads and sales. Internet marketers have rapidly discovered that the same need for strong offers exists in the online world.

For B2C marketers, one offer that seems to work well is "10/10"—either $10 or 10 percent off the list price when the consumer orders on the spot. Free gifts with an order also work, as does the accumulation of bonus points—the amount of which is based on the size of the order—good for a discount on future purchases or a free gift.

For business-to-business (B2B) marketers, downloads of software demos and white papers (usually in pdf) can work well. If you have an informative or useful e-zine (online newsletter), you can offer a free subscription in exchange for people giving you their e-mail address and other information about themselves.

9. **Be clear.** Clarity is important in the offline world and absolutely essential in the online world. In the offline world, if the prospect doesn't get what you are saying, she quickly loses interest. And it's frighteningly easy for her to stop reading your ad and turn the page, toss your sales letter in the garbage, or hang up on your telemarketing representative.

I think the online-customer's attention span is even shorter, and her patience even thinner. If your website becomes the least bit unclear or uninteresting, your visitor can jump to another site with just a click of a mouse—an action that burns, I believe, less than one-tenth of a calorie.

In an era where readers are suffering from information overload, their tolerance for lack of clarity or deliberate obfuscation falls to near-zero levels. Every word on your Internet documents must speak, in clear, easy-to-follow language, to the needs and interests of your target audience. The minute you veer off track or slip into jargon, the reader is gone.

10. **Make it easy to respond.** Always have a clear, easy, and direct link between an online offer and the response mechanism.

For instance, say you are sending out an e-mail offering a free interior design consultation for the first ten people who fill out and submit a form posted on your website. Your message should include a hyperlink to a URL. This URL should go directly to the form, not your home page. If you send people to your home page, hoping that they will work their way around your site to the form, you will find a dramatic decline in click-through rates. The easier and more direct the response, the greater the replies you will receive.

Notice that none of these tips is unique to the Internet. These are proven principles of persuasion, based on decades of tested offline direct-marketing experience. They are directly transferable to the Web and in fact work particularly well online. Using these simple principles in your Web marketing can give you a big advantage over your competitors. Why?

Offline direct marketing is filled with a lot of gray-haired Matures and Baby Boomers, like me, who have decades of experience and therefore draw on a large database of what works and what doesn't. I know what I'm doing, but the advantage this gives me is somewhat negated by the fact that my fellow offline direct marketers, for the most part, do too.

But the online world has a large population of Web marketers who, whizzes though they may be in Visual Basic or Front Page, have not been exposed to decades of direct-marketing test results. The Internet marketing programs they produce work on a technical level but often fall short in generating the desired sales results because they have not constructed effective offers, appeals, headlines, or copy. By applying the time-tested direct-response principles of print that are transferable to the Internet, you gain an edge, producing Web marketing that is more powerful, compelling, and effective.

But Print and the Internet Are Not the Same

Having said that people are people and they stay basically the same whether they are reading a newspaper or browsing a website, I would be an idiot to suggest that print and the Internet are identical, or that writing direct mail is exactly the same as writing e-mail.

We have briefly discussed the highlights of what works in the offline world and how these are directly transferable to the online world; here are some of the key differences between offline and online marketing.

Keep It Short

Copy length is an issue of great debate in the offline world, with some direct marketers claiming that long copy works best, while others insist that it should be short. Outside of direct marketing, in the world of general advertising, the consensus seems to be that consumers don't read, and the shorter the copy, the better.

While opinions vary, as a rule, we strive for shorter copy in online marketing rather than longer. If we can get our message across in fewer words, we do—cutting out unnecessary words without sacrificing clarity.

"In general, online text should be half as long as printed text, maybe even shorter," says Kathy Henning, giving what seems to me to be a sensible rule of thumb. Why this "keep-it-brief" imperative in the online world? Part of it is the Net environment itself. People today are busier than ever, and the Internet is the physical embodiment of what sociologist Barbara Ehrenreich calls "the cult of busyness." People treat their busyness as a status symbol; the personal digital assistant (PDA) and wireless phone—both of which offer Internet connectivity—are the visible representations of that status symbol. Therefore, when people are on the Internet they are in a busy, no-nonsense mode, and you have to get right to the point, or you risk losing them.

Follow the Rules of Netiquette

The Internet has its own culture. The original Internet culture was an environment of free information sharing and dissemination for educational and intellectual purposes. With the rise of e-business, the Internet is rapidly transforming to a culture of commerce. But the influence of the early Internet culture has created a certain standard or code of behavior for online communication, known as *netiquette* (Internet etiquette).

Those most concerned with netiquette are often hardcore Internet users and other technophiles who are frequently not your customers. Newer Internet users are often unaware and unconcerned with netiquette or its violations. Yet you, as an Internet marketer, should be aware of the rules of netiquette and strive not to violate them.

You never know when a breach of netiquette may enrage or incite someone, and the hardcore Internet users are sometimes extreme in their behavior. They may go to great lengths to discipline or even wreak havoc with a business that has violated the accepted rules of Internet behavior.

This kind of ire can stir up more trouble for you than you think. Some hardcore Internet users can find ways to harass you, whether it's bombarding your website with complaint messages, calling for an Internet user boycott of your site, or bad-mouthing you in discussion groups throughout the Internet. Some are technically proficient in coding and can even disrupt your site's operation. It's illegal and they can be prosecuted (if you can catch them), but who needs the headaches?

To avoid breaches of netiquette, just follow a few simple guidelines. First, don't spam people. (Spamming, the illegal sending of unsolicited promotional e-mails to people who do not want to get such messages, is covered in Chapter 8.) Do not advertise yourself or conduct unseemly and blatant self-promotion in forums, news groups, and other areas intended for noncommercial chat and exchange of ideas and information.

And stick by your word. If you promise to deliver in seven days and you are going to be late, send an e-mail explaining the delay, rather than have the customer complain that you are a crook and don't deliver merchandise. If you offer a money-back guarantee, give it directly, promptly, and without difficulty when someone asks for a refund.

Practice the Soft Sell

The Internet was originally conceived as a medium for information exchange, not commerce, and still has that flavor to it—even though e-commerce has become the next big thing on the Internet. (Forrester Research predicts annual online retail sales of $187.9 billion by 2004.)

You can therefore tap into the comfort zones of Internet buyers by couching many of your Internet promotions in the language of information dissemination, rather than sales. In other words, write your copy like you are sharing information, rather than selling.

Actually, giving product pitches in the guise of information is not unique to the online world. It is practiced on television with infomercials and on the radio with commercials written like parts of the program and read by the announcer who is also doing the program. Listen to Paul Harvey. It's difficult to tell where the show pauses and the paid pitch begins. And that's what makes the commercial so effective. You think it's news or objective information, rather than advertising. In direct mail, we have the "magalog," which is a direct-mail piece disguised to look like a magazine, newsletter, or special report rather than promotion.

The same practice works well in the online world. The line between content and promotion is already becoming increasingly thinner. And if you can make your promotion read like content, you reduce buyer resistance, increase their attention span, get them to read more, and persuade them to buy. We will explore this idea of writing promotions in the guise of information more fully in Chapters 3 and 7.

Practice Permission-Based Marketing

Bestselling author Seth Godin invented the term *permission marketing*, which means you don't send any marketing message to an online user without his or her permission. On the simplest level, you don't send marketing messages via the Internet to anyone who does not want to receive them.

On a broader scale, you continue to get and retain permission from prospects and customers to whom you target your Internet marketing campaigns. For instance, if they agree to receive an e-zine, every issue should remind them that they can ask to stop receiving it, and make it easy for them to do so online. You should also remind customers, when appropriate, that they gave you permission or requested online contact from you. For instance, an e-mail to visitors who registered on your site's guest page might begin, "You are receiving this e-mail because you registered on ILoveBuildingModels.com and indicated an interest in receiving information on model airplanes. If you do not want to receive further online notices of this type, hit REPLY and type 'Unsubscribe' in the subject line."

Use the Three Levels of Hyperlinks

In the 1970s, Ted Nelson wrote about hypertext, which was a method of communicating in nonlinear fashion, jumping from place to place in a document based on what subjects interested you.

A neat idea, hypertext never really caught on back then, because in print, it is cumbersome to execute. Occasionally, you read print documents based on the hypertext model, most notably novels for young readers that let you choose what happens next from among multiple plot pathways. These stories are usually clunky and rarely satisfying.

Now, Internet technology enables hypertext. Indeed, the Internet—with its ability to establish live hyperlinks that take you from place to place with a mouse click—is ideally suited to hypertext. To fully take advantage of this powerful feature of the Internet, you should use hyperlinks throughout your online marketing documents.

There are three ways to use hyperlinks.

1. **You can link within a document, allowing the reader to jump from section to section.** For instance, a long document can have a table of contents up front, where the section or chapter titles are live links to those segments of the document. You click on a subhead and are automatically taken to that section.

2. **You can link between documents.** If your Web's home page mentions a new product, the product name can be highlighted. Click on the name and you are immediately taken to a separate page or document dedicated to product description.

3. **You can go from one website to another.** You can have a separate page on your site with links to relevant sites, or you can embed these links on specific pages. For instance, if your new product is compatible with a new standard, you can include a link to the website of the professional organization that has written and maintains the standard.

Although it's tempting to pack your Web pages and other Internet documents with lots of links, don't overdo it. Too many links are distracting, and is the reader really going to check all of those cross-references? Links add a dimension that the printed page cannot match, but use them judiciously.

Modularize Your Copy

When we say copy on the Internet should be short, that's really not accurate. Websites for major manufacturers like IBM and Lucent Technologies often have a ton of information on any given product—quite often much more than appears in their printed brochures or catalogs. (IBM.com has 4.5 *million* pages.)

When people say Internet copy must be short, what they really mean is modular. Instead of cramming everything into one Web page or document, the content is broken into short sections and may appear in several pages or documents.

The assertion that online prospects, because they are on the Web, won't read a lot of copy about a product isn't true; what they don't want to read is long chunks of unbroken text on a single Web page or e-mail message. The solution is to make your copy modular, so the customer can browse and read it in short, bite-sized chunks.

For instance, in a brochure on a high-tech product or system, I might include benefits, features, theory of operations, applications, specifications, and selection guidelines in a single document. On a website, I would still have all this information, except each section would be on a single page: one Web page covering specs, another addressing key benefits, a third explaining the theory of operations, perhaps one page each describing the top five applications, and so on. Long copy, but in short chunks.

Increasingly, print documents are being written in this modular format. But the aversion to long single documents is perhaps greater on the Web than in the offline world.

Write to the Reading Habits of Internet Users

Knowing the aversion of online readers to big blocks of text, you should write so that what appears on the screen is pleasing to the eye and easy to read. "Online readers tend to scan, so help them by adding subheads, bulleted points, and clear navigational tools," says Henning. Use color, fonts, and pictures to add variety and eye-appeal to the online page.

Recognize That the Internet Is a Graphics-Oriented Medium

Printed-page readers are not, as a group, a visually oriented audience—we tend to gravitate toward words rather than pictures. But Internet users, like TV watchers, are "picture people."

"We live in the MTV society, where people's attention span is about as short as a newborn baby's," says copywriter Mike Pavlish. Think about how you can use graphics to communicate your message more effectively and dramatically. For instance, if you are selling stocks, show stock charts—both individual stocks and the markets— to illustrate recent performance. And let's face it: sex sells, especially on the Internet. If you are selling bras, show pictures of attractive models wearing them.

Take Advantage of the Medium's Interactivity

Unlike catalogs, which are static, Web marketing is dynamic. Logos can spin, product names can light up, sneakers can sprout wings and fly through space, fat people can morph on the website of a fitness consultant and become thin, and visitors to an astrology site can enter the date and time of their birth and get a personalized online horoscope.

The two basic modes of interactivity are audiovisual presentations and interactive online tools. In Chapter 4, we will learn how to write Flash presentations, which are online "movies"—with pictures and sound—that can be viewed with a Shockwave player. Shockwave is one of the most popular formats for writing audiovisual presentations for the Web.

You can also engage the viewer with interactive tools. For instance, a health site I visited asked me to enter my height, then automatically computed my ideal weight. Today, websites offer visitors a host of interactive tools ranging from free e-mail accounts to programs that automatically calculate the terms and monthly payments for equipment leases.

Take Advantage of the Medium's Audiovisual Components

Both print and the Web have the dimensions of text and graphics. The Web has a third dimension, often neglected: sound. If you sell fine art prints online, browsers can hear strains of Mozart as they stroll through your online gallery. A corporation can let its customers listen to a recording of a recent Web seminar or speech by the CEO.

Another element the Web has that print doesn't is animation. On Bonzi.com, an Internet portal, you download a purple monkey—BonziBUDDY—who periodically talks to you, giving you tips, special information, and special offers (such as free downloads), throughout the day. BonziBUDDY rolls his eyes, smiles, swings on a vine, and even juggles coconuts to get your attention. By the way, Bonzi.com is a good example of permission-based marketing. In exchange for downloading BonziBUDDY for free, you are asked to provide some personal information and indicate what types of products you are willing to receive online offers for.

Be dynamic—but don't overdo it. As a rule of thumb for copywriting, any attention-getting technique must be used judiciously or it loses its effectiveness. For example, if you underline a word or phrase on a page, the reader's eye will be drawn to it. So underlining can emphasize important information. But if you underline every other word or sentence, then nothing stands out.

If you are a hobbyist or computer enthusiast building your own website for fun, feel free to load your site with Flash presentations, rich media, and as much experimentation as your heart desires. On the other hand, those of us who use the Web for marketing should focus on prospect education, product information, and sales. "If you want to play in the new economy, you still have to play that tired old game of making a profit," writes Robert McKim in *DM News* (February 24, 2001, p. 24).

Will the Internet Make Print Obsolete?

Will print die in the twenty-first century? Advocates of CD-ROMs, software, the Internet, and electronic publishing are loudly proclaiming that print is dead. But futurists have been saying this for a long time—yet so far, it has not come to pass.

When Thomas Edison invented the phonograph (from the Greek words *sound* and *writing*) in 1876, he did it to bring music into the average American home. In his early model, the "records" were made of cylinders coated with tinfoil onto which the vibrations from sound waves were impressed with a needle.

Once he got a working model, Edison saw that his invention could be used to carry the spoken word as well as music. He publicly proclaimed that the book-on-record (precursor of today's audiobook industry) was a far superior learning tool to the printed page, and that by the end of the millennium, all college students would be learning by listening to recorded texts, and paper textbooks would be obsolete. In 1996, however, textbook sales in the United States grossed over $4 billion.

In 1964, when Sony introduced the CV-2000, the first home VCR, technologists proclaimed that the new videocassettes heralded the death of the printed word. Futurist and science fiction author Isaac Asimov responded with an essay describing what he called "the ultimate cassette."

Such a cassette, said Asimov, would be lightweight and portable. It would not require a player or need to be plugged into a power supply. It could be searched to look up specific information or access particular sections. And its per-unit cost should be low. At the end of the essay, he revealed that he was, in fact, describing a *book* to demonstrate that with all these advantages, print media might be supplemented by—but never replaced with—electronic media.

At the dawn of the new millennium, the fate of print is undecided. Working toward the demise of the printed word is the rising illiteracy rate and declining reading skills. According to an article in *Publisher's Weekly* magazine, four out of ten American eight year olds cannot read independently. Approximately 26 percent of Americans are illiterate, with another 16 percent classified as "functionally illiterate."

A recent Roper poll shows that 69 percent of Americans prefer to get their news from TV versus only 37 percent from newspapers. The average American household watches TV fifty hours a week. In 1980, 62.2 million newspapers were sold each day. In 1995, that figure had dropped to 59.3 million, a decline of 4.8 percent in fifteen years. During the same period, the number of daily newspapers in America dropped from 1,743 to 1,548—a decline of 11 percent.

In a 1979 interview, I asked fantasist, screenwriter, and TV critic Harlan Ellison if TV would replace print by the end of the century. Here was his reply:

I used to think that television could be potentially the most power-ful medium for the dissemination of knowledge that the world has ever known, it could be a very rich and rewarding thing if handled properly and that the problem was in the execution. I've now come, after ten years in the business, five years of which was as a televi-sion critic, to taking a very extreme viewpoint. I think television itself is bad.

The idea of television, the act of watching television kills the imagination. It's not like radio, with radio you had to listen, had to make things, you had to build things in your mind. Movies do that. Television is something else again. Television lays it all out there in a very prescribed way and the bare minimum of imagination on the part of the viewer is needed and I really fear for all of us.

Much of this argument applies today toward video and computer games and recreational websites. Although the multimedia presenta-tions are sophisticated—my son has a system in which the control vibrates in his hand when his character gets hit—they tend to focus on sex and violence, and the educational content is minimal. Chil-dren's books that compete against video games for attention often lose out, the Harry Potter series being a shining exception. As with TV, the more time children spend at Nintendo and PlayStation, the less time they spend playing outdoors, reading books, or playing with toys.

Newspaper columnist Charles Krauthammer is even gloomier, predicting that print will all but vanish in the next century. "The Gutenberg age will end with the twentieth century," he writes. "First to go will be the newspaper. Then the magazine. Then the book. Their paper versions, that is. They will all find a new life on screen, on disk, on line. What is dying is printing, not writing. It is our way of trans-mitting words—not words themselves—that is obsolete."

Are consumers proving Krauthammer right? According to Dan Poynter, author of *The Self-Publishing Manual*, 80 percent of U.S. families did not buy or read a book last year. He also notes that 70 percent of U.S. adults have not been in a bookstore in the last five years, and 58 percent of the adult population never reads another book after high school.

On the other hand, says Poynter, U.S. adults spent $25.6 billion on books in 1996—almost five times the $5.4 billion they spent going to the movies. "The pessimist says our market is smaller than we thought," Poynter tells book lovers. "The optimist says our potential market is larger than we thought."

In a 1997 interview with *Publisher's Weekly*, Nicholas Negroponte, author of *Being Digital*, predicted the demise of the printed word in the new millennium: "In the future, the act of printing words on paper will be as common as writing in stone is today.

"By the year 2050, paper will be rare because it will be far too expensive, and it will be difficult to use. A three-year-old child of that year will have to be told why paper doesn't make sounds, show movies, or read a story to him by itself when he's ready to doze off."

If you are a lover of the printed word, of course, your emotional reaction to the "death of print" is different than Negroponte's.

Novelist Umberto Eco, in *World Press Review*, disagrees with Negroponte's and Krauthammer's assertions that electronic media will make print media disappear, leaning toward Poynter's optimism.

"The appearance of new means of information does not destroy earlier ones; it frees them from one kind of constraint or another," observes Eco, noting that painting and drawing did not die with the invention of photography and cinema. He says that of the two types of books—reference books versus books meant to be read—only the former are likely to be replaced by the Internet and CD-ROMs.

"There is no doubt that the new media will eliminate the books in the first category," writes Eco. "Today, you can have the entire *Encyclopedia Britannica* on CD-ROM or access it on the Internet for very little money. We will save a lot of paper, and will preserve trees."

"But we cannot get rid of books that we sit down to read—from the *Iliad* to the latest novel," Eco says. "Reading them cover-to-cover on the screen would be tiring." Eco agrees with Asimov that the book is one of those inventions (like the hammer, spoon, and fork) for which no better ergonomic substitute has been found. "The book fits well in the hand, and one can read it in almost any situation, including in bed."

Content as a Marketing Tool

In the old model of printed publishing, information was produced as books and articles and sold to the reader for a fee. In the new model of the Internet, content is published on websites and given away for free for a variety of purposes: as a public service, to promote a viewpoint, to market goods and services, and to attract traffic to those websites.

The idea of publishing and giving away free content is not new. Drug companies, for example, have long been publishing and disseminating free patient information booklets (e.g., *Coping with Depression*) to promote prescription drugs targeted at the conditions described in the booklets. But the Internet has certainly accelerated this trend.

Look, for example, at VitaminShoppe.com or any website selling nutritional supplements. Many give away reams of research and writing on alternative medicine. One wonders if consumers will continue to buy health books at the bookstore if they can get the same information free from the Web. Content for free definitely competes with content for money.

As a copywriter, I frequently hear marketers ask themselves whether they can eliminate printed materials altogether and offer product information solely on the Web. The consensus seems to be not now.

We had a discussion at a major e-business solutions provider's training class that made the point clear. One marketing manager suggested not producing a printed catalog this year. All the products were on the website, and producing and printing a color catalog is costly. And, the prospects surely were all Internet-enabled, so access was not a barrier.

Another manager vehemently disagreed. "I don't want to have to log onto the Internet to read about your product," he said to his colleague. "That way, you're making me do the work." Also, many marketers feel that Internet and print have a synergistic effect—they complement rather than compete with each other.

A case in point is traditional paper direct mail (snail mail) versus e-mail. E-mail marketing has become widely accepted as a highly responsive direct-marketing medium. Some wonder if they should choose e-mail marketing in lieu of postal marketing.

In our book *Internet Direct Mail*, Steve Roberts, Michelle Feit, and I recommend doing e-mail marketing *in addition* to postal marketing versus instead of postal marketing. Why? The fact is that each method provides marketers with different advantages in reaching their intended targets. By combining the advantages of both, through a process we refer to as "multimailing," marketers can realize outstanding results.

Postal mail pieces tend to affect the buying process differently from e-mailing. Postal direct mail, in the form of catalogs, brochures, and circulars, tends to stay on the desk for a while. People can hold it, view it, refer it, file it, and (you hope) respond to it.

E-mail is more immediate. It appeals to our impulsive nature. Either the recipient will respond to it or he won't. By following up your direct-mail campaign with e-mail, you can influence the undecided person who is holding on to your brochure or who has forgotten about using your product or service.

One thing we have learned is that we should offer people more than one way to respond to us. Targeting with both a postal and e-mail campaign gives your prospects or clients two different ways to respond to you in a method and at a time and place of their choosing. This makes it easier for them to reply.

What's more, sending your offer twice, in two different ways, offers an opportunity to raise the visibility of your company and reinforce its message—making it more likely that prospects will respond. Aside from higher total response, other benefits of multimailing include timeliness, lower costs, as well as the ability to do one-to-one personalization.

The bottom line: paper marketing materials aren't going away anytime soon. According to the Direct Marketing Association, an industry trade group, the catalog market—estimated at $78.3 billion in 1997—is expected to reach $106.8 billion by 2002. That's a compound growth rate of 6.3 percent. In 1997, 257,900 Americans were employed in the catalog industry, which mailed more than thirteen billion catalogs. By 2002, catalog marketers will employ 485,400 people.

By the way, Lester Wunderman literally invented the direct-response industry, coining the term "direct marketing" in the 1960s. He has probably created more successful mail-order ads and direct-mail packages than anyone in the country. His creations include the Columbia Record Club, American Express, L.L. Bean, and Gevalia

Kaffe, the first mail-order coffee. Wunderman sees the future of direct marketing based in electronics, not paper. In his autobiography, *On Being Direct*, Wunderman writes:

> Video on demand, home shopping, on-line games, and directory services will become increasingly convenient and less costly. We can see the beginning of a revolutionary new communication, information, and entertainment shopping system. The information superhighway will likely be some combination of telephone, broadcast and cable TV, and local area computer networks. It is not clear who will pay for what, but the consumer will be empowered as never before. Video on demand, advertising on demand, and shopping on demand will change the way consumers shop.

Content as a Product

"Content as a product" means the information you create is not written to promote some other cause or sell some tangible product; the product is the information itself. Authors, freelance writers, publishers, and information marketers all follow this model. A publisher of financial newsletters, for instance, publishes reports on stocks—which she sells as advice to paying subscribers. A brokerage also publishes reports on stocks, but these are distributed free to clients to persuade them to buy the stock—and the broker makes his money from commissions on stock orders.

When content is the product, there are a number of perceived advantages, not the least of which is objectivity. Since you are paying for the advice up front, the writer's sole interest is giving good advice; otherwise, you'll cancel your subscription. Therefore, we assume the financial newsletter's advice is objective and unprejudiced; there's no hidden agenda, no product to sell. The brokerage, on the other hand, is trying to sell shares of the specific stock, especially if they are the underwriters. So their advice is not neutral. But, it is free. And many investors think, "Why pay for financial advice when it's free on my broker's website?" In fact, you can even get real-time stock quotes online for free on the Netscape home page.

The competition of content for free versus content for fee is one factor contributing to the diminished perceived value of and market for paid information. Another is technology. Before the computer, you needed a typesetter and graphic designer to produce professional quality publications for sale; now any PC with desktop publishing software or even Word can produce pages that look equivalent to typeset. Suddenly everyone is a publisher.

The Internet and e-books further increase the ease and reduce the cost of publishing information. Paper and printing, the major costs of producing information products in the pre-electronic age, are eliminated.

Elimination of cost as a barrier allows more and more people to self-publish, avoiding the problem of selling manuscripts to mainstream media (such as newspapers, magazines, book publishers). Self-publishing sidesteps the traditional editorial process, "democratizing" information dissemination and allowing everyone to become a "published writer."

The democratization process solves problems, but it creates them, too. "The best thing about the Internet is that everyone can publish to it," comments a columnist in *Maximum PC* magazine. "And the worst thing about the Internet is that everyone can publish to it."

As the barriers to entry vanish and the numbers of small publishers (including individuals) increase, the market becomes cluttered and what small quality checks were in place before disappear.

A friend's mother, an artist, recently commented to me, "How do you know the information you get on the Internet is any good?" And I didn't have a definitive answer for her. Despite all its frequently voiced flaws, traditional publishing with its editorial committees at least evaluated manuscripts for clarity and content. Without this control in place, the amount of poor-quality information disseminated increases exponentially.

The Internet makes publishing child's play. You don't even need a printer or a garage to store the copies; just type your manuscript and post it on the Web for all to read. But what check do we have that ensures even a minimal level of quality and accuracy in all this new Web-based material? We used to believe that if something was in print it was true. While this was sometimes an erroneous belief, it's even more apt to be untrue when applied to Web-based content.

Another Internet phenomenon affecting communications is the shift in value away from content and to the media. With the Internet, information can be stored and retrieved in ways previously not possible. Therefore, the speed and accuracy of the data-search mechanism is often more important to the user than the quality of the text. As an ad for Compaq observes, "What good is wonderful content if no one can get to it?"

The emphasis today is on how quickly one can find information, not necessarily on the quality of the prose. As a result, writers and even subject-matter experts have diminished in importance. The entrepreneurs envision new ways to use the new media and the technologists' programming makes them a reality, and they get the glory and the money in the Internet age.

Content creators who write pages of text in English, instead of lines of code in Visual Basic, are the wage slaves of the new economy—the least valued and the most poorly paid. Therefore, communication skills are valued less and technology skills are highly revered. Network managers command six-figure salaries while journalists at local town papers earn not much more than minimum wage. Article writing has never been a lucrative profession and the Internet has not changed that. Websites hiring freelancers to produce articles pay slave wages, often $100 an article or less.

Ubiquitous Delivery

Journalism has always been a deadline-oriented business, but with the rise of the Internet, that deadline is measured in minutes instead of days. As technology enables speedier production, it also enables speedier delivery.

In his report *The Rules of the New Millennium*, Australian marketing consultant Winston Marsh writes: "Information is the product, technology is the tool. With the development of more powerful computers, the Internet, e-mail, and cellular phones, more and more information will be soaked up by a world ever anxious to have more. As more of this new technology becomes available, people will use more of the information it provides more quickly and more often than ever."

For example, a survey of business-to-business newsletter publishers from the Newsletter and Electronic Publishers Association shows that one-third of business newsletter publishers now offer alerts or updates via e-mail to their subscribers.

Wired communications will increasingly be augmented by wireless. Cell phones abound. Computers proliferate. But in the new millennium, a new trend in communication is combining the best of both technologies. The trend? *Wireless data.* Businesspeople and even consumers, carrying small data terminals, or "mobile end systems," will be able to send and receive spreadsheets, documents, e-mail, presentations, and even credit card orders over the air using built-in wireless modems.

According to Lucent Technologies, a manufacturer of wireless networks, four out of ten workers today have jobs that require some level of mobility, and there are more than thirteen million wireless data users. Vertical-industry and company-specific applications, such as field service and emergency dispatch, now account for 90 percent of wireless business data.

Michael Greenwood, a market development executive with IBM's Pervasive Computing Division, notes that in 2001, 40 percent of Internet access was from non-PC devices. These include mobile phones, cable TV, personal digital assistants, even automobile dashboards and household appliances. That means you can deliver content no matter where your customer is.

"But there's a downside to this newfound power," writes Megan Santosus in *CIO Web Business* magazine (June 1, 2000, p. 188). "Many of us are becoming obsessive control freaks. We agonize over every blip in the market, compulsively check eBay to make sure we're not missing out on a good deal, and furtively monitor the goings-on at Mercata in the hope of saving a few bucks. We may indeed be more informed and enjoy more power in our transactions, but at the same time we're losing control of our lives."

With information available everywhere, anywhere, at any time, will people continue to pay for it? According to market research by Webnoize, so far initial attempts at subscription models that sell content for money have failed. An article in the *Washington Post* concludes, "Consumers will stick with free sources of content until media companies get it right. . . . Content prices are [so far] too high and virtual environments lack compelling features."

Fundamentals of Persuasive Online Copy

WHAT ARE THE characteristics that make online copy persuasive? Why does one Web page make a lasting impression and sell merchandise, while another falls flat and doesn't generate enough revenue to pay its own cost?

To be persuasive, your copy must:

1. Gain attention

2. Focus on the customer

3. Stress benefits

4. Differentiate you from the competition

5. Prove its case

6. Establish credibility

7. Build value

8. Close with a call to action

9. Give the user a reason to act now instead of later

All online promotions do not need to have all nine characteristics in equal proportions. Depending on the situation, some of these elements will be dominant in your electronic document; others subordinate or omitted altogether.

Let's take telephone service. If you are AT&T, MCI, or Sprint, you have a long track record of success and enjoy a well-established reputation. Therefore, you will be naturally strong in elements five and six (proving your case and establishing your credibility).

A new telephone services provider, on the other hand, does not have a track record or reputation; therefore, these two elements will not be the dominant themes in their online marketing. Instead, the strongest element might be number three (benefits the service offers to customers) or perhaps number four (differentiation in service resulting from superior technology).

Each product or service has natural strengths and weaknesses. The strengths are emphasized and the weaknesses de-emphasized. But all nine elements must be present somewhere in your e-marketing campaign, to some degree, or sales effectiveness is reduced.

Here are the nine elements of persuasion discussed in a bit more detail, with examples of how to achieve each in your copy.

Element 1—Gain Attention

If a banner ad or Web page fails to gain attention, it fails totally. Unless you gain the prospect's attention, he or she won't read any of your copy. And if the prospect doesn't read your copy, he or she won't receive the persuasive message you've so carefully crafted.

There are numerous ways to gain attention. Sex certainly is one of them. Look at the number of products—abdominal exercisers, health clubs, cars, Club Med, clothes, beer, soft drinks, chewing gum—that feature attractive bodies in their ads and commercials. It may be sexist or base, but it works. And we know that a huge number of Internet users are interested in looking at dirty pictures. (According to a special report from CNET, pornography accounts for one out of every ten dollars in e-commerce revenues.)

Similarly, you can use visuals to get prospects to pay attention. Parents (and almost everyone else) are attracted to pictures of babies and young children. Puppies and kittens also strike a chord in our hearts. Appealing visuals can get your ad noticed. The Netscape home page typically features color photos of attractive movie, TV, and music stars.

Because so much advertising is vague and general, being specific in your copy will help to set it apart from other ads and create interest. A sales pitch promoting collection services to dental practices begins as follows:

How we collected over *$20 million* in unpaid bills over the past 2 years for thousands of dentists nationwide

In the past 2 years alone, IC Systems has collected more than *$20 million* in outstanding debt for dental practices nationwide.

That's $20 million these dentists might not otherwise have seen if they had not hired IC Systems to collect their past-due bills for them.

What gains your attention is the specific figure of $20 million. Every collection agency promises to collect money. But saying that you have gotten $20 million in results is specific, credible, and memorable.

Featuring an offer that is free, low in price, or unusually attractive is also an effective attention-getter. An ad from Guaranteed Term Life Insurance announces, "NOW . . . $1 a week buys Guaranteed Term Life Insurance for New Yorkers over 50." Not only does the $1 offer draw you in, but the headline also gains attention by targeting a specific group of buyers (New Yorkers older than 50).

You know that in public speaking, you can gain attention by shouting or talking loudly. This direct approach can work in copy, especially in retail marketing. An ad for Lord & Taylor department store proclaims in large, bold type: STARTS TODAY . . . ADDITIONAL 40% OFF WINTER FASHIONS." Not clever or fancy, but interesting to shoppers who are looking to save money.

Another method of engaging the prospect's attention is to ask a provocative question. *Bits & Pieces*, a management magazine, begins its subscription mailing with this headline, "What do Japanese managers have that American managers sometimes lack?" Don't you want to at least read the next sentence to find the answer?

A promotion for a book club has this headline on the first page of the document:

Why is the McGraw-Hill Chemical Engineers' Book Club giving away—practically for **FREE**—this special 50th Anniversary Edition of PERRY'S CHEMICAL ENGINEERS' HANDBOOK?

To chemical engineers, who know that Perry's costs about $125 per copy, the fact that someone would give it away is indeed a curiosity—and engineers, being curious people, want to get the answer.

Injecting news into your copy, or announcing something that is new or improved, is also a proven attention-getting technique. A promotion offering subscriptions to the newsletter *Dr. Atkins's Health Revelations* has this headline:

Here Are Astonishing Nutritional Therapies and Alternative Treatments You'll *Never* Hear About from the Medical Establishment, the FDA, Drug Companies, or Even Your Doctor . . .
   3 decades of medical research breakthroughs from the Atkins Center for Complementary Medicine . . . revealed at last!

The traditional Madison Avenue approach to copy—subtle wordplay and cleverness—often fails to get attention. Those browsing the Web may not get the joke or pun. Or if they do get it, they don't think it's that funny (or they think it's funny, but that doesn't compel them to read the ad or buy the product). An ad for a New Jersey hospital, promoting its facilities for treating kidney stones without surgery, carried this headline:

The End of the Stone Age.

Clever? Yes. But as former kidney stone patient, I can tell you that having kidney stones is not a fun, playful subject, and this headline misses the mark. The kidney stone sufferer wants to know he can go to his local hospital, get fast treatment, avoid an operation and a hospital stay, have a painless procedure, and get rid of the kidney stones that are causing his current discomfort. Therefore, the headline,

Get Rid of Painful Kidney Stones—Without Surgery!

while less clever, is more direct, and works better with this topic and audience. Which do you think works better as the subject line of an e-mail marketing message?

Element 2—Focus on the Customer

When writing copy, start with the prospect, not with the product. Your customers are interested primarily in themselves—their goals, problems, needs, hopes, fears, dreams, and aspirations. Your product or service is of secondary importance. The degree of concern is determined by the potential for the product or service to address one of the client's wants or needs or by its ability to solve one of her problems.

Effective copy speaks directly to a specific audience and identifies their preferences, quirks, behavior, attitudes, needs, or requirements.

Write from the customer's point of view—for example, not "Introducing our Guarda-Health Employee Benefit Program" but "At last you can combat the huge health insurance premiums threatening to put your small business *out* of business."

WEKA Publishing, in a campaign promoting the *Electronics Repair Manual*, a do-it-yourself guide for hobbyists and others who want to repair their own home and office electronics, uses copy that speaks directly to the personality type of the potential buyer:

> If you're *handy* . . . fascinated by *electronics* and the world of high-tech . . . are happiest with a *tool* in your hand . . . and respond to household problems and broken appliances with a defiant, "I'll do it myself" . . .
> . . . then fun, excitement, the thrill of discovery, time and money saved, and the satisfaction of a job well done await you when you preview our newly updated *Electronics Repair Manual* at no risk for a full 30 days.

A good way to ensure that you are focusing on the prospect, and not yourself or your product or your company, is to address the prospect directly in the copy as "you." For example:

> Dear Health Care Administrator:
>
> You know how tough it is to make a decent profit margin in today's world of managed care . . . and how the HMOs and other plans are putting even *more of a squeeze* on your margins to fill their own already-swelling coffers.
>
> But what you may *not* be aware of is the techniques health care providers nationwide are using to *fight back* . . . and get paid every dollar they deserve for the important work they do.

This copy—which successfully launched a new publication—works because it focuses on the prospects and their problems (making money from their health care business), and not on the publication, its editors, or its features or columns.

Copy that fails to focus on the prospect often does so because the copywriter does not understand the customer. If you are writing to metal shop managers, attend a metalworking trade show, read a few issues of the trade publications they subscribe to, spend some time on metal shop websites, and interview some of these prospects in person or over the phone. Attend live focus group sessions or study their transcripts, or even accompany salespeople on calls. The better you understand your target audience, the better feel you have for the way they think and what they think about. You will then be able to more effectively create copy that speaks to their concerns.

Element 3—Stress Benefits

Although, depending on your audience, your prospects may be interested both in the features and the benefits of your product or service, it is almost never sufficient to discuss features only.

Virtually all successful copy—on- or offline—discusses benefits. Copy aimed at a lay audience would primarily stress benefits, mentioning features mainly to convince the prospects that the product in fact delivers the benefits promised in the ad.

Copy aimed at specialists often gives equal play to features and benefits or may even primarily stress features. But whenever a feature is described, it must be linked to a customer benefit it provides. Buyers not only want to know what the product is and what it does, but they also want to know how it can help them achieve the benefits they want—such as saving money, saving time, making money, being happier, looking better, or feeling fitter.

In copy for technical products, clearly explain the feature to make the benefit more believable. Don't just say a product has greater capacity; explain what feature of the product allows it to deliver this increased capacity. A pdf document posted on the Lucent Technologies website to promote their wireless CDMA technology explains, "CDMA gives you up to 10 times the capacity of analog cellular with more efficient use of spectrum. Use of a wideband block of radio frequency (RF) spectrum for transmission (1.25 MHz) enables CDMA to support up to 60 or more simultaneous conversations on a given frequency allocation."

A website for a computer consulting firm tells corporate information systems (IS) managers how working with outside consultants can be more cost-effective than hiring staff, thus saving money.

> When you augment your IS department with our staff consultants, you pay our staff consultants only when they work for you. If the need ends tomorrow, so does the billing. In addition, various studies estimate the cost of hiring a new staff member at 30 to 60 percent or more of the annual salary (an executive search firm's fee alone can be 30 percent of the base pay). These expenditures are 100% eliminated when you staff through us.

In an online product description for a software package that creates letterhead using a PC and laser printer, the copy stresses the benefits of ease, convenience, and cost savings versus having to order stationery from a printer.

> Every day, law firms struggle with the expense and inconvenience of engraved and preprinted stationery.
>
> Now, in a sweeping trend to cut costs without sacrificing prestige, many are trading in their engraved letterhead for Instant Stationery desktop software from Design Forward Technologies.
>
> With Instant Stationery, you can laser print your Word documents and letterhead together on whatever grade of blank bond paper you choose. Envelopes, too. Which means you never

have to suffer the cost of expensive preprinted letterhead—or the inconvenience of loading stationery into your desktop printer—ever again.

Element 4—Differentiate Yourself from the Competition

Today your customer has more products and services to choose from than ever. Therefore, to make your product stand out in the buyer's mind, and convince him or her that it is better than and different from the competition, you must differentiate it from those other products in your copy. Crispix cereal, for example, was advertised as the cereal that "stays crisp in milk." Post Raisin Bran was advertised as the only raisin bran having "two scoops of raisins" in each box of cereal. Chips Ahoy recently ran a campaign promoting "1,000 chips" in every bag of chocolate chip cookies.

Companies that make a commodity product often differentiate themselves on the basis of service, expertise, or some other intangible. BOC Gases, for example, promotes itself as a superior vendor not because their product is better (they sell oxygen, and one oxygen molecule is the same as another), but in their ability to use oxygen and technology to benefit the customer's business. Here is copy aimed at steelmakers:

> An oxygen supplier who knows oxygen *and* EAF steelmaking can be the strategic partner who gives you a sustainable competitive advantage in today's metals markets. And that's where BOC Gases can help.

If your product is unique within its market niche, stress this in your copy. For example, there are dozens of stock market newsletters. But *IPO Insider* claims to be the only IPO bulletin aimed at the consumer (there are other IPO information services, but these target professional investors and money managers). In their subscription promotion the *IPO Insider* says:

> *IPO Insider* is the *only* independent research and analysis service in the country designed to help the *individual* investor generate greater-than-average stock market profits in select recommended IPOs.

Lucent Technologies competes with many other companies that manufacture telecommunications network equipment. They set themselves apart by stressing the tested reliability of their switch, which has been documented as superior to other switches in the industry. One online document explains:

> The 5ESS-2000 Switch is one of the most reliable digital switches available for wireless systems today. According to the U.S. Federal Communication Commission's (FCC) ARMIS report, the 5ESS-2000 Switch has the least down-time of any switch used in U.S. networks, exceeding Bellcore's reliability standards by 200%. With an installed base of more than 2,300 switches, the 5ESS-2000 Switch currently serves over 72 million lines in 49 countries.

Element 5—Prove Your Case

Element 4, just discussed, claims product differentiation. Element 3 claims substantial benefits to product purchasers. The reason why these elements cannot stand alone is precisely that they are advertising claims, made by the manufacturer. Therefore, skeptical consumers do not usually accept them at face value. If you say you are better, faster, or cheaper, and you do not back up your claims with proof, people won't believe you.

IC Systems convinces dentists it is qualified to handle their collections by presenting facts and statistics as follows:

> The nationwide leader in dental-practice collections, IC Systems has collected past-due accounts receivables for 45,717 dental practices since 1963. Over 20 state dental associations recommend our services to their members.
>
> *IC Systems can collect more of the money your patients owe you.* Our overall recovery rate for dental collections is 12.4% *higher* than the American Collectors' Association national average of 33.63%. (For many dental practices, we have achieved recovery rates even higher!)

BOC Gases tells customers that the gas mixtures they sell in cylinders are accurately blended, and therefore the composition listed on the label is what the buyer will find inside the container. They make this argument credible by explaining their blending and weighing methodology:

> Each mixture component is weighed into the cylinder on a high-capacity, high-sensitivity equal-arm balance having a typical precision of ±10 mg at 95 percent confidence. Balance accuracy is confirmed prior to weighing by calibration with NIST-traceable Class S weights. Electronic integration of the precision balance with an automated filling system provides extremely accurate mixtures with tight blend tolerances.

Many stock market newsletters promise big winners that will make the reader rich if he or she subscribes. Since everyone says it, the statement is usually greeted with skepticism. Table 2.1 shows how the newsletter *Gold Stocks Advisory* combats this skepticism by putting their recent successes in an easy-to-scan format:

Table 2.1 A Sample of Paul Sarnoff's Recent High-Profit Gold Stock Picks

Company	Purchase price	Year high	% increase/ time frame	Potential profit on 10,000 shares
Gold Canyon	C70 cents	C$10.50	2,793% in 14 months	C$195,500
Coral Gold	C$1.20	C$6.45	438% in 8 months	C$52,500
Bema Gold	C$2.20	C$13.05	439 in 20 months	C$108,500
Jordex	C70 cents	C$3.75	435% in 6 months	C$26,300
Glamis Gold	US$1	US$8.88	788% in 84 months	US$78,800
Barrick Gold	US$4.81	US$32.88	584% in 96 months	US$280,700

The most powerful tool for proving your case is to demonstrate a good track record in your field, showing that your product or service is successful in delivering the benefits and other results you promise. One way to create the perception of a favorable track record is to include case histories and success stories in your copy.

Testimonials from satisfied customers are another technique for convincing prospects that you can do what you say you can do. You can also impress clients by showing them a full or partial list of your customers.

Share with readers any results your firm has achieved for an individual or group of customers. IC Systems, for example, impressed dentists by telling them that the company has collected twenty million dollars in past-due bills over the past two years alone—a number that creates the perception of a service that works.

On websites, testimonials and user success stories are usually posted in separate sections. An online pdf document containing product description can be hyperlinked to those case studies featuring that particular product.

Element 6—Establish Credibility

In addition to the benefits you offer, the products and services you deliver that offer these advantages, and the results you have achieved, prospective buyers will ask, "Who are you?"

In terms of persuasion, of the three major topics you discuss in your marketing campaign—the prospect, the product, and the product vendor—the "corporate" story is usually the least important. The customer is primarily interested in himself and his problems and needs, and perceives your product or service only as a means of solving those problems or filling those needs. The client is interested in your company only as it relates to your ability to reliably make, deliver, install, and service the product he buys from you.

Yet, the source of the product or service—the company—still is a factor in influencing purchase decisions. In the early days of personal computing, IBM was the preferred brand—not because IBM necessarily made a superior computer at a better price, but because if something went wrong, IBM could be counted on for fast, reliable, effective service and support. As PCs became more of a commodity and local computer resellers and stores offered better service, the service and support reputation of IBM became less of an advantage, and their PC sales declined.

Here are some examples of copy in which the vendor gives credentials designed to make the consumer feel more comfortable in doing business with them.

We guarantee the best technical service and support. I was a compressor service technician at Ingersoll Rand, and in the last 20 years have personally serviced more than 250 compressors at over 80 companies.

For nearly 100 years, BOC Gases has provided innovative gas technology solutions to meet process and production needs. We have supplied more than 20,000 different gases and gas mixtures—in purities up to 99.99999 percent—to 2 million customers worldwide.

Lion Technology is different. For nearly two decades, we have dedicated ourselves 100% to training managers, engineers, and others in environmental compliance-related subjects. Since 1989, our firm has conducted more than 1,400 workshops nationwide on these topics.

You'll find some of Paul's fundamental research in precious metals summed up in his more than 60 bestselling books including *Silver Bulls* and *Trading with Gold*. Paul's unique blending of solid research, combined with an unprecedented record of success in picking gold stocks, may have been what moved one *New York Times* reporter to dub him "the dean of commodities researchers."

Consider listing the following credentials in your copy:

- Year founded
- Number of years in business
- Number of employees
- Annual revenues
- Number of locations
- Number of units sold
- Patents and product innovations
- Awards and commendations
- Publications
- Memberships and participation in professional societies
- Seals of approval and agency ratings
- Independent survey results
- Media coverage
- Number of customers
- In-house resources (financial, technological, and human).

In print copy, the problem was where to insert this credentializing copy in the piece. Senior executives often argued that it should be up front, while marketers insisted that this information was of secondary importance and should be in the back of a brochure or catalog.

The modularity of the World Wide Web neatly eliminates this dilemma. On most websites, the About the Company information is conveniently posted on a separate page, accessible from the main buttons on the home page.

Given the ethereal nature of the Internet and the shaky finances of so many dot-com companies, it's even more important to establish credibility when you are marketing online than when you are talking offline. Here are a few other techniques that can help you establish your credibility with online buyers:

• Show a picture of your building or establish a physical presence to prove you're more than just a mailbox. Promotions for Dr. Atkins's *Health Revelations* show a photograph of his impressive seven-story clinic in midtown Manhattan. The copy points out that tens of thousands of patients have been treated there.

• Link the specifics of the product manufacturer's or service provider's background to reasons why it enhances his value as a vendor. A promotion for *Forecasts & Strategies*, a financial advisory service with a Web presence, notes that editor Mark Skousen was once with the CIA, which gave him government insider contacts he still uses today to interpret the market for his readers. Likewise, promotions for *Technology Investing*, another financial advisory with a Web presence, point out that Michael Murphy's proximity to Silicon Valley enhances his ability to research high-tech companies firsthand.

• Cite any awards the company has won or favorable third-party reviews the product has garnered. It doesn't have to be the Malcom Baldridge Award; even a citation from the local chapter of your trade association is impressive.

• Get and use testimonials from customers and the media. The best testimonials are specific rather than superlative, and support the key points you are making in your copy.

- If you are selling professional services, for example as a consultant, stress the expert's credentials and experience. List the books she has written (and their publishers) and the periodicals in which her articles have appeared. Also list major conferences and speaking engagements as well as academic or business affiliations. Give the names of the TV and radio shows or stations that have featured the expert as a guest.

- Don't forget standard credibility stuff, like number of years in business or number of subscribers—especially if you have been in business a long time or have an unusually high number of customers. "Our fiftieth year" or "more than 100,000 sold" impresses some people. Also, look for other statistics that can boost your credibility. For example, perhaps you still have your first customer who bought from you twenty-eight years ago when you shipped your first product.

Element 7—Build Value

It's not enough to convince prospects you have a great product or a superior service. You must also show them that the value of your offer far exceeds the price you are asking for it. You may have the best widget in the $100 to $200 price range of medium-size widgets, but why should the prospect pay $200 for your widget when they can get another brand for half the price? One argument might be lower total cost of ownership. Although your widget costs more to buy, its greater reliability and performance save and make money for your firm that, over the long run, far exceeds the difference in price between you and brand X.

Stress cost of ownership versus cost of purchase. The purchase price is not the only cost of owning something. There is the cost of maintenance, support, repair, refurbishment, operation, and, when something wears out, replacement. Therefore, the product that costs the least to buy may not actually cost the least to own; oftentimes, it is the most expensive to own!

The following example illustrates this point. Several companies are now selling artificial bone substitutes for orthopedic surgeons to use in bone graft operations. As of this writing, a small container of the artificial bone substitute, containing enough material for one spine surgery, can cost $500 to $800.

The shortsighted buyer sees this as expensive, especially because a bone graft can be taken from other sites in the patient's own body, and there is no cost for this material. But is there really no cost? Collecting bone graft from the patient's own body adds about an hour to the surgical procedure. With operating room time at about $1,000 an hour, it makes sense to pay $750 for bone material and eliminate this extra hour in the operating room.

That's not all. Often removing the bone from a donor site causes problems that can result in an extra day's stay in the hospital. That's another $1,000 down the tubes. And the removal of bone from the donor site can cause infection, which must be treated with costly antibiotics. Also, the removal process can cause pain; how do you measure the cost of the patient's added suffering? So while $750 for a small vial of artificial bone may seem initially expensive, it is in fact a bargain when compared with the alternative (which, on the surface, appears to have zero cost).

Here's a simpler example. You need to buy a photocopier for your home office. Copier A costs $900. Copier B costs $1,200. The features are essentially the same, and the reputations of the brands are comparable. Both have an expected lifetime of 120,000 copies. Most people would say, "Everything's the same except price, so buy copier A and save $300." Copier A compares itself feature for feature with Copier B, and runs an ad with the headline, "Copier A vs. Our Competition . . . We Can Do Everything They Can Do . . . at 25% Off the Price."

But you are the copywriter for the makers of Copier B. You ask them what it costs to make a copy. Their cost per copy is 2¢. You investigate Copier A, and find out that the toner cartridges are more expensive, so that the cost per copy is 4¢. You can now advertise copies at "half the cost of our competitor."

What's more, a simple calculation shows that if Copier B is 2¢ a copy cheaper, and you use the machine to make 120,000 copies, your savings over the life of the machine is $2,400. Therefore, an investment in Copier B pays you back eight times the extra $300 it cost to buy. This is additional ammunition you can use in your copy to establish that purchase price is not the ultimate factor determining buying decisions, and that Copier B offers a greater overall value to the buyer.

If your product costs slightly more up front but actually saves money in the long run, stress this in your sales talk. Everyone knows that the cheapest product is not automatically the best buy; corporate buyers are becoming especially concerned with this cost of ownership concept. Only government business, which is awarded based on sealed proposals and bids, seems to still focus solely on the lowest purchase price. And even that is slowly changing.

The key to establishing value is to convince the customers that the price you ask is "a drop in the bucket" compared with the money your product will make or save them, or the other benefits it delivers. Here are some examples.

> What would you do if the EPA assessed a $685,000 fine against your company for noncompliance with environmental regulations you *weren't even aware existed*?
>
> Now get the special 50th Anniversary Edition of PERRY's CHEMICAL ENGINEERS' HANDBOOK . . .
>   . . . for only $4.97 (list price: $129.50) with your *No-Risk Trial Membership in McGraw-Hill's Chemical Engineers' Book Club*

Another way to establish value is to compare the cost of your product with more expensive products or services that address the same basic need:

> The cost of *The Novell Companion*, including the 800+ page reference binder and NetWare utilities on diskette, is normally $89 plus $6.50 for shipping and handling. *This is less than a NetWare consultant would charge to advise you for just one hour* . . . yet The Novell Companion is there to help you administer and manage your network, year after year.

If your product or service is used over a period of time, as most are, you can reduce the sticker shock that comes with quoting a high up-front price by showing the cost over the extended usage period. For instance, a life insurance policy with an annual premium of $200 "gives your loved ones protection for just 55¢ a day." The latter seems more affordable, although the two prices are equivalent.

Here are some other ways to convince the prospect that the value of your offer far outweighs the asking price.

• **Dramatize your point with a visual.** Visualize statistics instead of just presenting them. A promotion for a financial advisory service promoted the stock of a high-capacity data storage device manufacturer as "Get rich cleaning up the Internet data explosion." The key fact: the amount of Internet data doubles every six months, so this is a big opportunity. Copy translation: "Picture a company's data as a bag of marbles. If you have 100 today, in 5 years you will have 60,040." On your website, you can post a Flash presentation that shows a small pile of marbles. As the narrator talks, it grows into a huge mountain, with marbles tumbling down the side.

• **Make an apples-to-oranges comparison.** Don't compare your product to other products in its category; compare it to higher-level products and services. For instance, an ad campaign for Audi didn't position the Audi as just another car; Audi positioned their new auto as a "jet plane on wheels." Promotions for *American Speaker* (a resource guide for executives who give speeches) compare the $297 price to the $5,000 that a top speechwriter would charge to write just one speech. Leeb's Index Options Alert (an e-mail service on options trading) notes that the $2,950 it charges for its e-mails is like paying a 2.95 percent fee on a $100,000 managed options account—and that it's actually lower than the total fee such a managed account would charge.

• **Spread out the payments.** Rodale and Franklin Mint are well aware of the sales-closing benefits of offering several smaller payments instead asking for one large lump sum. This is common practice in fields such as mail order, where infomercials sell ab machines for "4 easy payments of $29.95"—and the elimination of one payment is offered as an incentive for immediate response. Collectibles are also sold on this basis. For instance, the Franklin Mint sold its Civil War chess set by the figure for $17.50—making it seem affordable and avoiding the need to state that a chess set, which has a total of thirty-two pieces, costs $560 at this price. If you are selling a service, subscription, or regular product shipments over the Internet, consider offering it for so much a month with credit card payment on a till forbid basis. That means that the buyer's credit card will be charged each month until she says "stop." After all, which sounds better— "$19.95 a month" or "$240 for one year of service"?

• **State the price in terms that make it seem smallest.** Even if you want full payment up front, state the price in your promotion in terms that make it seem smaller. A $59 annual subscription, for instance, gives the buyer access to vital information for just 21¢ a day. A term life insurance policy with a $150 annual premium "protects you and your loved ones all year long for just 41¢ a day." One technique for making your price seem small—especially if you charge more than your competitor does—is to stress the price differential in terms of the benefit. For example, "You get superior Acme quality and world-class reliability for just a dollar per unit more than conventional widgets that can't match our performance." Another technique is to help the reader mentally amortize the purchase price over the expected life of the product. For instance, if you buy a $25,000 car and own it ten years, your cost is $2,500 per year or $208 per month, which compares favorably with a monthly lease for the same vehicle. And of course, you own the car.

• **Value the component parts.** If you are selling an options trading course for $200, list the individual elements and show that the retail prices of each (videos, workbook, telephone hotline, website access) add up to much more than $200—therefore the course buyer is getting a great deal. Even better: position one or two of the product elements as premiums the buyer can keep even if he returns the product or cancels the subscription. Offering "keeper" premiums usually increases response. For example, instead of selling your eight-cassette audio album for $69, say it is a six-cassette album for $69, then position the other two cassettes as premiums.

• **Add an element that cannot easily be priced by the buyer.** Information products like books, reports, and loose-leaf services, for instance, face a built-in resistance from the buyer: "Why is it X dollars if it's just a book?" Supplements help differentiate from regular books, but publishers have found it even more effective to include a CD-ROM with the notebook. The CD-ROM is perceived as a high-value item with indeterminate retail price (software on a CD-ROM can cost anywhere from $19 to $499), so it destroys the book-to-book comparison between loose-leafs and ordinary books.

- **Show the value or return in comparison to the price.** Demonstrate that the fee you charge is a drop in the bucket compared to the value your product adds or the returns it generates. If your service helps buyers pass regulatory audits, talk about the cost of failing such an audit—fines, penalties, even facilities shutdowns. If your manual on energy efficiency in buildings cuts heating and cooling costs 10 to 20 percent a year, the reader with a $10,000 fuel bill for his commercial facility will save $1,000 to $2,000 this year and every year—more than justifying the $99 you are asking for your product.

- **Use statistics in your favor.** With intelligent manipulation, you can almost always make the numbers come out in support of your selling proposition. For example, a high-priced trading advisory specializes in aggressive trades with profits of around 20 to 30 percent with average holding periods of less than a month. The challenge: overcome resistance to paying a big price for modest-sounding returns. Solution: dramatize the profits the subscriber can make with numerous quick trades. The copy reminds readers, "If you could earn 5% each month for the next 10 years, a mere $10,000 investment would compound to a whopping $3.4 million. At 10%, it would be an almost unimaginable $912 million!"

- **Preempt the price objection.** Most mailings for expensive products build desire and perceived value, then reveal the price once the customer is sold. An opposite approach is to state the price up front, and use the exclusivity of a big number to weed out nonprospects. For example, "This service is for serious investors only. It costs $2,500 a year. If that price scares you, this is not for you." An element of exclusivity and snob appeal is at work here. This approach was best expressed in a *New Yorker* magazine cartoon where a salesman in a luxury auto dealership haughtily tells the customer in his showroom, "If you have to ask about the mileage, you can't afford it."

Element 8—Close with a Call to Action

Copy is written to bring about a change—that is, to cause prospects to change their opinion, attitude, beliefs, purchasing plans, brand preferences, or immediate buying actions.

To effect this change, your copy must be specific about the action the prospects should take if they are interested in what you've said and what to do to take advantage of your offer or at least find out more. Tell them to visit your home page, click on a link to a URL, fill out and submit your guest page, print out a discount coupon and take it to your retail outlet, request a free estimate, or whatever. Directly specify the next step in your copy or else few people will take it. Here are some examples.

> Go to www.collections.com/report to download a free copy of our new special report, "How to Get Better Results from Your Collection Efforts." You'll discover at least half a dozen of the techniques IC Systems uses—and you can use, too—to get more people to pay what they owe you.

> Think it's time to talk with a gas supplier that really knows your business and has real solutions to your problems? Call your BOC Gases representative today. Or visit our website at www.boc.com.

Element 9—Give the Reader a Reason to Act Now

It's just so easy for online prospects to click away. So, the sooner you can get them to fill in and submit your guest page—or take whatever other action you want them to take—the better. You will increase click-throughs and conversions by giving your online prospect reasons to respond now, instead of later.

Here are just some of the incentives you can offer:

- A free gift
- A free e-zine subscription
- Free access to password-protected segments of your website containing useful tools, content, or online communities
- A time-limited discount offer
- Free shipping and handling
- A free upgrade
- A special package offer (e.g., two for the price of one)
- An expiration date or other impending deadline (e.g., supplies are limited; first come first served)
- A sense of urgency (e.g., "Arrange for a free Internet security audit—your data are at risk.")
- Limited opportunity (e.g., "This special offer is limited to the first 1,000 users who respond to this e-mail.")

Table 2.2 indicates the relative effectiveness of act-now incentive offers in online marketing. More and more marketers are testing online promotions. Here's what promotions marketers are testing and their response to which promotion is most effective.

Table 2.2 Online Offers

Promotions	Recently tested	Rated most effective
Free merchandise	60%	31%
Sweepstakes	53%	20%
Free shipping	36%	16%
Coupons	64%	11%
Contests	11%	4%
External points programs	24%	2%
Price discounts	24%	2%
Gift certificates	20%	2%
Rebates	7%	2%
Referral programs	20%	0%
Internal points programs	11%	0%

Source: Forrester Research

DID YOU KNOW?

- 56 percent of U.S. residents use the Internet.
- 30 million U.S. children under age eighteen are online.
- 73 percent of kids between the ages of twelve and seventeen have online access.
- 50.6 percent of Internet users are women.
- Only 15 percent of Americans age sixty-five or older are on the Internet.
- 82 percent of families with an annual household income of more than $75,000 are on the Internet.

Source: *Infoworld*, February 26, 2001, p. 29

3

Adapting Existing
Print Copy to the Web

D<small>URING THE FORESEEABLE</small> future, and especially in the next five to ten years, companies are going to spend thousands of hours taking existing paper documents and posting them on the Web. These include everything from press releases, articles, and white papers, to data sheets, product literature, and annual reports.

"Realize efficiency and consistency by repurposing graphics and information from print and broadcast media," writes Larry Kacyon in *Metalworking Marketer* newsletter (August 1997, p. 5), "but make it a little different."

"A little different" is the issue here. Can (and should) these paper documents be transferred directly, word for word, to the Web? Or should they be modified to take advantage of both the inherent advantages of online communication as well as the reading habits of the Internet user? Common sense suggests, and experience indicates, that the latter course of action is the most sensible and effective.

In this chapter, we look at the steps involved in converting offline documents to online media. These steps are as follows:

1. Do a gross edit of the document.
2. Scan into an electronic file.

3. Update the technical content and check for accuracy.

4. Reduce the promotional content and tone.

5. Increase the informational content and tone.

6. Place strategic hyperlinks where useful.

7. Insert dynamic headlines and subheads.

8. Do a fine edit to tighten and strengthen the text.

9. Proofread.

10. Post the document on the website.

11. Ask for feedback.

Let's take a brief look at each of these steps.

Do a Gross Edit of the Document

A rough rule of thumb, presented in Chapter 1, is that online documents should be about half the length or less than offline documents. Reasons include the impatience of the online reader and the ease with which this reader can click away from your page.

Almost everything written on the planet today probably contains extra words whose deletion would only make the piece stronger and tighter. Corporate documents, written and reviewed by committee, tend to be more bloated than journalism and other types of writing. Therefore, even if the Internet didn't ask for less length, your current documents could probably benefit from pruning anyway. So it's a no-lose proposition either way.

Take a hard copy and sit in front of it with a red pen or pencil. This is a better method then deleting on screen, where stuff disappears once you delete it (except if you use Word's Track Changes or a similar revision tool, in which case you can get confused with too many different versions and colors).

First, cut out sections that are extraneous. For example, if you are editing a brochure for transition to an online document, you probably want to cut out the "about the company" section on the back cover. The reason is that your website already has an "about the company" page. The same logic may apply to the brochure's list of offices and addresses, which appears on your website's contact page, or the list of customers, which may also already be on your site.

Second, within major sections themselves, cut out paragraphs and sentences that are extraneous. Delete any text containing information that is unimportant or is covered through hyperlink to other documents. For example, a brochure on a software product might have two or three paragraphs on support. The same document posted on a website might have the sentence, "The price includes free *technical support* for 30 days." The words *technical support* are highlighted and link to a separate support page.

You'll also notice that a lot of your printed marketing documents contain a certain amount of "fluff"—empty words that sound nice but don't actually communicate any new information. Sometimes copywriters use fluff for dramatic effect or in an attempt to snare the reader's interest; sometimes it's to fill out a section that looked too short when the copy was laid out on the page. Slash these ruthlessly with your editor's red pencil.

Scan into an Electronic File

Make sure all of the above edits are clearly crossed out on your hard copy, then scan it into a text or Word file. The scanned document becomes the electronic document that you work with from this point on.

If you've done scanning before, you know that optical scanning is not perfect, and typos sometimes result. Clean these up now with a quick proofing before going on to the next step.

Check the scanned copy against the original for accuracy. If scanning errors have changed a number or moved a decimal in the copy, the only way to spot this is by comparing against the original.

Update the Technical Content and Check for Accuracy

In today's fast-paced business world, by the time most documents are printed they are already out of date. Webizing your paper documents is the ideal time to bring them up to date.

Work from the latest print version or electronic file (if it's a computer-based document). Show a copy or printout to engineers, product designers, brand managers, and product managers. Ask them to mark it up with a red pen, crossing out dated information and writing in updated content. Sometimes this is as simple as changing "version 3.0" to "version 3.1" in the copy and updating performance specifications. In other situations, it may require more extensive rework.

Be careful about posting online documents that have dated references in them. Although one of the biggest advantages of websites is that they can be updated quickly and at minimal expense, often they are not. For that reason, hunt for and remove dated references from print documents before converting them to online formats.

Examples of references that can quickly become dated include:

- Posting a seminar description from a printed invitation containing a date that has already passed.
- Documents citing standards, regulations, laws, and guidelines that are subject to change.
- Descriptions of sales figures, number of employees, branch offices, and other metrics reflecting your company size, especially for fast-growing firms. For instance, if your "about the company" page says "XYZ Corporation is a logistics firm with $103 million in annual revenue," that becomes obsolete when your sales the next year exceed $118 million. One solution is to say "more than $100 million in sales."
- Product pages mentioning special offers (free installation, free upgrades, extended warranties) that were temporary promotions and are no longer in force.

Reduce the Promotional Content and Tone

Although, as we discussed earlier, the Internet is gradually making a transition from an environment of scholarly and academic information exchange to a medium of commerce, the "hard sell" is, as of this writing, much more acceptable in print than online. Even when visitors log onto an e-commerce site, they hope to get useful information about the topic, not just product data or special offers.

Take a look at the paper documents you are converting for use online, especially brochures, ad copy, sales letters, and other marketing materials. Do you need to tone them down for the Internet? Well, yes and no.

No, in the sense that the Internet, like print, thrives on a sense of excitement and enthusiasm. Good marketing copy, whether in print or online, conveys that sense of excitement. At its best, copy sounds like one friend talking to another, telling him about this great product, service, or idea he discovered and wants to share. This kind of "hype" is welcome on the Internet. So don't edit it out of your copy.

Yes, in the sense that the Internet is an environment of discovery rather than salesmanship. The Internet prospect likes to feel she is learning, not being sold. In a retail ad for a beauty product, the copy might be, "Buy this face cream today!" On a Web page, the copy might read, "If you want to prevent flakiness, apply this particular cream twice a day after washing." The former is hard sell; the latter is information sharing.

Increase the Informational Content and Tone

As Internet marketing guru Joe Vitale points out, "Information is pure gold on the Internet." And what explorer doesn't like to find nuggets of sparkling gold on the trail? If you think of visitors to your site as Web explorers, you can see why beefing up the informational content can help you gain their interest and trust. According to an article in *Business Marketing* magazine (November 1999, p. 33), 64 percent of Internet users surveyed said they used the Internet to "obtain information about a hobby or personal interest."

Using information as a marketing tool is nothing new. In TV, it's done with the infomercial, which is a commercial (paid advertising message) produced to look like a show (unpaid entertainment, news, or information). Nobody is fooled—the viewer knows it's an infomercial—but putting the sales pitch in an information-rich environment makes it more credible, believable, and palatable . . . and gets more people to buy.

In print advertising, direct marketers have had much success with *editorial-style ads*—space ads disguised to look like articles. Whenever you see an article with the word *Advertisement* at the top in small type, you are looking at an editorial-style ad.

People are trained to be skeptical of advertising, but they believe what they read in newspapers and magazines and see on TV. Therefore, if you make your promotional copy look like editorial matter, you increase both readership and response.

This technique works especially well on the Internet, a medium that favors information over selling. A good example is the website for Engineered Software, EngineeredSoftware.com. The company makes and markets software that allows engineers to design piping systems on their computers.

The website is filled with articles and case histories on how to design piping systems. You think you are learning (and indeed you are learning) how to do this work, but really the editorial matter teaches you to use the firm's software by offering a demo version that can be downloaded free at the site. It's selling, but in an information-rich environment.

Place Strategic Hyperlinks Where Useful

Obviously, the printed version of your copy was not created to function as hypertext that can jump from one point to another at the reader's disgression. Yet, subjects are embedded within the text that are probably amplified or expanded upon in other pages on your site. Your job is to find these subjects and insert the logical links in your document now.

Hyperlinks should be short—usually just a word or two. For instance, in the sentence "fume hoods are available with optional HEPA filters," you could link *filters* to a description of them. If you have many different types of filters, you might want to link *HEPA filters* to the description to be clear.

Ideally, you want just a couple of links per screen—three or four at the most. The reason is that hyperlinks, like most communication devices, work best if not overused.

The ability to instantly link to details on key topics is a benefit to the customer. But if you insert a link in every other sentence or every other word, the reader is frustrated. You interrupt the natural flow of reading and induce anxiety. The client thinks he can't understand the next sentence or phrase without going to and reading the complete reference document you've linked to . . . and he soon gives up.

Hyperlink technology on the Web enables the hypertext that was invented by Ted Nelson in the 1960s. Nelson's idea was that reading and learning were limited by the linear format of conventional written text, and hypertext was created to allow the reader to jump around to various content at his whim. But it was clunky to implement on paper and didn't catch on.

The interactive nature of the Internet has finally allowed smooth implementation of hypertext, yet we find that most of today's readers are accustomed to—and more comfortable with—the linear presentation of print. And therefore they also read online text in linear fashion, even though the technology allows them not to (and they say they don't).

Academics theorize that the brains of youngsters today—the first generation growing up with the Internet—will become wired differently, so as to prefer nonlinear information. But for the near-term, your customer is still a linear reader. So offer links, but don't overdo it.

Some links take you from section to section within a page or document. For instance, Burlington Industries, a textile manufacturer, puts its proxy statements on the Web for shareholders to access. If you own stock, you know that proxy statements are long, dense documents, and most shareholders don't want to read every word.

Burlington puts an index to the sections of the proxy statement at the front of their html document. The index is interactive, so by clicking on the name of the section you are interested in, you go right to it in the document. The browser will also find a link to the index itself on every page. So you never get lost in the document and can always return to where you started.

Some links take you from page to page. For instance, a vitamin website might post an article on nutrition for improving eyesight. The article mentions taking bilberry as a supplement to improve night vision. Click on the word *bilberry* in the article, and you immediately jump to a page with a description and ordering information on the bilberry pill that the site sells.

Then there are links that take you from website to website. When you use a search engine, you are given a list of websites that match your interest. The names of the sites on the list are linked to the home pages of each website. You click on the name and go directly to the site. See Chapter 7 for more information on how to create a links page for your website.

Insert Dynamic Headlines and Subheads

"Visitors typically scan pages, rather than read them word for word," writes Marty Foley in *Opportunity World* (April 2001, p. 62). "Keeping this in mind, use descriptive headlines and subheads, write concisely, and make important points stand out by highlighting them or using different colored text."

The use of headlines catches the reader's attention as she surfs the Web, causing her to stop and start reading. The use of subheads breaks up the copy into sections, eliminating long chunks of text that lack eye appeal. They also allow for easy scanning, and with internal links in the document, they permit you to quickly jump to only those sections of interest. Subheads enable quick scanning, and if written informatively, (e.g., "Cutting pump size reduces energy costs") they can give you the gist of the page's contents without forcing you to read the whole text.

Do a Fine Edit to Tighten and Strengthen the Text

Now that you have taken out extraneous material, added or sharpened heads and subheads, and inserted appropriate links (indicated by the writer by underlining the word), make sure the whole thing reads smoothly.

When editing your online document, keep these points in mind:

• The rules of grammar and punctuation are the same whether you are on- or offline. Do not get sloppy simply because it's an online document and is not being printed.

• Continue your pruning process. Delete all extraneous words, phrases, paragraphs, and sections that still remain. When in doubt, take it out. (Because your document is online and not printed, you can always put it back later.)

• Keep sentences and paragraphs short. Give sentences the "breath test" by reading them aloud. If you run out of breath before you get to the end of the sentence, it's too long and should be broken into two or more sentences.

• Prefer short paragraphs (three to five lines on your screen) to longer paragraphs. Whenever you see a long paragraph, read it again. As soon as you come to a new thought or idea, start a new paragraph.

• With technical or scientific material, give your copy the "gist test." Give it to the least technical or scientific person you know, and ask him to read it. If he can't at least get the gist of what's going on (even though he may not know all the terms or concepts), it's probably not clear enough to post on the Internet.

Proofread

Proofread all Internet copy—Web pages and e-mails—before it is posted or transmitted. Many potential buyers are overly sensitive to grammatical and spelling errors. They feel if you are not careful about your writing, you may not be careful about their business.

Poor grammar is perhaps a symptom of our technological age where anybody with a keyboard can produce his or her own slick-looking printed materials. Many of these people don't seem to realize that they have—or perhaps they don't bother to use—the spell checker their e-mail service provides for checking text messages.

In addition to running a spell check, proof each document manually. Spell checkers miss many errors. Once, the training manager at

---

SPELL CHECKER

Eye halve a spelling chequer
It came with my pea sea
It plainly marques four my revue
Miss steaks eye kin knot sea.

Eye strike a key and type a word
And weight four it two say
Weather eye am wrong oar write
It shows me strait a weigh.

As soon as a mist ache is maid
It nose bee fore two long
And eye can put the error rite
Its rare lea ever wrong.

Eye have run this poem threw it
I am shore your pleased two no
Its letter perfect awl the weigh
My chequer tolled me sew.

—As seen on the Internet

---

a Big Six accounting firm hired me to teach business writing to his employees. He said, "Please stress proofreading in the seminar." He then showed me a proposal one of his employees submitted to a major client. The cover described the firm as "Certified Pubic Accounts."

"If you can't get someone to proof your cyber epistles, read them through yourself, at least once or twice, before clicking 'Send,'" advises Julie Meyer in an article in *Opportunity World* (October 1999, p. 46). "There's a reason computers still need people to operate them."

Post the Document on the Website

The next step is posting the document on your website, intranet, or extranet. And here we see another great advantage of the Internet over print: mistakes are easy to correct, and online documents are easily upgraded.

We've all lived through the horror of printing two hundred resumes, sending out one hundred cover letters, or getting a color brochure back from the printer, only to discover one or more typos. You then have to decide: leave it and hope no one notices, or throw out the documents, correct, and reprint.

You don't want to post documents on your website that have errors, of course. But if you do, it's not a disaster on the same level as a typo in a printed annual report, and you can correct it quickly and easily . . . and at no cost.

Ask for Feedback

A growing trend is to put a button on your website that asks visitors to give feedback. If you do, people may e-mail you to tell you about errors and typos in your online documents. They might also give you suggestions for adding content to existing documents or posting backup and supporting documents.

Making Your Online Documents More Persuasive with AIDA

In their book *Connections: A Guide to Online Writing*, Daniel Anderson, Bret Benjamin, and Bill Paredes-Holt divide online documents into two categories: informative and persuasive. "Informative writing seeks to present information as clearly as possible," they write. "Persuasive writing can be anything that moves someone else to action."

You are almost certain to have both persuasive and informative documents in your online marketing program. Sometimes there is a clear separation between giving information and persuasion; more often, Web pages, e-mails, and e-zines combine elements of information and persuasion within a single document.

Even a purely informative document has an agenda of persuasion when it is posted on a business website. After all, you are not in the business of giving away information; you are trying to sell the visitor your product.

The persuasive element of online documents can be made stronger by applying a formula originally invented for print. Perhaps you have heard it before—AIDA—Attention, Interest, Demand, and Action, a sequence of psychological reactions that happen in the mind of the reader as he is sold on your idea. Briefly, here's how it works.

First, the document gets the reader's attention with a hard-hitting lead paragraph that goes straight to the point or offers an element of intrigue.

Then, the copy hooks the reader's interest. The hook is often a clear statement of the reader's problems, needs, or wants. For example, if you are sending an e-mail to a customer who received damaged goods, acknowledge the problem and then offer a solution.

Next, create demand. Tell the reader how he or she will benefit from your offering. That creates a demand for your product.

Finally, call for action. Ask for the order, inquiry, and completion and submission of your online form, a click-through to your website.

Here are the steps:

Attention

Getting the reader's attention is a tough job. If your copy is boring, pompous, or says nothing interesting, you'll lose the reader. One attention-getting technique used by successful writers is to open with an intriguing question or statement—a teaser that grabs the individual's attention and compels her to read on. A banner ad using this technique flashed the message, "How to get telemarketing firms to stop calling you." An e-mail offering an e-zine subscription has the subject line, "What never to eat on an airplane."

Interest

Once you get the reader's attention, you've got to provide a hook—a promise to solve problems, answer questions, or satisfy needs—to create real interest in your subject and keep him reading. The hook is often written in a two-paragraph format. The first paragraph is a clear statement of the reader's needs, while the second shows how the writer can satisfy these needs.

A principal rule of persuasive writing is to remember that the reader isn't interested in you. The reader is interested in *the reader.* And because we want to hear about ourselves, the following—although obviously a promotion—was particularly effective in gaining and holding my interest:

> As you may already know, we have been doing some work for people who have the same last name as you do. Finally, after months of work, my new book, THE AMAZING STORY OF THE BLYS IN AMERICA, is ready for printing and you are in it!
>
> The Bly name is very rare and our research has shown that less than two one thousandths of one percent of the people in America share the Bly name.

Desire

Get attention. Hook the reader's interest. Then create the desire to buy what you're selling. Don't write to impress—write to express. State the facts, features, and benefits of your offer in plain, simple English. Give the reader reasons why he or she should buy your product, visit your site, sign on as a member of your online community, or join your association. Create a desire for what you're offering.

Action

If you've carried AIDA this far, you've gained attention, created interest, and turned that interest into desire. The reader wants what you're selling, or at least he or she has been persuaded to see your point of view. Now comes the last step—asking for action. To move things along, determine the action you want your letter to generate and tell the reader about it.

Formulas have their limitations, and you can't force fit every online document into the AIDA framework. The contact page on your site, for example, doesn't require this degree of persuasiveness. But when you're faced with more sophisticated writing—an e-mail marketing campaign, a home page—AIDA can help. Get attention. Hook the reader's interest. Create a desire. Ask for action. And your Web copy will get better results.

Critiquing Online Documents

H. G. Wells once said, "There is no human urge greater than the urge to change someone else's copy." And Ken Weissman, a colleague who ran a general advertising agency in the 1980s, once told me, "Subjective judgment is the bane of the advertising industry."

Internet marketers give each other opinions every day. Consultants tell clients they are doing everything wrong and should follow the consultant's advice. Content editors complain that marketing's draft is full of fluff, and that marketing doesn't understand the subscribers. Copywriters ride roughshod over clients and say "Don't change a word; I know what it takes to make winners." HTML designers show their clients the fancy spinning logos and take offense whenever their aesthetic judgment is challenged. But can the writers and designers guarantee a winner for that particular client and product, right then and there?

In her book *The 7th Sense*, Doris Wild Helmering presents criteria to distinguish constructive (i.e., helpful and useful) criticism from nonconstructive (i.e., petty, denigrating, and useless) criticism. Her criteria are meant for general criticism of creative work but certainly apply to creation and evaluation of online marketing campaigns.

According to Helmering, constructive criticism has the following three components:

1. There is a contract between the people involved. The person who is making the critical comment is involved with the project, has some authority, and has been invited to do so.

2. The negative feedback addresses a specific issue (e.g., "This e-mail blast ignores the current slump in tech stocks" versus "This stinks.").

3. There is direction for change (e.g., "Why not talk about why now is a time to pick up good stocks at bargain prices before the market picks up again?").

To be constructive, your criticism must have all three components. Inappropriate criticism, on the other hand, has one or more of the following characteristics:

1. It is uninvited. There is no contract. It is unsolicited.

2. The feedback is nonspecific or broad based.

3. The commentary is without direction for change.

A recent Dilbert comic strip gives a tongue-in-cheek illustration of inappropriate criticism:

Boss: Everyone says our website is ugly.
Web master: Really, every person on Earth said that? Even Tibetan monks?
Boss: Maybe it was just one person.
Web master: And you confused him with the entire planet?

When giving negative criticism, say what you like about the work before you say what you don't like. This preserves the recipient's ego, softens the blow, and ensures a positive working environment.

In a course I took while an employee at Westinghouse, my boss Terry Smith taught the following method for criticizing creative work. First say, "Here's what I liked" and recap at least three positive points. (If you look hard enough, it's impossible not to find at least three good things to say about almost anything.)

Then, say "Now, if it were mine to do. . . ." and proceed with your list of specific criticisms. This phrase implies that what you are telling the recipient is your opinion, and not an accusation of incompetence or shoddy work on his or her part.

If someone gives you inappropriate criticism, especially comments that attack you as a person or demean you as a professional, say to that person, "Is there a purpose for you saying this to me?" This alerts the person that you are aware of his or her demeaning tone and you want it to cease.

Also keep these points in mind:

• In marketing, the most useful criticism comes from the knowledge of what's working in your marketplace right now, based on recent test results the copywriter or agency may be unaware of.

• The second most useful form of criticism is sharing your knowledge of what has worked in the past in your online marketing campaigns, based on your test experience.

• Beware of sources offering you unsolicited advice, the basis of which is that your current website stinks and they have great ideas for improving it. If they're so smart, why do they spend time going around to people and giving free advice?

• If a major campaign element is a point of contention—$10 discount versus a free gift with purchase over $40, for instance—consider an A/B test to get the answer. An A/B split means testing two promotions to see which pulls best.

In particular, direct marketers (the subgroup of marketers to which I belong) like to brag that our discipline isn't subjective like general advertising because test results prove what works. But the process of creating and determining what to test in the first place is loaded with subjective decisions at every step, from initial copy and concept through design and execution selection.

By giving criticism more effectively during the creative process, we can help ensure that an Internet marketing campaign has the best chance of succeeding in the test phase—and therefore the best chance of being rolled out profitably.

Reaching the Non-U.S. Internet User

Efforts to target international Web customers are on the rise. Forty-four percent of retailers' sites are currently accessible outside the United States, and another 24 percent plan to offer Internet commerce to international customers. Manufacturers are even more aggressive:

39 percent of their sites are available outside the United States, and 46 percent will soon be able to take orders from international customers.

The strategies are already generating sales. Forty percent of U.S. companies with internationally accessible sites say some of their Internet orders are from global customers.

The Internet eases many traditional barriers for international customers, according to Jeffery Grayson, Lands' End's export business manager. "It provides free contact for global users, who would otherwise have to pay for a call to order merchandise." Customers receive order confirmation via the Net and can check which items are in stock when ordering. "We're also using the Net to give international customers access to closeouts," Grayson continues. "In the past, we haven't mailed liquidation pages to international customers. Now, every customer has the same opportunity to get at sale merchandise. We don't incur the print costs and we can take it off our site as soon as items are sold."

U.S. companies aren't the only ones using the Web. Shanghai's municipal government is constructing the Shanghai Infoport, which is designed to link businesses in the city via a high-speed network that also connects to the Internet.

Seattle-based iCat Corp., which provides commerce-ready web-sites for companies, recently launched ten commerce-enabled sites in Europe, among them sites for U.S.-based Toys 'R' Us, as well as Europe-based Cotswold and Bridgewater.

Although much of the Internet's growth is centered in the United States, Europe and Asia are expected to post sharp increases.

Markets for some products appear well developed. Barnes & Noble, which launched its site in 1997, projects that an immense, untapped international market for books in English could catapult its Internet sales to as high as 30 percent of overall business. Opportunities for international sales in the gift market are also significant, according to direct sales pioneer 1-800-FLOWERS.

The majority of executives surveyed (39 percent) are focusing their efforts on Europe. Slightly more than one-third will target the Asia/Pacific region, and 31 percent will target Canada. The lower priority given to Latin American and African countries reflects the low level of Internet penetration in the two regions.

Does this mean your website must be multilingual? According to an article in *CIO Web Business* (December 1, 1999, p. 18), English is still the dominant language of the Internet, with the majority of Web users—57.4 percent—speaking English as their native language.

But that may soon change. *Business 2.0* magazine (November 1999, p. 1) says that today 70 percent of websites are based in the United States and most are in English, the language in which 96 percent of all e-commerce is conducted. However, within three years, North America's share of Internet users will be halved to less than 35 percent. Europe is the fastest growing region, expected to have nearly 30 percent of Internet users by 2002. Not far behind Europe is the Asia/Pacific rim, which will have about 22 percent of the world's Internet surfers.

For the immediate future, plan to write and post your Internet documents in English, unless you are a non-U.S. marketer serving your own local country or region (e.g., a German marketer serving German customers).

Typically translating an English marketing document to another language increases the length by 10 to 20 percent. This is a problem with print documents, especially those with tight layouts and no more room on the page. It is not usually a factor in Web marketing where the extra copy length is more easily accommodated.

Push Yourself to Do One More Edit

Here is an easy way to make your online copy at least 10 percent better, sharper, clearer, and more interesting. Before you post the document on your website, run it through your word processor one more time for one last edit.

There is a definite correlation between the number of times a piece of copy is rewritten or edited by its author and the quality of the writing. E. B. White, author of the children's classic *Charlotte's Web*, is said to have revised every book eight or nine times before handing it in to his publisher.

Because the Internet is an "instant publishing" medium, the emphasis is often on speed at the expense of quality for written communication. Today, marketers face the pressure of achieving faster time to market, and that is often accompanied by faster time to publish with marketing communications. Speed is important, but quality counts too, and the trick is to find balance between the two.

Each time you come back to the document after a good night's sleep, you approach it with a fresh eye. As you read and edit, you almost always find ways to make it better—moving a sentence from here to there, cutting an unnecessary word, sharpening a phrase, adding a fact. This one-more-time edit almost always pays off.

In his privately published "Letter to a New Copywriter," Alan Rosenspan advises, "Push yourself. You're probably the very best judge of your own work. You know when you've done a great job, or a not-so-great job. You know when you've tried your hardest, and when you've just coasted. In fact, you're the only one who really knows. And the more you push yourself now, the more successful you'll be, and the faster you'll get there."

If you follow this one-more-edit routine, will your copy reach the peak of perfection? No. It will get better. But almost everything made by the hand of man or woman could always be a little bit better—even if the creator was a master who gave the work his or her very best effort.

But don't despair. "We never write as well as we want to," said copywriter Lou Redmond, "We only write as well as we can.

4

Illustrating Your Web Copy

THE WEB IS a medium with a dynamic visual component, so even if you are a writer, like I am, you can't avoid the subject of illustrating your online writing.

While the technology and file formats of Web graphics are beyond the scope of this book, this chapter will give writers some idea of what visuals they should create or recommend to illustrate their writing.

Visuals communicate at a glance, making it easy for your readers to better understand your message. Always be on the lookout for opportunities where you can supplement text with visuals such as charts, tables, pictures, and other types of information graphics. These add interest to your online publications and help readers quickly and easily grasp relationships, comparisons, and sequences.

Words Versus Pictures

Everyone likes to say that pictures and words are complementary, yet there is often a barely hidden animosity between word people and picture people.

Simply put, many word people (including me) think the words get more of the message across than the pictures. Many of the picture people think the opposite. They believe visuals communicate more effectively than words. "The current generation was raised on TV," they say. "Computer users find words boring. They need graphics and lots of interactivity."

There are two myths concerning words and pictures that have carried over to the online medium. And to communicate effectively online, we must replace myth with truth.

Myth 1: People Don't Read

Anyone who has eyes and looks around can see that this simply isn't true.

There are more than ten thousand newspapers in the United States, eight thousand magazines, more than a million websites, and sixty thousand books published every year. If people didn't read, no one would buy these publications or click onto the websites. Measure activity on your own website. You can see that visitors spend a considerable amount of time on pages that are mostly text.

When folks say, "People don't read," what they really mean is, "People don't have time to read all the stuff they want or even need to read." Eliminating the written word is not the solution. Rather, the challenge is to make your copy interesting, relevant, and concise enough for the prospect to pay attention to it, start reading, and stick with it all the way.

Myth 2: A Picture Is Worth a Thousand Words

There are those who believe that pictures communicate more effectively than words.

The most eloquent debunker of this myth is Rudolf Flesch, and here is what he says on this subject in his classic book *The Art of Readable Writing*:

> "Easy writing's vile hard reading," wrote Sheridan. The reverse is equally true; easy reading is difficult to write. In fact, it seems to be so difficult that most people would rather try anything else but write when they face a job of simple explanation. They escape from words

into pictures, symbols, graphs, charts, diagrams—anything at all as long as it's "visual." They point to the movies, the comics, the picture magazines. Obviously, they say, the trend nowadays is away from reading. People would rather just look.

That may be so; but unfortunately the idea that you can explain things without explaining them in *words* is pure superstition. A favorite proverb of the picture-and-diagram lovers is "One picture is worth more than a thousand words." It simply isn't so. Try to teach people with a picture and you may find that you need a thousand words to tell them exactly what to look at and why.

If that surprises you, look at the evidence. There's the psychologist, for instance, who tried to find out whether children understood the charts and diagrams in the *Britannica Junior Encyclopedia*. It turned out that they did not. Most of the devices used blithely by the encyclopedia writers were way over the heads of the children. They had been taught how to read, but nobody had ever bothered to tell them anything about how to look at flow charts, statistical graphs, process diagrams, and the like. (Unfortunately, the experiment didn't show whether a normal child, reading an encyclopedia, will even stop and look at a diagram. I suspect he won't; the temptation to skip what is baffling is too great.)

Naturally, that doesn't mean that you should never illustrate visually what you have to say. Not at all; anything pictorial or graphic does help *as long as there is enough text to back it up*. I don't mean captions; I mean that the running text has to tell the reader what the illustration means, how he should look at it, and why. Tell the reader what to see. Remember that graph-and-chart reading is not one of the three R's.

Painter, scientist, and Yale professor David Gelertner, writing in *Commentary* (April 2001, pp. 36–37), contends that people are not naturally visual nor have they been properly trained to appreciate visual communication.

"Nearly everyone has been moved by a story at one time or another, but relatively few people have ever been moved by a painting," says Gelertner. "We believe ours to be some sort of visual age, but painting is today the least popular of the arts. For the most part, crowds at big shows barely look at the paintings; there are more people gathered around the signs and labels than the pictures.

"For many of these people, words are easier to read than painted images. Perhaps the human visual sense tends to be poorly developed because we tend not to bother developing it." How can we make sure such people interpret our graphics correctly?

When you show a picture in an html e-mail or website, tell the reader what he is looking at and what it means to him. Do not expect him to draw the impression or conclusion from the visual that you intended; usually he won't.

In addition, it's easy for corporate types using T-1 (a high-speed digital transmitter link) to forget that their customers may not be able to download large multimedia files as quickly as they can. "Don't make your website so complicated that it takes a long time to download," according to direct-marketing copywriter Dennison Hatch. "Go for the lowest common technological denominator. Make up for razzle-dazzle graphics with gripping copy."

Having said that, let's look at the types of visuals you can use to enhance your online documents.

Photographs

Photos are the most obvious visual for the Web. Unlike in print, where four-color process—which duplicates photos in full color—is the most expensive printing method, it costs no more to post a color photo of your product on your site than it does a black and white one. So overwhelmingly, color photos are used on the Web. Millions are posted, a large percentage of which are naked people (but that's another story).

The photo is the most easily understood visual and perhaps the only visual inherently clearer, in some applications, than words. For instance, if you describe an aardvark to someone who has never seen one, the chances are slim that she will develop the same mental picture you have. But show her a photo, and communication of the animal's appearance is complete, accurate, and instantaneous.

People want to see what your product looks like, so show pictures on your website and in your html e-mails. Some buyers will not order the product unless they can see a picture of it on your site.

What else can you illustrate with photos aside from products? Applications, manufacturing, research and development labs, quality control procedures, facilities, personnel, customers using the product, exploded diagrams showing interior components—whatever helps convince the visitor that you're the one he should buy from.

Tables

Tables make it easy for readers to make instant side-by-side comparisons of information organized in rows and columns. Information that would be lost as words in a paragraph becomes obvious when placed in a table.

Table information, or *data*, is placed in cells that occur at the intersections of rows and columns. Tables are often surrounded on all four sides by borders. Internal gridlines separate the cells. Headers identify the information in the individual rows and columns.

When formatting tables, use the minimum number of graphic elements necessary to organize the data. Often, major improvements in the appearance of a table can be achieved by eliminating unnecessary borders and gridlines. Other times, you can improve contrast by reversing headers.

Another way you can improve the appearance of tables is by using shaded backgrounds (or fills). These can be placed behind alternating rows or columns, or groups of two or five rows or columns. Shaded fills behind rows guide the reader's eyes horizontally across the table so they don't lose their place as they search for information associated with each row's header.

Last name	First name	Mailbox	Phone	E-mail
Anderson	Peggy	Landsdown 321	555-0308	panders@firm.com
Billings	William	Harlow 445	555-1319	wbilling@firm.com
Caslon	William	Type Hall 110	555-1233	wcaslon@firm.com
Dartmouth	Peter	Hitchcock 201	555-1414	pdartmou@firm.com
Exeter	Gary	Landsdown 409	555-0101	gexeter@firm.com
Fairfield	Susan	Harlow 600	555-0091	sfairfie@firm.com
Hills	Juan	Type Hall 211	555-0090	jhills@firm.com
Norma	Wilson	Landsdown 408	555-0200	Nwilson@firm.com
Parker	Roger	Empire 100	555-0000	Rparker@firm.com

Categories

Categories can be considered a simplified form of tables. Categories help pave the way for a more in-depth analysis to follow, providing a useful overview. Unlike tables, categories don't tell the whole story, they just provide a visual frame of reference for the information to be described in greater detail in the adjacent text.

Accented Points

Accented point graphs are yet another table variation, one that permits you to visually introduce categories that summarize the impor-

ACCENTED POINTS	
Accentuates the main points	
Economy	No down payment required 60-month financing available Fuel economy: 18 mph city, 26 mph highway
Economy	0 to 60, 5.8 seconds Standard 4-wheel ABS 4-wheel drive and traction available
Economy	Air conditioning and heated seats Power sunroof 1,000-watt audio with 12-disc CD player

tant points to be discussed in the adjacent body copy. At a glance, readers can catch the high points of information that would otherwise not lend itself to an interesting visual display.

Circle Ratings

Circle ratings are another type of business graphic based on the row and column arrangement found in tables. Circle ratings use omitted,

CIRCLE RATINGS					
Compare products at a glance					
	Color	Bouquet	Flavor	Selection	Value
California	◒	○	◒	◒	●
Washington State	◒	●	◒	◒	●
Oregon	○	◒	◒	○	○
France	◒	◒	●	●	○

empty, filled or partially filled-in circles to communicate quality comparisons at a glance. The goal is to introduce and summarize the items being compared and provide a quick overview of how they perform in important areas.

Pro and Con Charts

Pro and con charts permit you to quickly compare the advantages and disadvantages of two sides of an issue, introducing and summarizing points discussed in detail in the adjacent body copy. Pro and con charts simplify complex arguments and direct attention to key conclusions. You can add color to the oversized plus and minus signs introducing each argument to add further interest to your print or online page.

PROS & CONS	
For highlighting two sides of an issue	
Advantages	**Disadvantages**
+ Few competitors + High profit margins + Opens new markets + Increases stock value + Resell past customers	− High initial investment − Unproven technology − Time to market

Quadrants

Quadrants permit you to compare multiple product or performance characteristics. Two-dimensional quadrant charts allow products to be positioned along an X-Y axis. In many cases, the X, or vertical, axis ranges from inexpensive to expensive while the horizontal axis displays performance attributes—such as miles-per-hour, miles-per-gallon, uncomfortable to comfortable, and so forth.

As an option, the circles representing each brand can be drawn larger or smaller depending on yet a third characteristic, such as market share.

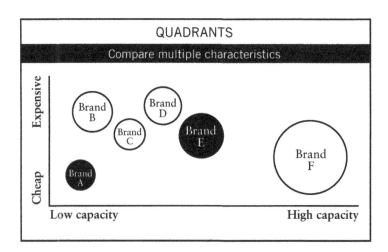

Using Visuals to Display Relationships

There are several ways you can visually represent relationships. These relationships can be hierarchical or sequential. Or, the visuals can display cause and effect relationships.

The information graphics permit you to visually represent relationships that you can discuss in greater detail in the adjacent body copy. In these cases, the information graphic adds visual interest to otherwise boring pages, acting as "advertisements" attracting your reader's interest and making your message more memorable.

Organization Charts Display Hierarchy

Organization charts permit you to display an organization's structure; who is responsible to whom. There are two types of organization charts.

The standard organization chart emphasizes departments or positions. The structure of even the most complicated organization can be understood at a glance. When the focus is on positions, the names of the individuals may or may not be displayed.

Team charts are a more sophisticated form of organization chart. These display not only the structure of an organization but also the names of the individuals who are responsible to each department or

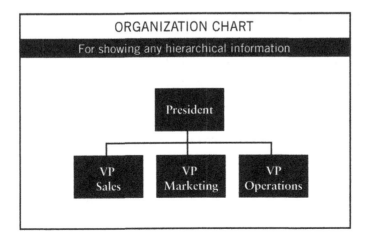

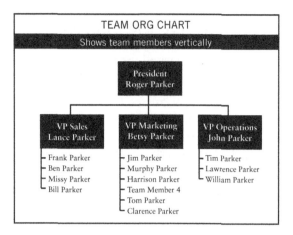

division head. By omitting boxes and just listing names next to vertical lines, team charts make it easier to read the names.

Consider a combination of organization and team charts. Use a simplified organization chart to provide an overview of your firm's structure. But, because organization charts can often become complicated and hard to read (i.e., as the number of layers in an organization chart goes up, the type size goes down), break the big chart up into smaller, individual team charts.

Use the organization chart to provide an overview of your firm's structure and use two, or more, individual team charts to show specific departments or divisions.

Visuals That Communicate Sequence

There are several types of visuals that can help your reader visualize sequence or cause-and-effect events. Employing these graphics will not only add visual interest to proposals and formal business documents, but they will also emphasize your message and make it more memorable.

You can greatly enhance your online publication's ability to communicate the order in which events occur by using visuals like flow charts, cycle charts, Gantt charts, and time lines. These visuals greatly simplify your message and attract readers who might not otherwise read the body copy.

Flow Chart

A flow chart is the easiest way to represent time relationships between events. Flow charts simplify complex processes and help readers understand procedures that take place only once.

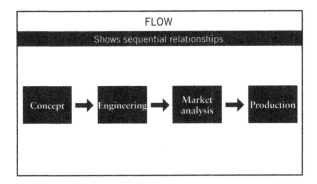

Cycle Chart

Use a cycle chart to emphasize repeating procedures that begin again after the last step has taken place. The completion of one cycle begins another.

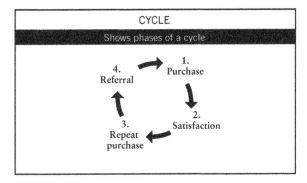

Gantt Chart

Gantt charts help you communicate when procedures take place. Gantt charts not only show the order in which steps occur but also how long each step takes. Completion dates are automatically updated if steps take longer or shorter.

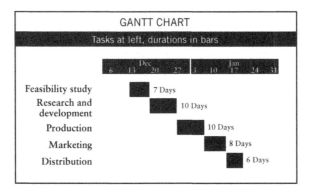

Time Line

Time lines permit you to visually communicate a historical perspective showing the order events took place and the environmental (i.e., competitive, economic, social, or historical) events that were occurring at the time.

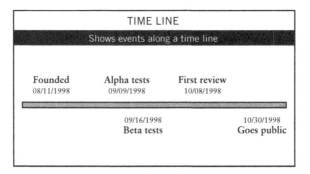

Although often displayed horizontally, time lines can be organized vertically.

Visuals That Represent Cause and Effect

In addition to hierarchy and sequence, information graphics can be used to display the environment in which an event occurs as well as cause and effect relationships.

Orbit Chart

An orbit chart allows you to display the environment in which an event or a procedure takes place. Orbit charts display the various forces acting on an individual, government, or business. For example, a business is influenced by the world economy, the weather, competition, and government regulations.

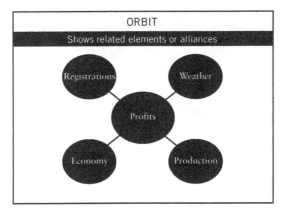

Flow-In Chart

A flow-in chart displays the resources or inputs needed for something to happen—for example, a concert to be performed, a meeting to take place, a sale to be made. A flow-in chart can illustrate the necessary requirements for the successful completion of a project or procedure.

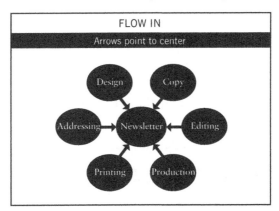

Flow-Out Chart

A flow-out chart displays individuals or groups of people who are influenced by an event, product, or service. It can describe the buyers of a product, the readers of a publication, or the market segments who purchase a product or service.

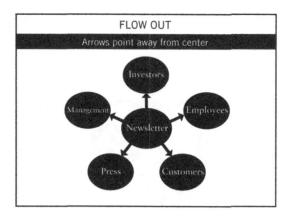

Creating Visual Metaphors

You can create visual metaphors by replacing words with visuals. These help you translate words into visual concepts and can add a great deal of eye appeal to your online document.

More important, when you translate words into visuals, you drive home the importance of the message you want to communicate. The following types of information graphics can be considered metaphors because they visually represent the meaning of the message they communicate.

Triad

Choose a triad when you want to emphasize three words of equal importance. A triad emphasizes the three important points you want to make and demonstrates that the three words (or phrases) are of equal importance.

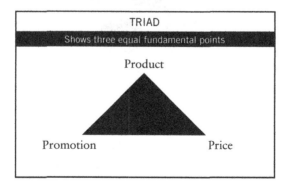

Pyramid

Use a pyramid when you want your ideas to visually build upon each other. Whereas the elements of a triad are of equal importance, a pyramid prioritizes your ideas and makes it easy to identify which ones are fundamental to those that build upon them.

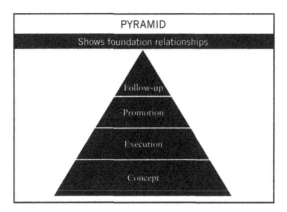

Puzzle

Use a puzzle to represent interlocking ideas. The puzzle emphasizes that no one idea, or component of a process, is more important than the others; the whole is the sum of the parts. Triads, pyramids, and puzzles can create visual themes.

For example, you can show the entire puzzle on your website's home page. Then each main page contains a graphic of the piece of the puzzle that applies to it.

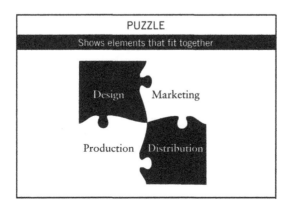

Number Charts and Graphs

Numbers make for boring reading. It is very difficult to gauge the importance of numbers contained within paragraphs of body copy or to evaluate their importance or relationship to other numbers.

The starting point for translating numbers into visuals is to choose the right type of chart or graph. Each type of chart or graph is best suited for representing a different type of information.

Pie Chart

Use pie charts to represent part-whole relationships. Pie charts make it easy for readers to evaluate the relative importance of each slice representing the various elements that make up the whole.

Pie charts use different colors, shades of gray, or textures to represent each slice.

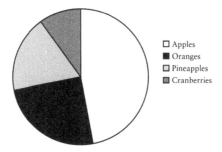

The legend, which can be located above, below, or to the left or right of the pie chart, helps readers understand the information represented in each slice.

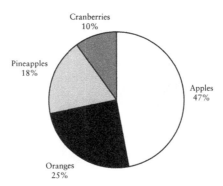

You can improve the appearance of your pie charts by keeping information as close to the slices as possible. For example, if size permits, replace the legend with data labels adjacent to each slice. These can indicate both the information displayed as well as the quantity or percentage of the whole the slice represents.

Using data labels helps readers avoid having to glance back and forth between the chart and the legend to understand the significance of each of the slices.

Titles are an easy way to enhance all types of charts and graphs. Never leave it up to your readers to figure out the significance of your chart or graph. Consider using borders and white space to isolate and draw attention to them.

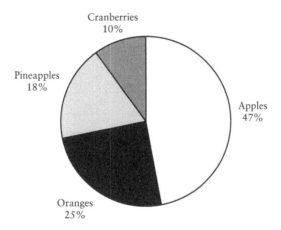

MOST POPULAR FRUITS AMONG
COLLEGE STUDENTS

Cranberries
10%

Pineapples
18%

Apples
47%

Oranges
25%

Avoid pie charts containing too many slices. This results in small slices that can easily get lost. Most charting software programs permit you to create a call-out bar or pie chart which groups together the smallest segments of the pie chart.

Bar Chart

Use horizontal bar charts to display side-by-side categories of information. Bar charts without data labels help readers make relative comparisons.

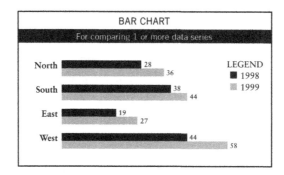

Add data labels to the bars if the exact quantity displayed by the bar is important to your message.

As always, keep your chart as simple as possible by eliminating as many unnecessary horizontal and vertical grid lines as possible. Often, white space between the data series is sufficient to organize the chart.

Stacked Bar Chart

A stacked bar chart is a more sophisticated form that permits you to display relative contributions as well as totals. A stacked bar chart, for example, can show not only the total performance of each of your

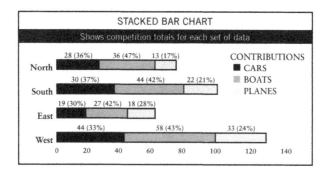

sales territories but also the relative contribution various products made to each territory's sales.

Column Chart

A column chart is ideal for showing changes of multiple variables over time.

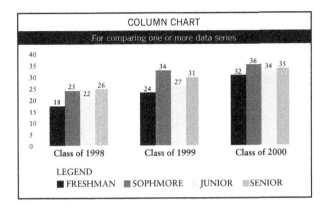

Again, a legend is used to identify each column and you can add data labels if the exact numbers are important to your message.

White space and logical proximity improve the appearance of column charts.

By selectively grouping columns and adding extra white space between categories, you can create simple, yet effective charts without the clutter often caused by unnecessary vertical grid lines.

Line Chart

A line, or fever, chart shows changes in data over time. Without data labels, trends become easily obvious. Different colored lines indicate each data series. If you add data labels, you can review the exact quantities displayed at each interval. Depending on the image you want to

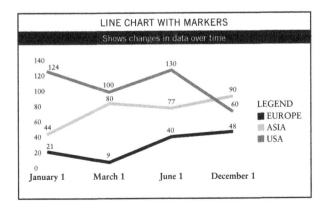

communicate, you can use curved, instead of straight lines to link the data points.

To avoid confronting your readers with charts that resemble spaghetti, however, limit yourself to a maximum of six lines—preferably fewer.

Area Chart

Use an area chart to emphasize changes in quantity, totals, or volume. Area charts combine the characteristics of stacked columns and line charts. You can observe the trends over time as well as the relative contributions made by different products, profit centers, or departments.

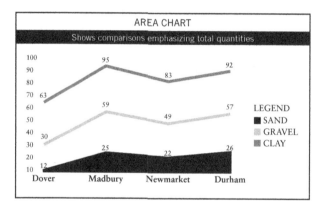

Start by adding the data series with the lowest values. Narrow elements look best grouped at the bottom of the chart rather than at the top.

Other Chart Options

There are several specialized types of charts and graphs that you should consider using, especially if your design work is financial or highly technical:

• **High-low charts** to display changes in data over fixed time periods. (Use the area option to emphasize the range of data.) Note: many software programs permit you to add bars to display opening and closing prices.

• **Radar charts** permit you to display information plotted against a number of criteria (for example product comparisons or survey results). Avoid radar charts with multiple comparisons when results are similar, as the chart elements may overlap each other.

• **Scattered point charts** show the relationship between sets of data to identify patterns. (Most software programs permit you to connect the points or add trend lines to emphasize the direction of change.)

Making the Most of Number Charts and Graphs

Simplicity is always a virtue when working with charts and graphs. The fewer elements you include, the easier it will be for readers to understand your message.

One of the biggest challenges you face is eliminating clutter, which can consist of unnecessary horizontal or vertical grid lines or tick marks. Tick marks can be added to the vertical axis of a chart to indicate increments between the major divisions indicated by grid lines. For example, if your chart contains grid lines at increments of 100, you can add tick marks to the inside of the vertical axis at increments of 10, and tick marks along the outside of the vertical axis at increments of 50.

Be careful when using the three-dimensional capabilities of your charting or graphing program. Although three-dimensional charts and

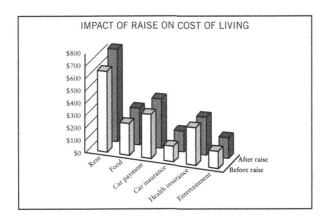

graphs can be very eye-catching, they often distort the chart's message. Small elements located along the front of the chart can become exaggerated in size. Three-dimensional charts can also hide information that gets pushed behind foreground elements.

Small, hard-to-read data labels are always a problem. When data labels are added to the columns of a chart, they often are both hard to read and detract from the reader's ability to get an overall view of the trend.

The solution to cluttered data labels is to slightly reduce the chart or graph's size and include the data in a table next to the chart. This gives readers the option of looking at the chart to gain an overall view of the trends, then analyzing the detailed data in the table. The combination of a simplified chart and an easy-to-read table permits both comparisons and detailed analysis.

Once you get in the habit of supplementing text with visuals, you'll undoubtedly notice more and more opportunities to do so.

For example, if you find yourself describing a schedule of upcoming events, instead of listing the events and their dates in text paragraphs, create a calendar showing the dates when important events occur. The calendar will help your readers relate "event" to "date" at a glance.

To add impact to your calendar, use a black or colored background to emphasize the important dates and reverse the date and text describing the event. Use a bold, sans-serif typeface to help the text stand out.

More information on creating charts and graphs can be found in Roger C. Parker's *One-Minute Designer*.

Flash Presentations

As a computer user, you occasionally (but with increasing frequency) see presentations that are dynamic—that is, that incorporate animation and sound, much like a video or a movie.

The most common of these is the Flash presentation, which is a short animated audiovisual presentation made and viewed using a program called Shockwave.

If you have ever written a video, a Flash presentation is not much different. Unlike CD-ROMs, which are often interactive, Flash presentations usually play straight through like a PowerPoint slide show or a video. The running time is short, typically one to three minutes.

To justify the time, effort, and expense of creating a Flash presentation, it should ideally use the animation to illustrate, dramatize, or explain a point, concept, or feature more effectively than could be done on a static Web page or print document.

For example, in writing a Flash presentation on submarine fiber-optic networks, I used stock video of ocean-floor footage to dramatize the great depths at which these networks are installed under the sea.

In another Flash presentation on a different fiber-optic network, the main sales point was that the dispersion of optical signals was reduced by the fiber, resulting in a clearer signal over a longer distance. To illustrate the concept of dispersion, I showed a video of drops of ink falling into a beaker and being stirred.

Many advocates of Flash presentations recommend using them simply because they are animated and therefore different and attention-getting. But the visitors going to your site are actively seeking information on a particular topic, so using a Flash presentation simply for the sake of being different may actually annoy them—Flash presentations are not as informative and as easy to follow as clearly written html pages.

As with other Web techniques—links, streaming video, streaming audio—Flash should only be used when it communicates a concept more engagingly and powerful than a straight text-and-graphics page would.

For instance, in one script, I had to make the point that an industrial spray dryer atomized the liquid, creating a fine mist. The benefit was that the small droplets had a large combined surface area, making the chemical reaction take place faster and more completely.

I asked the product manager how much surface area would be created by atomizing a gallon of water using the system. It turned out that running ten gallons of liquid would create a total surface area equivalent to a football field. In order to dramatize this, I showed a ten-gallon fish tank—an image everyone can relate to. We then showed the liquid being poured into the spray dryer and the spray dryer operating. We then cut to a video of a football field. Narration explained to the viewer that the ten gallons, atomized into mist, had the combined surface area of the field.

Most audiovisual scriptwriters prefer a two-column format, with the visual in the left column and the audio in the right (see Figure 4.1). You do not need special script-writing software, although such software is available; you can simply use a two-column page format in Word.

When you are writing the visual portion, turn your mind into a mental movie camera. View the images as if you were a camera oper-

Visual	Audio
Title—"Optical Fiber Networks by Lucent Technologies"—against a background of blue sky	MUSIC
Camera dives below clouds into a crowded city with lots of roads, traffic, and buildings.	Whether it's dense metro area networks serving millions of users in crowded cities . . .
Camera flies out of city over country-side and mountains	. . . . long haul networks crossing thousands of miles . . .
Camera zooms out over ocean, then below surface and down to ocean floor	. . . . or submarine networks dives operating at the crushing depths of the ocean floor . . .
Picture of fiberoptic cable with split ends lit up.	You can bet that Lucent Technologies—the world leader in fiberoptics—makes a cable that's right for the job.

Figure 4.1 Portion of a Sample Script for a Flash Presentation

ator on a film crew. "As writer of the script, you have to show the client—and through them, the audience—the images that make up the story you want to tell," writes Barry Hampe in his book *Video Scriptwriting*. "You'll write a lot of words in the script to describe the pictures the audience will see."

In the video column of your script, don't be afraid to give very specific directions to the art director or programmer producing your script. Indicate when you want to zoom in, zoom out, have a close-up, pan, or other camera angles. Take the time to describe scenes, colors, and special effects in detail. The result will be a finished Flash presentation that more closely represents what you envisioned in your mind's eye when you wrote it.

When you have finished your script, read the audio portion aloud. Doing so helps you catch phrases that look OK in print but sound awkward when spoken. Edit to smooth the language so the reading sounds complete natural, with no awkward phrases or transitions. Even better, have someone else read it aloud; this reading will shine a painful spotlight on any remaining awkwardness.

PART II

WEB COPYWRITING TASKS

THIS SECTION GIVES copywriting tips for specific online marketing documents. Chapters 5 through 7 cover websites, Chapter 8 details e-mail marketing, and Chapter 9 deals with online advertising. In Chapter 10, you learn how to write and publish an electronic newsletter, or e-zine, Chapter 11 covers Web documents and special considerations for technology marketers. In Chapter 12, you'll learn how to write promotions that drive traffic to your website.

5

Creating an Effective Website

FOR MOST ONLINE marketers, their website is the centerpiece of their Internet marketing program. In fact, because the most effective response mechanism to an online promotion is to send the prospect to a website, not having one significantly reduces the response rates to banner ads, e-mail, and other Internet marketing efforts.

What's in a (Domain) Name?

The first step in establishing a Web presence and building a website is to select and register your domain name. Choosing a domain name is not a trivial decision; it is as important as coming up with a strong company or product name.

According to a recent article in *CIO Web Business*, there are more than 550 billion individual pages posted on the World Wide Web. Network Solutions, a major online registration service, registered 840,000 domain names last year alone.

Although the Internet presents users with a wonderful tool for research, entertainment, communication, and commerce, we are faced today with the problems of clutter and overload. There is too much information for the consumer to digest, too many websites competing for his attention, and too many online stores and brands competing for his dollars.

For this reason, online marketers are—quite appropriately—incredibly choosy about the domain names they adopt for their websites. The domain name is an essential element—perhaps the most essential—in establishing and communicating an online brand.

Businesses tend to gravitate toward a particular domain name for three major reasons.

1. **Positioning and branding.** It might be a variation of their product name or product category.

2. **Association.** The Internet marketer believes Internet surfers would go to the name when looking for information on that specific topic. For instance, a porn site operator might register topless.com based on the assumption that Web surfers looking for a pornography site would try that URL.

3. **Memorability.** The Internet marketer believes that visitors will find the domain name easy to remember. This is the reason why a printer with a four-color press might decide to register the domain name colorprinting.com.

Choosing Your Domain Name

What makes for a good name on a website? Debate rages, but here are three criteria that are hard to disagree with:

1. **Memorable.** Why is an online bookstore called Amazon.com? Simply because it's easy to remember. Same thing with the portal called Yahoo!

2. **Logical.** Another tactic that works is to select a name that logically ties in with what you do. Some examples include printing.com for a printer and flowers.com for a florist. Or, simply make the domain name the same as your company name. For example, IBM's domain name is IBM.com. And Sprint Graphics, a New York City printer, uses sprintgraphics.com.

3. **Short.** Some marketers prefer longer domain names because they can be more descriptive. For instance, one printer has a website printingforless.com. It gets a message across, but will you really remember that when you are online and need printing? Although domain names can be as long as sixty-seven characters, shorter—like printer.com—is better. Think about the website URLs you can recall off the top of your head without going to your bookmarks. How many of them are more than one word long? It's no coincidence that one of the most popular online retailers is Amazon.com.

As for what not to do, just a couple of tips:

• Try to avoid having and in a domain name. I can never remember if it's Barnes&Noble.com or BarnesandNoble.com. I bet lots of other folks can't either.

• Having the last letter of your first word the same as the first letter of your last word also creates problems, because people can't figure out whether to use the letter once or twice. To convert my name into a domain name, would people be more apt to think bobly.com or bobbly.com? I solved the problem by registering the shorter and simpler bly.com. People frequently comment on how easy it is to remember.

• Make sure your URL is easy to say. People will remember it if it's repeated on TV commercials, plastered on billboards, or sung in a radio jingle. Sheraton had great success promoting a toll-free reservations number with a catchy TV jingle. Can you remember? "Eight-oh-oh, three-*two*-five; three-five, three-five."

• Avoid domain names that are difficult to remember or figure out how to spell. If your last name is Pasterittinelli, avoid pasterittin elli.com. People are likely to get confused and try pastteritineli.com or pasteritineli.com.

You can't copyright, patent, or register human names and book titles, which means multiple people can have the same name, and different books can have the same title.

But domain names, like phone numbers, are unique. So when in doubt, it pays to register any name you might want and hold it, rather than risk letting it go to someone else. Register your Internet domain name early. When in doubt about a name, register it anyway.

But if someone else registers the name you want, you may have to pay dearly to get the individual to sell it to you. Recently, drugs.com sold for $823,456. And a Texas entrepreneur recently sold business .com to a California company for $7.5 million. Two years earlier, he had bought the name from someone else for $150,000.

According to an article in *Business 2.0* (August 22, 2000, p. 32), a Scandinavian financial services company recently spent more than $1 million to register 3,080 domain names. "While registering thousands of names may be unusual, many large companies do log all possible combinations of their names and product—including possible misspellings," the article notes.

Some marketers, finding the domain name they want is already taken, do a close variation with a small typographical change. For instance, WorldclassMedia.com of Australia used attmexico.com, which gives the impression of being from AT&T.

According to *Writer's Digest* (March 2001, p. 48), under current trademark law, a domain name is not a trademark. Using the domain name does not automatically make it a trademark. If this is your intention, search trademark records to see whether the domain name has already been licensed. This can be done on idnames.com. If the domain name is not being used as a trademark, an application should be filed.

Will we ever run out of good domain names the way we exhausted the supply of available 800 numbers? Network Solutions registers a new domain name every 3.9 seconds. So the shorter, more logical-sounding .com domain names are rapidly being taken.

But there is another solution: registering the same domain name you wanted as a .com with an alternative extension. These alternatives include Top Level Domain names (TLDs) and Country Code Top Level Domain (CCTLD) names. The latter are available on the Network Solutions site idnames.com.

Right now, the major domain name suffixes—the letters after the last period—are .com, .org, and .edu. These suffixes are TLDs.

At a recent meeting in Japan, the Internet Corporation for Assigned Names and Numbers (ICANN) said it will create new TLDs to be determined, making many more domain names possible. They are even running radio commercials advertising the new TLDs on the Howard Stern radio show!

If consult.com is taken, maybe you can grab *consult* with one of the new TLDs when they become available. These include .biz, .info, .aero, .pro, and .museum.

But as always on the domain name front, it's first come, first served.

A far bigger inventory of alternative extensions is the CCTLDs. These are extensions you can get based on the name of the nation from which the domain originates. But in dozens of cases, you do not have to have a physical presence or even operate in that country to use their domain name extension. CCTLDs are plentiful and available for registration even as you read this.

There are 243 country-specific domain extensions (such as .de for Germany, .fr for France, .jp for Japan). These domains have been in existence for many years, but in the past several years have become popular in local areas and as a way for cybersquatters and potential competitors to cause confusion in top Internet markets. In fact, total registrations in CCTLDs have increased from just under one million in 1998 to nearly four million in early 2000, a jump which until last year had gone relatively unnoticed.

One possible reason for the rapid increase is because ICANN's dispute policy is not used or adopted by any country code as of this writing. Each country is free to register domain names in any manner they see fit. In fact, a 1999 study concluded that only half of the top twenty-five country-code registries even have a formal dispute policy. The half that do have a policy merely stating that "all disputes are between the parties." In summary: "See you in court."

The delegated 243 country-code domains are not all controlled by sovereigns, although a fair number of these CCTLDs are issued by tiny islands that barely qualify as having nation status. Typically, an Internet entrepreneur with deep funding approaches the nation, offering to market its CCTLD for domain name registration in exchange for part of the revenues—which these poor nations sorely need. It's a win-win situation for the entrepreneur, the domain name buyers, and the country.

The country-code domains can be classified as follows. Of the 243 assigned country codes, 184 are actively registering names. Of the 184 active country codes, 100 are classified as "restricted" and require a local presence or specific legal documentation in order to register (China, Japan, and France, for example).

The remaining 84 are classified as free market or "unrestricted." Anyone from anywhere can register, just like in the .com, .net, and .org domains. No local presence is needed. Examples include the United Kingdom, Mexico, Denmark, Israel, and South Africa.

To further confuse you, some countries require that applicants register in specific subdomains. In other words, in the United Kingdom, one must register as "name.co.uk"; the .co being reserved for commercial interests in the United Kingdom domain. It would not be possible to register as "name.uk."

In other countries, like Mexico, one must register as "name.com .mx," the .com part having nothing to do with the well-known .com generic domain. In Germany, there are no subdomains, so all must register as "name.de." These naming conventions have not stopped an onslaught of registration and marketing activity in these domains.

Why don't more organizations register a CCTLD in the United States (.us) domain? Because the .us domain is among the least marketing-friendly domains on the planet.

All domains registered must be geographically specific. One must register as name.city.state.us. It is not possible to register name.us. Obviously an address like name.city.state.us would be certainly hard to market and remember. Thus the .us domain is seldom used by serious marketers and has little commercial value.

You may have heard about the .cc domain. Contrary to some reports, it is not new. It has been around for years, just like .com and the other 242 domain extensions. What is new is how it's being marketed—as an alternative to .com for those that could not get their choice of names in the .com domain.

The .cc country code is delegated to and associated with the Cocos and Keeling Islands, located one thousand miles northwest of

Australia. The .cc domain has attracted a small number of registrants compared to "name-brand" country codes like Germany and the United Kingdom, places where people actually live and buy things over the Internet.

Because many nations actively market their own country-code domains, or have Internet entrepreneurs do it for them, certain names are becoming more visible and popular than others. Moldova, for example, is fortunate to have as its domain extension .md. This domain extension is, for obvious reasons, a popular choice with medical and health care websites. The small island nation of Micronesia has the extension .fm, which is naturally appealing to FM radio stations establishing their own websites. Western Samoa's .ws, which has the same initials as website (WS), is being touted as a direct substitute for .com. Niue, another small nation, has the domain .nu, which connotes "new" and is being marketed on that basis. The small nation of Tuzalu is actively marketing its CCTLD, .tv, especially for new economy and media-oriented websites.

Other CCTLDs now being aggressively marketed include Romania (.ro), Russia (.ru), the Dominican Republic (.do), Mexico (.mx), and Tonga (.to).

Keep Your Site's Objective in Mind

The tone and content of your website copy should be consistent with its marketing objective.

According to Network Solutions, there are five stages of website evolution. Each calls for a slightly different copy approach.

Stage One: Online Identity

Sixty-three percent of the 840,000 domain names Network Solutions registered one year ago are in stage one. These companies have their Web address and perhaps have some rudimentary home page posted, but nothing beyond that.

These rudimentary home pages should have a banner exclaiming, "Website under construction." The copy should explain that the URL is the future Web home of your company, give a brief overview of your organization and what you offer, and encourage the visitor to return when the site is completed.

Stage Two: Billboard Website

Approximately 31 percent of sites registered with Network Solutions are in this stage and are often called "promotional sites." They contain general company or product information, but do not allow visitors to order online.

The copy tone of these pages should be similar to a well-written sales sheet or brochure, only more concise. Highlight the features, benefits, and applications of the products described. Give product description, service details, options, and reasons why people should buy.

Stage Three: E-Commerce Enabled

Four percent of sites are truly e-commerce enabled. These allow visitors to order directly on the Web. Obvious examples are Amazon.com and cdnow.com. For your site to be in stage three, add an order mechanism, such as a shopping cart or an online order form. (See Chapter 7.) Also add buttons and banners that announce discounts, monthly sales, specials, and other incentives to buy now instead of later.

Stage Four: Provide E-Commerce and Customer Relationship Management

About 1 percent of companies are using their site to develop and maintain a relationship with their customers. Sites in this stage have Web-enabled key business processes on an intranet or extranet—for instance, allowing distributors to check product inventory online.

Good copy in print usually has a warm, personal, me-to-you tone, and this friendly, conversational style should be used in all websites, but especially for those in stage four. Technology that allows for personalization is one facet of building good customer relationships on the Web and copy that delivers it framed in helpful, encouraging words is another. Table 5.1 shows a variety of ideas implemented by stage-four websites.

Table 5.1 Ideas for E-Commerce Websites

Category	Marketing idea	Concept	Example
Enhanced Selling Process	Customer Input	The involvement of customers in our development process will lead to better new products.	Ford has put its design studio online to obtain the feedback of selected customers.
	Customer Targeting	Tracking customer status enables us to offer the relevant product, at the relevant time.	Amazon.com notifies customers of new book-buying options based on a profile of their previous purchases.
	Customer Aggregation	We have the ability to reach and serve a geographically dispersed customer segment.	eHobbies uses the Internet as a channel to reach model-train enthusiasts around the world.
	Benefit Selling	We can improve the way we illustrate to the customer the benefits our product provides.	Timex provides a downloadable simulation of its novel i-Control watch-setting system.
	Achievement Selling	Loyalty is strengthened when we show customers our track record of meeting commitments.	W. W. Grainger tracks and documents savings made by its corporate customers for maintenance supplies.
Enhanced Customer Buying Experience	Solutions-Specifier Proposition	We advise customers on the types of products required to meet their needs.	Home Depot provides customers with everything that they will need to carry out their do-it-yourself project.
	One-Stop Shopping Proposition	Through links with providers of complementary products, we meet more of the customer's needs.	Office Depot links to sites such as stamps .com, TelePost.com to increase its coverage of overall customer needs.

(continued)

Table 5.1 (continued)

Category	Marketing idea	Concept	Example
	System-Design Proposition	Our facilities enable the customer to design the overall system to which our products contribute.	Herman Miller's "room planner" enables design of new furniture for existing office layouts.
	Fastest-Source Proposition	We offer the customers the best chance of getting what they want quickly, with minimum hassle.	The core of Amazon .com's book-buying proposition and many other Internet offerings.
	Product-Specifier Proposition	We help customers understand the optimal product specifications for their needs.	Lands' End allows the customers to create a "personal model" on which they can test the fit and look of clothing.
	Tailored-Product Proposition	We rapidly deliver to the customer's individual product specification.	Chipshot.com allows expert golfers to configure clubs to their own preferred specification.
Enhanced Customer Usage Experience	Added-Service Proposition	As well as providing product, we help improve some aspect of the customer's operational activity.	Lonely Planet publications provides an online "travel vault" for storage of travelers' critical information.
	Tailored-Support Proposition	The support services for our products are tailored to reflect the customer's needs and practices.	A Dell corporate customer has a "Premier Page" online for users to access the agreed level of support.

Stage Five: Offer Service Application Model

The final 1 percent of websites are in this category. These sites use the most advanced Internet technologies to offer real-time business processing for functions such as financial management and human resources. Clarity is a requisite of any piece of copy and is especially important here: If your text does not clearly explain how to use the systems, you will get lots of user complaints and low levels of satisfaction.

Write Copy to Fit the Buyer's Mood and Intent

According to an article in the *MIT Sloan Management Review* (Winter 2001, p. 8), website visitors fall into one of the following four categories.

1. **Directed-purchase visitors.** These consumers are ready to purchase right away. Banners and buttons advertising "Special of the Month" and "Order Now" work well. Insert a link to the order mechanism on every page.

2. **Search-and-deliberation visitors.** These consumers are searching for the merchandise and terms with the intention to purchase in the near future. Include plenty of facts and specs in a clear presentation, such as a table or bulleted list. Make sure you show everything the prospect needs to know to make a purchase; if you leave out a key spec and your competitor's website has it, the shopper will buy from them.

3. **Hedonic-browsing visitors.** These consumers are doing electronic window-shopping—that is, shopping for pleasure or recreation. Add some fun to your website. Some examples are photos of attractive models or beautiful locations, games, quizzes, contests, incentives, interactive tools.

4. **Knowledge-building visitors.** This consumer is engaged in exploratory browsing to learn more about the marketplace. Add

how-to and educational resources to your website. For example, a website selling vitamins and nutritional supplements should have a library of articles on alternative medicine relating to the products being sold. Also consider adding a community of interest, such as a forum or chat room, where people can congregate to discuss the topic of your site.

Account for Different Communications Styles

In the offline world, we are taught that different people communicate in different ways. Some like to read; others prefer pictures; others prefer hands-on activities. To maximize communication, deliver your message to the individual in the manner in which he learns best.

In the online world, people also absorb information in different ways, as outlined in Table 5.2. In an article in *Target Marketing* magazine, Cliff Blake writes, "Good human interface design should embrace all these styles and should be redundant enough to allow people a choice of how they will interact with the system depending on circumstances. Most people use all these different browsing styles at one time or another, but one generally predominates over others, and people approach new and unfamiliar sites using that style." Design your site so there is something for everyone. Don't limit it to bulleted lists just because that's how *you* like to take in information. What about the prospect who prefers diagrams?

Write What Your Prospects Want to Know

Any website whose purpose is to sell must, to be effective, have these two components:

1. Information your prospects need to know in order to buy from you.

2. Information you know that will convince prospects to buy from you.

Table 5.2 Web Browsing Styles and Presentation Techniques

Style	What they like	Website layout tips
Artist	Artists are graphical users. It's easier for them to find what they're looking for from a picture than from a list of words.	Lay out text in digestible chunks to please these users, giving them space between text blocks for visual relief.
Writer	It's easier for writers to find what they're looking for from a list of words than from a picture.	Be sure graphics don't delay your load times. Don't make these users derive meaning from graphics; tell them in words.
Explorer	Explorers like to take time to investigate their surroundings. Most people are explorers the first time they enter a site.	Give explorers plenty of content. They like many different areas to visit.
Seeker	Seekers want to go in, get what they want, and get out again in the shortest time. People familiar with a site tend to become seekers.	Give seekers one-click access to what they want whenever possible. Your most valuable repeat visitors are very likely to behave as seekers.
Recognizer	Recognizers like to pick from a list rather than coming up with tactics on their own.	Be sure to include pull-down menus of choices, and charts for product comparisons, to please recognizers.
Requester	Requesters like to be in control. They prefer to type in their request.	Include fields in which these users can type in requests.
Verifier	Verifiers are analysts. They will test each feature on your site, and will e-mail you with suggestions and changes.	Keep your content current, accurate, and synchronized. Check the quality of your site thoroughly.

The information your prospects need to know is what the serious potential buyer is likely to ask for, including:

- **An overview of your products or services**—This is usually found on your home page or an "about us" page.
- **Pages on individual products and services**—One per product should do the trick.
- **Additional product information**—This might include specs, features, options, accessories, models, ratings, or upgrades.
- **Customers**—Who buys from you?
- **Projects**—What are some of the major projects your firm has handled?
- **Applications**—What applications is your product used for? What industries do you serve?
- **Testimonials**—Are customers satisfied? What do they say about you?

Product information can be provided in several ways. A common technique is to post product brochures on the site.

Converting a printed color brochure to an html file can sometimes be tricky. One company used typography printed over color photos in their printed brochures, which was difficult to read when put on a Web page.

The Web designer changed the design for the html versions, so that the copy was taken off the photo background and printed in black against a white background next to the pictures for greater legibility.

In industrial companies, it is common to photocopy product brochures and circulate copies to different decision makers while evaluating potential vendors. If you serve such a market, consider posting your product data sheets as pdf files which, when printed, look remarkably similar to a printed brochure.

Allow viewers to "drill down" to the level of detail they need. One chemical company has links in its product brochures to Material Safety Data, or MSDs, that describe the safe handling of each chemical they sell. A prospect with a particular safety concern can get her question immediately answered by accessing the MSD sheets online.

Why Should Customers Buy from You and Not Your Competitors?

Your website should not only contain everything the prospect wants and needs to know about you—but also everything *you want to tell them.*

There are certain facts and pieces of information that prospects may not look for or ask about, but that you would want to tell them, nonetheless. These are items that establish credibility and expertise—and convince people to buy from you instead of your competitors.

Many products are, to a large extent, commodities, with little to differentiate your goods from another vendor's. What determines whether the customer buys from you is whether you can convince her that you are reliable, trustworthy, knowledgeable, and competent. In other words, you know what you're doing, better than your competitors.

Jericho Communications, a New York PR firm, has a large button on its site labeled "Awards." Through that link, you can find all the PR awards Jericho has won. Although you may be more interested in PR results than awards, Jericho knows you'll be impressed.

They also offer a document called "Five Point Equation for Ideas That Work." Even though you may not intend to ask how they come up with PR ideas, they proactively tell you. The method establishes believability—they have a system for producing ideas—and makes you feel you have learned something about creativity when you read it.

On the website for my freelance copywriting practice, bly.com, I post samples of my work—because potential clients want to see promotions I've written for other companies before making the decision to hire me.

They can also click on a page showing color images of the covers of the many books I've written on marketing. That's what I want them to see, because it increases their comfort level regarding my expertise in my craft.

Posting content on your site—useful information, such as white papers or how-to articles—is another, more subtle way of convincing potential customers that you are the qualified source. After all, if they read and are impressed with your article on how to select a hydraulic pump, they're more likely to buy the pump from you than another seller.

One technique you might consider is a button on your home page for recommended vendors. It opens to an html file or database of resources, in fields allied with yours, that your visitors might find useful. For example, as a copywriter, my vendors list includes graphic designers and html programmers whom I recommend.

When you post a regularly updated, recommended vendors section, visitors come to view your site as a useful resource. Knowing that they can find, on your site, the other products and services they need to complete their project, increases the likelihood of them buying your product as well.

Create a Site Map That Meets Your Marketing Objectives

Just as a technical writer wouldn't start writing a manual before creating an outline, and a book author's first step is to come up with a rough table of contents, you should have a plan for creating your website too.

The most popular format for planning websites is a tool known as the site map, which is a block diagram—similar in appearance to an organizational chart.

In each block you write the topic or title of a page that you want to post on the site. Then you use solid lines to indicate the hierarchy of page organization. For instance, the home page would be on top, and all major sections would appear under it.

For those of us less visually inclined, a good old-fashioned outline, with Roman numerals and letters (I, II, IIA, IIB) shows the same information without the bother of drawings.

But that's just the mechanics. The real issue is how to create a website plan or strategy that will achieve your marketing objectives.

For hobbyists, enthusiasts, and artists, just having an attractive website might be the goal. For your business, however, a website is just a means to an end—increased sales. It's a waste of money to put up a site unless it is designed to increase revenues or achieve some other marketing goal.

Burlington Industries, a textile manufacturer, posts its annual report and proxy statements online. Shareholders can read proxy materials and vote their shares electronically, eliminating bulky paper documents and mailings. The objective is to promote a modern and professional corporate image. The online proxy distribution and voting makes Burlington look Internet savvy. It also provides better service and convenience to shareholders.

Although a well-written, well-designed website with great content can make a positive impression on your prospects, the design should focus on getting the visitor to take the action you want.

On one site for a company selling nutritional supplements, html images of recommended health books were plastered all over the pages. Clicking on the images sent the visitor to Amazon.com where he could purchase the book. The owner of the site felt—quite correctly—that highlighting recent books on topics related to his supplements added value for the customer. Unfortunately, clicking on the book link took people away from his site, and put them on Amazon, where they bought books, not his supplements.

Eight Steps to Consider Before Writing Website Copy

How can you make sure your website is a powerful marketing tool and not pretty html pictures posted on a server that people can look at for free? Here are some simple steps.

1. **Write down your marketing objective.** Is it to generate leads? Build a database of names with e-mail addresses? Give your business a storefront on the Web? Put your product catalog online to eliminate the time and expense of mailing print catalogs?

2. **Quantify your objectives.** Do you think having an e-commerce site can increase your sales 10 to 15 percent? Are you looking to attract a million visitors a month? If you don't know what these numbers should be, make your best guess.

3. **Make sure your website has the information your visitors need.** If you are selling a product, the prospect won't buy it unless there's a clear description of each item along with its features and benefits. If you are selling a service, the customer must be able to get a price on the site or at least be given a phone number or e-mail address to contact for an estimate.

4. **The prospect must be able to get all his questions answered while on your site.** The easiest way to do this is with a frequently asked questions, or FAQ, page. The FAQ page lists the most common questions visitors ask along with the answers. A number of software products now allow visitors to interact with a customer service rep while viewing sites, either via e-mail or on the telephone.

5. **Use tools that can quantitatively measure site activity.** Compare actual performance against your stated numerical objectives. An increasing number of applications can measure everything from how long visitors spend on each page on the site, to how much and how often they buy.

6. **Add strategic hyperlinks and site maps to guide visitors.** For instance, if you sell mixers and have an articles library on mixing, you might link articles about specific applications to pages describing the particular models that handle each application best. Don't be afraid to aggressively lead the visitor toward the solution you want to sell, not just the nice free stuff you give away.

7. **Study competitive sites carefully.** Creatively plagiarize site features and Web techniques they are using to sell products similar to yours. There's no need to reinvent the wheel. Despite the emphasis on creativity among programmers and designers, creative adaptation of marketing techniques that are already working for others is more likely to result in your own success. Of course, avoid stealing or plagiarizing copyrighted content or artwork.

8. **Take a tip from the Yellow Pages.** When people open the Yellow Pages, they have an immediate need and are looking for a solution. So the ads are heavy on content, light on fancy design or marketing fluff. Your site visitor may not have as immediate a need as the Yellow Pages user, but she still has some interest or she wouldn't

have come to your site. So while prize-winning Web design is fine, copy and content that *sell* are even more important.

Pictures Versus Words Revisited

In Chapter 4, we discussed the issue of pictures versus words in online communication. If you are a picture person and like to load up your site with graphics, here's another reason why you should do so with extreme caution.

A survey from the Boston Consulting Group, published in *American Demographics* (August 2000, p. 46), reveals that slow downloading drives visitors crazy. Almost half of online shoppers surveyed said they left sites when pages took too long to download.

According to Zona Research, Web pages take anywhere from three to eleven seconds to download, depending on the user's modem and Internet connection. The average viewer will bail out—click off the site onto another—if a page takes more than eight seconds to download.

Zona estimates these bail-outs cost e-businesses $4.35 billion annually in when people bail out of sites. Speed makes the difference; one site decreased bail-out rate from 30 percent to 8 percent just by reducing its download time by one second per page. One study found that 84 percent of websites examined downloaded too slowly.

Obviously, as people migrate to broadband (cable modem, DSL, T-1) these problems become less of an issue. But a common mistake is to judge website appearance and performance by viewing it only with your own computer. Keep in mind that millions of Internet users have older, slower machines. Your site must look good and perform reasonably well, whether being accessed from a sophisticated workstation or an IBM 486 with a 28Kbps modem.

Use the Word *Free*—A Lot

Despite the rise in e-commerce, the culture of the Internet is rooted in free and open exchange of ideas and information without payment. This continues today as Internet users expect and demand free stuff—and lots of it—on the sites they visit.

My kids love Cartoon Network and Nickelodeon. They frequently visit both sites, where they can play for free—and to their heart's content—cool computer games that rival the cartridges they pay to rent or buy. These sites also sponsor frequent contests with big prizes.

A new report from the Annenberg Public Policy Center shows that approximately one out of five kids age ten to seventeen would happily provide personal information—including their name and address—to their favorite websites in exchange for a free gift of an undisclosed amount. If you offer a gift valued at $100, nearly half the kids will share private data with you.

Whenever Internet users give you something—information, permission to market to them, an order—they usually expect something in return. Therefore, offering rewards can help motivate your prospect to take the action you want. For example, as I was writing this chapter, I paused to call Sprint and redeem my bonus points for a free gift. At the end of the conversation, the Sprint telephone operator offered me five hundred bonus points for free in exchange for my e-mail address—a clever and inexpensive way for them to add e-mail addresses to their customer database.

The biggest giveaway on the Internet, even more so than prizes and cash, is content—free information on topics ranging from aromatherapy to zoology. Marketers are wrestling with the challenge of how to make money giving away information, so people who come to the site for the freebies stay to make a purchase.

Bestselling horror writer Stephen King, who has sold two works of fiction on the Internet, *Riding the Bullet* and *The Plant*, recently commented, "Internet users see the Internet as a great big candy store, and they have to be made to realize that not all the candy is free."

And IBM CEO Lou Gerstner Jr. says, "The Internet is about business, not browsing; and about conducting real commerce, not merely accessing a bottomless reservoir of content."

Stress the Benefits

Whatever you offer your visitors, present it in a website that's easy on the eye and enticing to read. Everything—pictures, words, buttons, functions—should be designed to give customers what they need and want.

"Go back to the roots of the product or service being offered," says Web copywriter Scott T. Smith. "Why does it exist in today's world, and why does your company sell it?" A good website communicates this proposition and the product benefits to the visitors.

Ivan Levison, another first-rate Web copywriter, says many sites commit the deadly sin of being flat, sober, and boring, because they think Internet users are averse to being sold. He advises his clients to make their websites lively and exciting.

"The Web today is a text-based medium and you've got to quickly capture the reader's interest and attention," says Levison. "You have to establish a relationship with the reader and therefore write with energy, enthusiasm, and personality."

One way to do this, says Smith, is to stress benefits instead of features in product descriptions. The benefits should be linked to the features that enable the product to deliver the benefit to the user. "A benefit is anything that will make a customer's life better by using your product or service," explains Smith.

Smith also recommends giving visitors an incentive to order now, from the website. This could be a limited-time offer, free shipping and handling, a special bonus gift, or an extended warranty.

Discounts also work. Tell online shoppers that you offer them lower prices than you do through offline channels of distribution. Explain the rationale. Doing business online reduces your costs, and you pass on some of the savings to the customer as lower prices. It's a win-win situation.

Send out an e-mail and post a banner on your home page offering the special of the week or month at $10 to $20 off. ToyTime.com offered as its Christmas promotion a $20 coupon good for the next purchase when the customer spent $75 or more at the site. The marketing objective was to motivate the customer to return for a second visit and purchase.

To encourage a purchase of more than one item, you can offer a free gift for purchases over $40 or a similar dollar amount. Free shipping and handling also works to stimulate e-commerce sales.

Periodic contests and events can train people to check in at your site regularly, and notifying them of these specials by e-mail will increase traffic even more.

One site promised a sale day with an unusual twist. For a brief period during that day, anything you bought would be free—your credit card wouldn't be charged. Of course, the exact time was kept a secret. The marketer reports that site visits tripled that day and for the next several days even after the event was over.

Not sure what discount to include in your copy? Remember the Rule of 10/10. You do not need a large discount in consumer marketing to get a substantial boost in online response. Offer at least a $10 discount or 10 percent off the list price, and sales can increase substantially.

Understand the Three Cs of Web Marketing

Web marketers often speak of the Three Cs of websites—commerce, community, and content.

Commerce

Commerce is the ability to take orders over the Internet. Even though e-business is the hot buzzword in business today, the fact is, according to Network Solutions, only about one in twenty websites can accept orders online.

Community

Community means the site provides a forum, chat group, bulletin board, or other mechanism for visitors to share thoughts, opinions, and information about the subject of the site.

Now, Web marketers today are increasingly talking about making their sites "stickier." What does that mean? And how does community affect this measurement? Some define stickiness as how long people stay on your site during a visit. The theory is the longer Web surfers stay on a particular site or even a particular page, the more engaging and effective it must be.

Others gauge stickiness by how many times Web surfers return to the site. When they revisit five times in three days, obviously there's something that piques their interest.

Thomas H. Davenport, professor of Management Systems at Boston University School of Management, offers a better definition of stickiness. Writing in *CIO Web Business* (February 1, 2000, p. 58), Davenport defines stickiness as "a measure of how much attention a website gets over time."

The metric, then, would be overall number of minutes a viewer devotes to your site over a given time period, for example, a month. The total time is increased both by length of visit as well as frequency of visits, but it doesn't matter which is the prime contributor.

According to an article in *American Demographics* magazine (June 2000, pp. 39–40), consumers who participate in online communities are more likely do make online purchases than noncommunity users. And of the commercial websites surveyed by Forrester Research, 94 percent said they provided an online community on their site to drive repeat traffic.

A "community of interest" on the Web is a group of like-minded people sharing information, experiences, and anecdotes on a topic of common interest. Why should you consider establishing such a community of interest on your site? Here's what's in it for you.

- **Community increases website stickiness.** If your website is not merely a place to buy products or read articles, but rather a place to gather, visitors will stay longer and come more often. To understand the importance of a gathering place in marketing, merely visit any Starbucks. People come for the coffee but stay for the environment.

- **You can add community features at modest cost.** It's a lot of added value for a small investment.

- **As the supervisor or manager of your online community, you see and hear everything that goes on.** This can tell you a lot about your visitors and what they want.

There are very few online communities that target every Internet user. Those few which are able become portals.

Most online communities focus on a specific topic aimed at a specific audience. For example, kibu.com aims at generating sales for its sponsors by becoming a community—they call it a "digital hangout"—for teenage girls. Experts in areas such as fashion, wellness, and relationships moderate chats on these topics in which the girls can participate.

CyberSite Inc. oversees about twenty communities of interest. Their most popular is AncientSites, which is aimed at pre-Medieval history enthusiasts and has ninety thousand registered members. "It (the community of interest) is a superior environment for selling merchandise," says CyberSite's COO Keith Halper.

When I was putting together my new website, mychemset.com, html programmers quoted me a high price to create custom software that would build the online community I wanted—for instance, a chat room, message forum, and online polling.

I wondered whether it was really necessary for these custom html programmers to reinvent the wheel for each new client. Turns out, it's not. A lot of the online community functionality you want for your site is available as free Common Gateway Interface (CGI) shareware scripts. CGI is a standard for running external programs from a Web server. An interface-creation scripting program, CGI allows Web pages to be made on the fly based on information from buttons, checkboxes, and text input. For this reason, most interactive forms for building online communities are created using CGI.

To improve performance, Netscape devised NSAPI and Microsoft developed ISAPI. These standards allow CGI-like tasks to run as part of the main server process, thus avoiding the overhead of creating a new process to handle each CGI invocation.

Programmers have created large libraries of CGI scripts that you may use to create community-of-interest type functionality on your website. One such library is available at scriptsearch.com. There is usually no fee to use most of these scripts. Some allow free use in exchange for running their banners on your site.

The key to creating community on your website is having some kind of mechanism where visitors can exchange ideas, information, opinions, and resources on the topic of your site. For instance, if you sell welding equipment, your community should deal with tips, techniques, and problems encountered in welding. *Welding*—not your particular product line—is the focus of the community. What promotes your product line is the fact that this community exists on your site. When participants need welding equipment or supplies, and their community is on your site, they are likely to look there first to fulfill their needs.

To the online marketer, community may be the most important of the three Cs. The greater the sense of community, the stronger the relationship between the users and the website.

Therefore, the users who have registered as members of your community and are on your e-list (and you can get almost all of them to opt-in by requiring them to register to use chat rooms, forums, and other favorite site features) have a great relationship with the site. This maximizes their receptiveness and willingness to receive e-marketing messages sent both by you and by other companies you allow to rent your e-list.

Content

Content is the information available to visitors on the site. Many people—Web experts as well as users—believe that on the Internet "content is king." The very essence of Internet culture is the sharing of information, traditionally freely and without charge. The notion of using the Internet to actually make money is a fairly recent development, albeit one that is rapidly revolutionizing the business world.

As one of the three Cs, content is critical to your website's success. People who come to your site expect to learn something or take away free information when they leave. The more free content you offer, the more likely they'll visit again and again.

Content is not terribly difficult to come by. You don't have to write your own content or even post original material. For instance, if you are a therapist and have written self-help articles for local newspapers, scan these articles and post them in a "how-to articles library" on your website. Almost all your print publications—everything from rotary club speeches to that unpublished book—can be recycled for the Web in this way.

You can post content from other sources, often for free, simply by asking. Many authors will grant permission for you to post their articles on your website, in exchange for a link from the article to their own site. Most will even e-mail you the text as an electronic file upon request.

Soon, other website owners will be calling or e-mailing you, asking to post your articles on their sites. If you hold the copyright, you should grant permission in exchange for a link to your site. You can generate lots of traffic and even sales at zero cost this way.

Stuck for content? Here's a secret very few people know. The U.S. government publishes tons of free information on all sorts of business and consumer topics, and almost none of it is copyrighted. You can just zip over to a website, such as pueblo.gsa.com; find a report or booklet you like; and make this content available on your site to your visitors. They'll appreciate it because they'd never find the information on their own. All that Uncle Sam asks in return is that you acknowledge the government as the source.

More Ideas for Your Website

Here are some additional techniques for building a community of interest on your site.

- **Polls.** People love to give their opinion. You can use CGI scripts to do online surveys on your site. The scripts instantly tally the results and display them numerically and graphically, so you can learn how your opinions compare with other members of the online community.

- **Voting.** Voting is a variation of the online survey, the difference being the vote asks for an opinion on a single issue, while the survey has multiple questions. The results are tabulated and displayed after the individual votes.

- **Tests and quizzes.** In addition to giving opinions, visitors like to test their knowledge of your site's topic. Giving and scoring an online quiz adds an element of fun and challenge to the site. Be sure to change the quiz frequently so people come back for the new ones.

- **Message boards.** On a message board, forum, or bulletin board, people can post and reply to messages on various topics. By reviewing the content of these discussions, which remain posted on the board, you can learn a lot about your visitors and their interests.

- **Chat rooms.** A chat room is a live discussion on a topic. Messages are not posted and left for consideration; they are typed and immediately responded to by people who are online at that moment.

- **Guest books.** You can invite visitors to your online community to join as official members by filling out and submitting an online registration form or guest book. By doing so, they qualify themselves by providing a lot more information (address, company, phone number) than just their IP address.

- **Bonus point program.** Another technique that can boost orders and visits is a bonus point program, where site registrants build bonus points toward future discounts or gifts based on purchases. Show visitors their points via a counter on the screen. Load the counter right at the start—before they have even made a purchase—with some free points (one hundred to five hundred to start). Once people have a bonus "account" already loaded with points, they will be more inclined to visit and use the site, to check and add to their point total—people hate wasting bonus points once they have them.

Post the rewards (discounts, merchandise, other incentives) you offer for different levels of bonus point accumulation. Change the rewards monthly or more frequently. This encourages frequent visits. Bonus point customers must check in periodically to see what new offers they can get.

E-Commerce and Special Offers

There are three phases in enabling purchasing on your site, and you can start with phase I right away, then gradually evolve your capability as your site expands.

Phase I: Pricing and Ordering Information

In phase I, you go from merely having product descriptions posted on your website to giving actual prices. You also include ordering instructions along with shipping and handling options.

In a phase I site, you take orders offline. Website visitors can call an 800 number posted on your Web pages, the way they do in your offline catalog.

Add an html or pdf order form to your website. Encourage people to print the order form, fill it out, and fax or mail it to order—again, just like an order form in a catalog.

Phase II: Taking Online Orders

In phase II, you replace the pdf or html order form with an online order form that is interactive.

Visitors no longer have to print the order form and fill it in by hand. They can enter information to fill-in fields on the screen and click boxes to indicate their preferences (e.g., regular versus priority shipping). When they are finished, they submit the order form with their payment, which is typically credit card information.

On your end, you have to run the credit card number manually to get approval. You may also have to transfer the customer information to a database to keep a record of the transaction. If there is a problem with the credit card, you can send an e-mail to notify the customer and resolve it. You do not have to create such an interactive online order form yourself. You can find several at scriptsearch.com. Pick one and download it for use on your own site.

A few points to keep in mind regarding pricing in phase II and higher sites:

- Supermarket pricing works best—$49.95 seems more affordable than $50.
- Discounts attract Internet buyers—they like "10% off," "save $10," "buy 2, get 1 free," and similar offers.
- Taking a credit card online allows extended payment plans that can increase sales by lowering price resistance and sticker shock—instead of "$240 for a one-year subscription" you can say "just $19.95 a month."

Phase III: Full-Service Shopping

In phase III, you have a full-fledged online catalog or shopping cart system on your website, similar to Amazon.com or other high-traffic commerce sites such as Victoria's Secret.

Phase III is the online equivalent of a mail-order catalog or retail store. You can flip through the pages or walk the aisles, pick the merchandise you want, put it in your cart or on your order form, then check out at a cash register to finalize your purchase.

Unlike phase II, a phase III e-commerce site usually checks, authorizes, and charges the credit card automatically, eliminating the need to do this manually. If there is a problem with the credit card, the site automatically notifies the customer and does not accept the order until it is corrected.

Almost all e-commerce websites, whether in phase I, II, or III, offer online shoppers a money-back guarantee of satisfaction. If you do not, online buyers will go elsewhere.

When you implement e-commerce phase I, II, or III, promote your product sales on your website. One way to do this is with banners that pop up announcing specials and sales.

Web consultant Amy Africa says special offers should appear in the upper-right-hand corner of your home page, because this is the most read area of your site. Africa advises making some noticeable change to your home page frequently—every eight to ten days. These changes can include new banners announcing new specials, news items, or graphics. Basic colors and navigation tools should not be changed.

For example, National Geographic surveyed its online gift shop to determine the most popular item, which turned out to be greeting cards. They then sent out e-mails featuring html images of four of the cards. The e-mail encourages the recipients to go to the National Geographic site, view the full selection of cards, and then e-mail them to friends.

The click-through rate was 32 percent. And National Geographic added 25,000 new names to its opt-in database within three weeks.

6

Home Pages and Splash Pages

ONE CAN ARGUE that the home page is the most important page of any site. Why? Because it's the first thing the user sees when she logs onto your site. There's an old saying, "You never get a second chance to make a first impression." Well, the home page—like the cover of a book or CD, the theme song to a TV sitcom, the headline of an ad— is the first impression your visitors get. If it repulses them instead of attracts them, you may never get a second chance, period.

In this chapter, we'll look at how to write an effective home page for your website, focusing on the elements to include, messages to communicate, objectives you want your home page to accomplish, and how to design the page. We'll also examine how to carry the look and feel of the home page through the rest of the site and why that's important.

But first, let's look at the second cousin of the home page—the splash page.

Splash Pages

A splash page is the page you see on a website *before* you get to the home page. It's sort of like the outer envelope teaser of a direct-mail package, the trailer for a motion picture, the dust jacket of a hardcover book, the outer wrapper on a magazine.

The visitor sees the splash page before he is allowed to proceed to the real home page. It often consists of a company name, an attractive graphic, and the words *Click Here to Enter*—nothing more.

"A splash page is basically a digital version of a traditional book cover," reports an article in *Webmaster Tips Newsletter* (October 2000). "Its purpose is to set a mood for the rest of the site or to reinforce a brand." Many splash pages I see do not seem to accomplish these goals. I think many people use splash pages simply to display a large, attention-getting color graphic across the screen that they cannot fit on their regular home page. The belief of the Web designer might be that the pretty pictures and color will attract the person's attention.

But to me, using a splash page is like sending a direct-mail package with an extra envelope, sealed with superglue that's almost impossible to open. It slows down the communication process, frustrates the visitor, and puts an extra step between the user and the content he's trying to access on your site. According to the newsletter's article, "Some sites that have tried splash pages have found that more than 25 percent of their visitors have left the site immediately."

"Splash pages are useless and annoying," says Jakob Nielsen, a recognized expert in website usability and design. "In general, every time you see a splash page, the reaction is, 'Oh no, here comes a site that doesn't respect my time.'"

Even if you agree that a splash page gets attention or is a nice design element—and I don't—it is an annoyance to any user who is not a first-time visitor to your site. And for first-time visitors, it adds a useless step between them and whatever purpose brought them to your site in the first place. So it annoys them and wastes their time, too.

Another problem cited in the *Webmaster Tips Newsletter* article is that most search engines rank pages based on a combination of html code elements, page content, and the number of sites that link to the page. Splash pages, often deficient in all three areas, are harder for search engines to find and list, which can hurt your site's ranking on these engines.

My personal preference is to not use splash pages, and I advise most site creators to follow this rule. If you have one already, you might want to get rid of it. After all, the splash page puts another layer between the user and the information he wants to get at.

However, when I e-mailed my friend Roger C. Parker, author of numerous books on Web marketing and design, and asked his opinion of splash pages, I was surprised by his positive reply.

> I think that splash pages can fill a very important role: that is, emphasizing a "new and different" or "current" limited-time offering without detracting from a site's home page.
>
> Consider the way the Handel and Hayden Society uses them. When you reach their home page, handelandhayden.org, a small splash screen typically shows up describing their next concert. The day after the concert the splash screen disappears and is usually replaced by a new page for the next concert. This allows their home page to contain links about the enduring aspects of the Handel and Hayden Society—their philosophy, performers, outreach programs, and year-long schedule—while adding immediacy.
>
> Splash screens permit you to add immediacy to your website without constantly redesigning your home page or overemphasizing just one of the topics you want to introduce on your home page. Splash screens can be considered "teasers" and thus should contain a link to a page that describes the topic in greater detail and, equally important, splash pages should automatically disappear after a few seconds. In any event, they should contain a text link along the lines of "click here to go to home page" to allow visitors to immediately proceed past them.

Although the idea of using a splash page as a teaser sounds sensible, my preference would be to add a banner to the home page describing the temporary event or special offer. I still think a splash page gets in the user's way and wastes too much of his time.

Michael Montoure, writing on his website, webmutant.com, has a different take on why he likes splash pages.

"Splash pages give you a moment to *orient* yourself," writes Montoure. "To establish a style, a tone, a mood, a purpose. This moment to take a breath is, I think, important on the Web, where the process of moving from link to link and site to site is so inherently seamless that it all becomes a blur; your website doesn't necessarily feel like a distinct place to a user, but simply a part of their entire Web-surfing experience."

If you are going to use a splash page (and I recommend that you don't), have a definite purpose, such as a teaser, like Roger suggests. Don't use a splash page, as so many website designers do, just because you think it looks cool.

Home Pages

The way people and businesses design their home pages is no secret. A quick surf through the World Wide Web will show you hundreds of different home pages, each with a different design and structure. Which will you emulate? What should you feature on your home page? What's the purpose of a home page, anyway?

As the name implies, a *home* page should make your visitor feel at home on your site. Because visitors access so many sites, don't try to be all things to all people. Your home page should establish you as *the* Internet resource for your particular niche topic or product.

Here, for example, is the lead copy from the home page for espeakonline.com, a website on communication:

WELCOME TO THE WORLD OF ESPEAK!

An online forum and resource for people concerned about the Internet and its impact on writing, publishing, information marketing, and communication—in print and on the web.

The purpose of this Website is to serve as a forum and community for discussing "communication in the Internet age." Together we will explore issues relating to how the rise of the Internet is changing the way we communicate (write, speak, and publish) both online and offline.

Examples: Will people still read printed books 20 years from now? Will the Net put newspapers out of business? Can you skip checking your spelling and grammar when e-mailing a colleague? Do people now think in hypertext instead of linearly?

Visitors should get the idea that if they want to know more about communications—or cuckoo clocks, index funds, or whatever your specialty—your site is the premier source of ideas and information for that topic on the Web.

Your home page, at minimum, should contain the following eight elements:

1. **A strong headline.** The headline can welcome visitors to the site ("Welcome to the world of espeak"), reinforce the company positioning ("your online one-stop printing shop"), or state a benefit ("Find a job fast").

2. **A site introduction.** Two to three paragraphs directly under your headline should explain your site's reason for being, who can benefit, and what those benefits are. The introduction should orient the reader to where she is on the Internet (your site) and why she came (the information or help you offer).

3. **A site menu.** Provide a series of buttons the reader can use to access the various sections or pages of the site. These should remain at the sides, top, or bottom of the screen as the user navigates.

4. **What's new?** Internet users are always looking for what's new, so highlight news and new features on your home page, either with a "what's new?" button or a banner advertising special offers and new information.

5. **Contact information.** Make it easy for the visitor to find your Internet, snail mail, and e-mail addresses and your phone and fax numbers. You never know when or how a potential customer may want to contact you. A buyer with an immediate need may want to speak with a live person on the spot and not wait for e-mail reply.

6. **Instant e-mail reply.** On the home page and elsewhere display a click-on button that lets visitors instantly send e-mail to you. Be sure someone in your office reads the incoming e-mails at least daily.

7. **Privacy statement.** Show visitors that you respect their electronic privacy by posting a privacy statement on your home page. Nike's privacy statement reads, "OK, so you're on your computer

minding your own business and you get an e-mail telling you about a special offer from Nike for free shoes, or some other golden opportunity. Don't believe it. It's not real. For the record, Nike doesn't send out unsolicited e-mails. From time to time we'll notify consumers who let us know they want to hear from us. Otherwise, any information on the Internet from Nike to the public comes on www.nike.com or www.nikebiz.com."

8. **Copyright notice.** Your home page should contain a copyright notice along these lines: "Copyright © 2002 XYZ Company. All Rights Reserved." Also, the name that you give your site is technically a service mark, which means it can and should be trademarked if it is available and not used by someone else.

If you make your home page more interactive, then more visitors will get involved. The more involved they get, the longer they'll stay and the more likely they will be to make a purchase.

Netscape's home page continually changes the featured news articles, so visitors know they can always get the latest news. Think about what's important in your field to the visitor and give it to him. If you're a financial website, people who click onto your home page should get a summary of the day's market activity along with your analysis so they can be instantly informed and guided.

Another technique that works is to display a link to an online survey on your home page. People love to tell you their opinions. With online polling, you can display the results in real time, so that visitors get valuable information. In one poll, I found out that 67 percent of the responding parents agreed with me that Britney Spears's act contains too much sexual innuendo.

If your site attracts groups of like-minded people—systems analysts, contractors, resellers—put a link to a message board on your home page. Invite them to discuss issues of the day with their peers. Make your home page a true home for them on the Internet, and they'll come home to it again and again.

In an article in *Newsletter Industry Monitor* (February 2001, p. 7), Craig Huey gives the following tips for writing a home page that increases your website's ability to generate leads and sales:

• **Your home page should have a strong, clear welcome that tracks with the primary purpose the prospect has in visiting your site.** The welcome acknowledges the reason for visiting the site and gives benefits for reading on. Then the prospect is clear on what to expect.

• **The welcome needs personality or your home page will be a dud.** The personality can be simply a voice that is compatible with the marketing that has brought the person to the site. It can also be the image you that you want to project. Better yet, make the personality an actual individual: the president, publisher, or editor, who is a spokesperson for the site. Depending on your publication and audience, you may even want to use a photo to increase interest, believability, and correlation.

• **The home page should have one clear theme without multiple distractions.** The prospects are coming to the home page because they have one purpose in mind: to find out about whatever it is that drove them to your site.

For example, you are marketing to people in the paper industry and you're highlighting price increases. Prospects want to learn about price increases in the paper industry on your home page. They don't care about the site map. They don't care about all the other publications you may have. They don't even care about other issues involved in the paper industry. Their only interest is to navigate so that they can find out about pricing issues in the paper industry. Other options will distract, misdirect, and lower response.

• **The copy used on the home page must be warm, personal, direct response copy.** Use short words of six characters or fewer, short sentences with no more than eight words, and short paragraphs with no more than six lines. And it is imperative that the copy turns features into benefits. Just like a powerful direct-mail letter, your copy can draw and boost response—weak copy can kill your sale.

• **The graphics should not delay the site in coming on the screen.** Nor should the graphics in any way detract visual attention from where you want the prospect's eye to flow—to a headline and then to the body copy of the welcome page. Anything else that draws the prospect's eye is counterproductive and could lower response.

• **The home page must encourage and motivate prospects and tell them why they need to read on.** Again, it goes back to the reason why they came to the site in the first place. They must be encouraged by the benefits and see why it's in their interest to spend one more second on your site versus going somewhere else. Time is of the essence. Who are you? What will they learn? What are your benefits? Why should they care? Why can't they learn this information elsewhere?

The Three Home-Page Styles: Splash, Ad, and Tabloid

Although you will find an almost infinite variety of copy and design styles on home pages, Web masters seem to choose three basic formats: *splash-page style, ad style,* and *tabloid style.*

The first is a home page that looks like a splash page, with minimal text and one large, eye-catching graphic dominating the screen. The only difference between this single-graphic home page and a splash page is the addition of a navigation bar that lets you select the section of the site you want to move to next (splash pages usually only offer a single option, "Click here to enter").

The second format is a page with a strong positioning headline, a lead-in section of introductory copy, and a navigation bar with buttons leading to the major site sections. We can call this ad style because the home page resembles a print ad in design and content. For an example, visit bly.com or mychemset.com.

The third home-page format has multiple headings and text blocks. Often one of the text blocks is a short but complete article that starts on the home page and requires a click to continue. The other headers and text blocks are one-paragraph abstracts or summaries of articles; you can click on the title to read the full text. This tabloid-style format resembles the front page of a tabloid-size newspaper. For an example, visit useit.com, the website of usability expert Jakob Nielsen. Or, see Roger C. Parker's newentrepreneur.com.

"Most websites fail because their home page consists of a single large, slow-loading graphic rather than fast-loading html text that contains news value," says Parker, who is a proponent of the tabloid-style format and not in favor of applying splash-page style to an actual home page.

How can you create an effective tabloid- or ad-style home page? Roger's advice: think small instead of large, so you can include more information on your home page, particularly the top half, which is what most of your website visitors encounter first.

In many ways, the top half of the home page is the most important part of your website. Your home page represents the first—and sometimes only—chance you have to make a good impression and ensure that readers will spend a lot of time at your website.

A well-designed home page tells a lot about your business and should have six essential characteristics. It should:

1. Introduce your business

2. Describe the products or services you offer

3. Share your firm's philosophy or positioning, i.e., the customer benefits or unique selling propositions that set your firm apart from the competition

4. Project an appropriate image through your choice of words, colors, typeface, and layout

5. Start a relationship (which, you hope, will become a sale) by capturing the visitor's e-mail address and offering visitors reasons to spend time at your site and return frequently

6. Communicate urgency by offering fresh information and meaningful reasons for visitors to act now

Many home pages sabotage the website they introduce because the text and graphic elements are too large and they look like splash pages. On a home page, large is bad because the larger the size of the objects occupying the screen, the fewer the number of objects that can fit into the space.

Also, very large graphics take a long time to download. If you are a corporate type, it is easy to forget that most customers do not have the same high-speed T-1 connection to the Internet that you do. According to an article in *Iconoclast* newsletter (August 2000), 93 percent of at-home Internet users in the United States have dial-up connections that are 56 kbps or slower. Only 7 percent of home users have high-speed access such as DSL or cable modem.

"Speed must be the overriding design criterion," writes Jakob Nielsen in his *Alertbox* (March 1, 1997). "To keep page sizes small, graphics should be kept to a minimum and multimedia effects should be used only when they truly add to the user's understanding of the information."

Too often, the top half of a home page consists of a large logo plus the firm's address and phone number, without any further selling of the firm's position, products, or services. Switching from a splash-style to ad-style home page can solve this problem.

Another common mistake on the home-page design is having links that are only visible if the site visitor scrolls down the page—which few visitors will bother to do unless the top half of the page gives them a reason to.

Links are frequently too large and vertically arranged in a single row below the firm's logo. This limits the number of links visible at a single time. A better alternative is to use smaller links and arrange them in a two- or three-column table, thus permitting more links to be visible at once.

When viewing your website on their computer monitors, your visitors' attention is focused on a relatively small area. Unlike a newspaper ad, which must be large to be noticed, big online logos and headlines aren't needed to compete with adjacent ads and editorial matter.

In a tabloid-style home page, you have many more smaller items than an ad-style home page, which usually has one major heading and lead-in section. The advantages include the ability to include more items on the home page, each of which can appeal to a different segment of your visitors, as well as faster-loading text and graphics.

If you choose the tabloid-style home page, think of the top half of your home page as the front cover of a magazine. Most magazines

MEASURING WEBSITE SUCCESS

WebSiteStory (websitestory.com), a San Diego–based company specializing in Internet technologies, services, and sites, created both of these.

Statmarket.com: Accurate Internet statistics and user trends in real time.

Services include e-data mining. StatMarket presents raw data computed from millions of daily Internet visitors to websites monitored by WebSiteStory Technology. StatMarket.com is the most accurate source of data on Internet user trends.

HitBOX.com: Website traffic counter and analysis tool

HitBOX (and its high-end counterpart StatMarket eData Mining) remotely and anonymously collects and warehouses data from visitors to websites. In other words, it monitors the "who, what, when, and where" of every visit.

Hundreds of thousands of websites analyze their traffic with the HitBOX technology. Through the company's massive in-house network operating center, WebSiteStory analyzes and stores data from billions of visitors to these sites every month. This has created an immense warehouse of data on Internet users—the largest of its kind. WebSite Story converts the massive amounts of raw Internet user data it collects into useable information.

HitBOX is the most popular and comprehensive Web-traffic analysis service and is the largest community of independent websites ranked by traffic.

list the titles of several articles inside the issue, as well as a prominent photograph or teaser promoting a feature article inside. In addition, there's often a tagline positioning the magazine apart from the competition, e.g., "Slot car racing—and only slot car racing."

The top half of a tabloid-style home page performs basically the same functions. Roger C. Parker favors a crowded tabloid appearance with a lot of stories, each containing a link to the full text.

"The more options you offer, the more likely visitors are to click one of your links," says Roger. "Accordingly, as many links as possible should appear on your home page." One option is to group the links along the top or left-hand edge of your home page.

The Home Page Sets the Website's Tone and Style

The home page sets up an expectation on the part of the visitor as to what he will get when he goes deeper into the site. If the home page is folksy, he'll expect a warm, down-home site with perhaps a community of peers and straight, inside talk about the topic. If the home page reads like an annual report, the visitor will expect hard facts—and maybe some hard sell—inside.

The tone and style of the home page should, to a reasonable degree, be carried out throughout the other pages on the site. A white paper, of course, doesn't have to sound exactly like an e-zine—nor should it. But overall, tone and style on a website should be consistent from page to page, just like a group of ads that make up a unified ad campaign have a similar graphic style, typeface, theme, and slogan.

"Style, and style guides, are perennial hot topics in the online business," writes online content specialist Amy Gahran. "Many content professionals seem preoccupied with finding the ultimate, authoritative source with the final word on whether 'Internet' should be capitalized, or whether 'Web site' is one word or two."

"But in reality," says Gahran, "where you put the punctuation doesn't matter nearly as much as how you shape and deliver your messages."

Among the key issues to consider before you create your home page:

• **Who are your key target audiences?** Isolate out each key group. Don't forget about journalists, investors, and other important secondary audiences, too.

• **Which types of content are of primary interest to each of your key online audiences?** Should you target certain sections of your site (or even certain e-mail newsletters) to cater to specific audience segments?

• **Which channels or formats does each key audience segment prefer and use?** Do they prefer text-only e-mail? Do they welcome and use access to downloadable files, searchable databases, or multimedia? Make sure you offer content options and channels that make sense for your audience. Also, make sure you understand what the most appropriate least common denominator for content delivery should be across all of your audience segments.

• **What is the "mindset" of each of your audiences?** Do they want details? Are they skeptical? Can you assume that they know anything about your organization, what you do, and how you do it? Are they experts who would understand a lot of the jargon of your field?

• **Which tone is most appropriate for each of your key online audiences?** Do they prefer a strictly business approach, or will a more chatty or casual tone succeed? Can you employ sarcasm or humor at all? What would likely offend or alienate the groups you wish to attract?

Home Page Buttons

Almost every home page has—usually at the left or bottom of the screen—a series of buttons. By clicking on these, visitors can activate certain buttons or access various pages or sections of the site.

What buttons should you have on your home page? What should their labels be? What should they allow the visitor to do?

In her article titled "Web Site Planning" in *Intercom* magazine (December 1997, pp. 14–15), technical writer Theresa Wilkinson suggests this useful exercise. Make a list of the things people are coming to your site to do. These tasks might include:

• Obtaining information on products and services
• Obtaining information about your company

- Reading press releases
- Finding out about new products
- Downloading software
- Obtaining product documentation (such as manuals)
- Getting customer support
- Buying products online with a credit card
- Getting price quotations
- Finding out shipping options and prices
- Requesting a proposal by sending you a request for proposal (RFP) electronically
- Learning how a product or technology works
- Returning a product for refund or credit
- Checking their order or account status
- Obtaining stock quotes
- Finding a calendar of upcoming events
- Reading case studies or success stories of customers in their industry using your product
- Learning how your product can be used in their application
- Downloading or printing hard copy of product literature

Look at this task list when it is complete. You probably want to make sure the most important tasks are accessible directly with one click off the home page. For example, if most customers want to read about success stories, your home page should have a small section or button that says "Click here for our latest customer success stories."

One exercise you might find helpful is to write a brief description of your site—an overview—before sitting down to write the actual home-page copy.

The website description you create in this exercise is not for publication. This is not home-page copy but rather a preliminary plan. This description should include:

- The intended audience for the site
- The objective of the site
- The content it will present
- How people will use the site
- The benefits of using the site

Here is a sample website description.

Global Stocks on U.S Exchanges (GSUSE) eliminates the frustration that investors and investment advisors encounter in finding good information about foreign companies at an affordable price.

Our database contains information on global companies with shares traded on U.S exchanges. Information on these companies is presented in two formats; (1) a website the URL of which is www.gsuse.com, and (2) a CD-ROM disc that is updated quarterly. The website is available to subscribers for a monthly subscription price of only $29.95.

The site lets the user group and review companies by country, region, or industry. Current quotes, news, and charts are provided for each company. For each company, the user can choose either a one-page or a four-page summary of financial information. The user can download the financial pages from the annual and interim reports of each of the companies.

The site also gives information on financial markets around the globe, updated daily, as well as currency exchange rates, also updated daily. Links are provided to over fifty exchanges around the world.

OECD statistics and publications are available on the site, organized by country. Financial reports on most of the companies prepared by Thomsons can be ordered from the site.

The Elements of Style on Your Home Page and on the Web

Given these parameters and the variations in them between one website and the next, is there any "right" style for writing copy for your home page and the rest of your website? For a commercial site—one that has marketing as its purpose—I think the answer is "yes." And the style you should use is *conversational style.*

Conversational style does not mean your writing is a transcription of spoken language, with its awkward pauses, repetition, ums, and uhs. It simply means writing in plain English, and avoiding jargon and "corporatese."

A recent bestselling book *The Cluetrain Manifesto* (by Christopher Locke, et al.), and its supporting website (cluetrain.com), make two claims. First, "markets are conversations." The second claim is that "the Internet is enabling conversations that were simply not possible in the era of mass media." The manifesto then notes: "Conversations among human beings sound human. They are conducted in a human voice. Whether delivering information, opinions, perspectives, dissenting arguments, or humorous asides, the human voice is typically open, natural, uncontrived."

If markets are conversations, and conversations are conducted in a human voice, then marketing documents should be written with this human, conversational sound. Since Web pages are online marketing documents, it follows that your home page and other Web pages should be written in this conversational style.

How do you get into the groove of writing in this conversational style? Write naturally. Pretend you are talking to a friend, telling him or her about an exciting new product or idea you discovered. You wouldn't sound like an annual report or a letter to shareholders. You'd be animated, enthusiastic, even a bit excited.

Do not be afraid to let your personality shine through in your online writing. The best online writers not only get their information across clearly, but they also give the reader a sense of who they are as a person (or, in the case of a corporate website, the personality and character of the company). This book, for example, is written in conversational style.

Within the conversational style, there are many gradations. Your website may have a particularly laid-back style if you are selling to ordinary folks. It may lean toward being slightly more academic if your market is college professors or technical if you are selling to engineers. If you are trying to position your site as *the* place on the Web for users to get definitive information on your topic, you may have to take on a more authoritative tone.

"A smart writer can make a very real difference by discovering a true voice for the company that really does engage both the company's customers and employees," writes Internet copywriting expert Nick Usborne. He also observes that selling on the Internet, once forbidden, is now gaining wide acceptance. This means it's becoming OK to write persuasively and sell a product or service openly on the Web.

"It's OK to sell from your site," says Usborne. "In fact, when you refuse to sell, many of your visitors will get confused and wonder what the heck is going on. They expect to be sold to. It's the design they are waiting for. It tells them, 'Hey, here's the spot where I say "Yes."'

"To take the view that selling with copy online is wrong is an insult to the intelligence of your visitors. Customers aren't stupid. They get it. They read what you're saying and apply the appropriate grade of 'ad-talk' filtering."

Tips for Setting the Conversational Tone

Even though selling online is acceptable, copywriters know that the more their copy sounds like a blatant sales pitch, the more skeptical and resistant the consumer will be. Therefore, we often go to great pains to make our copy sound like useful information, rather than selling. An example is the infomercial, which—although it's a paid advertisement—is produced like a TV program rather than a commercial.

As Usborne points out, the customer is not fooled. She knows the infomercial is really a commercial, not a TV show. She knows your Web page is there to promote your product, not as a public service.

But, when you can make marketing sound like a real conversation between human beings, as the *Cluetrain Manifesto* folks suggest, it's more effective. The customer knows she is being sold, but because you treat her like a person instead of a prospect, she is more willing to listen.

The following pointers can help your home page and other Web pages sound more like a genuine conversation, less like pure ad copy:

Put the reader first. When you write, think about your readers. Ask yourself, will my reader understand what I have written? Does he or she know the special terminology I have used? Does my copy tell them something important or new or useful? If I were the reader, would this copy persuade me to buy the product?

One technique to help you write for the reader is to address them directly as *you* in the copy—just as I am writing to you in this book. Copywriters call this the "you-orientation." Print copywriters know its power, yet the you-orientation is underused on the Web today.

The left-hand column shows examples of copy written from the advertiser's point of view. The right-hand column shows the copy revised toward a you-orientation.

Advertiser-Oriented Copy	**Reader-Oriented Copy**
Bank Plan is the state-of-the-art in user-friendly, sophisticated financial software for small business accounts receivable, accounts payable, and for general ledger applications.	Bank Plan can help you balance your books, manage your cash flow, and keep track of customers who haven't paid their bills. Best of all, the program is easy to use—no special training is required.
The objective of the daily cash accumulation fund is to seek the maximum current income that is consistent with low capital risk and the maintenance of total liquidity.	The cash fund gives you the maximum return on your investment dollar with the lowest risk. And, you can take out as much money as you like—whenever you like.
To cancel an order, return the merchandise to us in its original container. Upon receipt of the book in good condition, we will inform our Accounting Department that your invoice is canceled.	If you're not satisfied with the book, simply return it to us and tear up your invoice. You won't owe us a cent. What could be fairer than that?

Make your copy interesting. Generate enthusiasm for the product by telling a story, disseminating news, and showing how your product will improve the consumer's life. Remember, you can't bore people into buying your product.

Don't talk about yourself. Don't tell the reader what you did, what you achieved, what you like or don't like. That's not important to him. What's important to him is what *he* likes, what *he* needs, what *he* wants. Make sure your copy discusses facts that are relevant to the reader's self-interest.

Divide the copy into short sections. If the content of your page can be organized as a series of sales points, you can cover each point in a separate section of copy. This is the tabloid-style home page we discussed earlier.

Why are short sections better than long ones? As length increases, copy becomes more difficult to read. Breaking the text into several short sections makes it easier to understand. On the Web especially, users find long blocks of unbroken text on a page cumbersome.

What's the best way to divide the text into sections? If you have a series of sections where one point follows logically from the previous point, or where the sales points are listed in order of importance, use numbers.

If there is no particular order of importance or logical sequence between the sales points, use bullets, asterisks, or dashes to set off each new section. Or place them within separate frames within a page.

If you have a lot of copy under each section, use subheads in your page (as we've done in this book). Paragraphs within each section should also be kept short. Long, unbroken chunks of type intimidate readers. A page filled with a solid column of tiny type says, "This is going to be boring!"

When you edit your copy, use subheads to separate major sections. Leave space between paragraphs. And break long paragraphs into shorter paragraphs. A paragraph of five sentences can usually be broken into two or three shorter ones. Find the places where a new thought or idea has been introduced and begin the new paragraph there.

Use short sentences. Short sentences are easier to read than long sentences. All professional writers—newspaper reporters, publicists, magazine writers, copywriters—are taught to write in crisp, short, snappy sentences.

Long sentences tire and puzzle your readers. By the time they get to the end of a lengthy sentence, they don't remember what was at the beginning. How can you reduce sentence length? There are several techniques.

Break long sentences into two or more separate sentences whenever possible:

Today every penny of profit counts and Gorman-Rupp wants your pumps to work for all they're worth.	Today every penny of profit counts. And Gorman-Rupp wants your pumps to work for all they're worth.

Use punctuation to divide a long sentence into two parts:

One purpose is to enable you to recognize and acknowledge the contributions of all of your fellow employees from the company president right down to the newest foreman.	One purpose is to enable you to recognize and acknowledge the importance of all of your fellow employees—from the company president right down to the newest foreman.
The outcome is presentations that don't do their job and that can make others wonder whether you're doing *yours*.	The outcome is presentations that don't do their job . . . and that can make others wonder whether you're doing *yours*.

Vary sentence length to make your writing flow. Copy becomes dull when all sentences are the same length. Even if you frequently write longer sentences, you can reduce the overall length in your copy by interspersing the occasional short sentence or sentence fragment:

Over 30,000 aerospace engineers are members now. To join them, send your check for $46 with the coupon below and become a member *today*.	Over 30,000 aerospace engineers are members now. Join them. Send your check for $46 with the coupon below. And become a member *today*.
Now, discover the Splint-Lock System, an effective and versatile chairside splinting technique that helps you stabilize teeth quickly, easily, and economically.	Now, discover the Splint-Lock System . . . an effective and versatile chairside splinting technique that helps you stabilize teeth. Quickly. Easily. And economically.

Sentence fragments—concise clauses that grammatically are not complete sentences—can be used to keep your sentence to an appropriate length. And sentence fragments can add drama and rhythm to your copy.

Basic Eye Emphasizer does it all. It's the one eye makeup everyone needs. The only one.

Not one of the Fortune 1000 companies even comes close to our rate of growth. And no wonder. Computers are the hottest products of the 1990s, with no end to demand in sight.

It doesn't take much to block the door to success. A flash of an idea that slips your mind. A note that never gets written.

Train yourself to write in crisp, short sentences. When you have finished a thought, stop. Start the next sentence with a new thought. When you edit, your pencil should automatically seek out sentences that can be broken in two.

Use jargon sparingly. Should you use jargon? It depends. If your website is designed primarily for specialists, a certain amount of technical terminology may be acceptable, even desirable. On the other hand, use jargon sparingly when writing to an audience that doesn't speak your special language. Jargon is useful for communicating within a small group of experts. But used in copy aimed at outsiders, it can confuse the reader and obscure the selling message.

Computer and data communications professionals, for example, have created a new language—LAN/WAN internetworking, data warehouse, GUI, PDA, client/server, dumb terminal, remote node. But not everybody knows the vocabulary. A business executive may know the meaning of *software* and *hardware* but not understand terms like *bindery, bandwidth, directory,* and *computer telephony.* And even a customer with a technical background may be baffled by a brochure that refers to *interprocess message buffers, asynchronous software interrupts,* and *four-byte integer data types.* When you use jargon, you risk turning off readers who don't understand this technical shorthand.

Computer experts aren't alone in baffling us with their lingo. Wall Streeters use an alien tongue when they speak of *downside ticks, standstills, sideways consolidation,* and *revenue enhancements.* Hospital administrators, too, have a language all their own: *cost outliers, prospective payments, catchment areas, diagnostic-related groups, ICD-9 codes.* Because advertisers are specialists, it is they—not their copywriters—who most often inflict jargon on the readers. One of my clients rewrote a product description so that their storage silo didn't merely *dump* grain—the grain was "gravimetrically conveyed." Another, a manufacturer of dental products, informed me that their dental splints did not "keep loose teeth in place"; they "stabilized mobile dentition."

When is it OK to use technical terms, and when is it best to explain the concept in plain English? Don't use a technical term unless 95 percent or more of your readers will understand it. If you do use jargon that is unfamiliar to your readers, define these terms in your copy.

Don't use a technical term unless it is the best choice. We would use *software* because there is no better way to say it. But instead of using *deplane*, we would just say, "get off the plane."

Your prospects should not have to figure out what you mean. It is *your* job to say what you mean in plain, simple English. Use short sentences, short paragraphs, small words. Be clear.

Be concise. Good copy is concise. Unnecessary words waste the reader's time, dilute the sales message, and take up space that could be put to better use.

People have more information to absorb today than ever before, and less time to absorb it. Your prospects are in a hurry and have shorter attention spans than they did ten or twenty years ago. One study reported that in 1968 political election coverage, the length of the average TV sound byte was 42.3 seconds. Today it is less than 8 seconds. On the Internet, if your page takes more than 8 seconds to download, your prospects won't wait—they'll click onto another site.

Rewriting is the key to producing concise copy. When you write your first draft, the words sometimes pour out, and you can't help being chatty. In the editing stage, unnecessary words are deleted to make the writing sparkle with vigor and clarity.

One copywriter describes her copy as a "velvet slide"—a smooth path leading the prospect from initial interest to final sale. Excess words are bumps and obstacles that block the slide. Tell your story in as few words as possible. When you are finished, stop.

Be specific. Internet users are hungry for facts. The more facts you include in your online copy, the better. Online writers who don't bother to dig for specifics produce vague, weak, meaningless copy.

"If those who have studied the art of writing are in accord on any one point," write Strunk and White in *The Elements of Style*, "it is this: the surest way to arouse and hold the attention of the reader is by being specific, definite, and concrete. The greatest writers—Homer, Dante, Shakespeare—are effective largely because they deal in particulars and report the details that matter."

When you sit down to write copy, your file of background information should have at least twice as much material as you will end up using in the final version of your ad. When you have a warehouse of facts to choose from, writing copy is easy. You just select the most important facts and describe them in a clear, concise, direct fashion. But when copywriters have little or nothing to say, they fall back on inflated language to fill the page. The words sound nice, but say nothing. And the ad doesn't sell because it doesn't inform.

Here are some examples of vague versus specific copy.

Vague Copy	*Specific Copy*
He is associated in various teaching capacities with several local educational institutions.	He teaches copywriting at New York University and technical writing at Brooklyn Polytech.
Adverse weather conditions will not result in structural degradation.	The roof won't leak if it rains.
Good Housekeeping is one of the best-read publications in America.	Each month, more than five million readers pick up the latest issue of *Good Housekeeping* magazine.

The more specific you are, the less the chance that your readers will misunderstand you. Some computer users, for example, called a support line to complain that the manual often told them "hit any key" and they could not find a key labeled "any." At last report, the computer manufacturer was planning to rewrite the manuals so they specified "hit the RETURN key"—eliminating the user's uncertainty.

Get to the point. If the headline is the most important part of your home page, then the lead paragraph is surely the second most important part. The lead either lures the reader into the text by fulfilling the promise of the headline, or bores her with uninteresting, irrelevant, unnecessary words.

Start selling with the very first line of copy. If you feel the need to "warm up" as you type your thoughts into your PC, do so. But delete these warm-ups from your final draft. The finished copy should sell from the first word to the last.

Creating the Conversational Copy

Ann Landers is one of the most widely read columnists in the country. Why does she think her column is so popular? "I was taught to write like I talk," says Ann. "Some people like it." Writing in a conversational style produces copy that engages your readers.

Conversational tone is especially important online, where the Internet is an economical substitute for a salesperson. A light, conversational style is much easier to read than the stiff, formal prose of business, science, and academia. And when you write simply, you become the reader's friend. When you write pompously, you become a bore.

For example, IBM's famous Charlie Chaplin ads and commercials helped make the IBM PC a bestseller in the early 1980s. This ad series was a model of friendly, helpful, conversational copy. Here's a sample:

> There's a world of information just waiting for you. But to use it, study it, enjoy it, and profit from it, you first have to get at it.
>
> Yet the facts can literally be right at your fingertips—with your own telephone, a modem, and the IBM Personal Computer.

Note the use of colloquial expressions ("a world of information," "at your fingertips") and the informal language ("just waiting for you," "you first have to get at it"). IBM seems to want to help us on a person-to-person level, and their copy has the sound of one friend talking to another.

How do you achieve a conversational style in your online writing? An article in the *Wall Street Journal* recommends this simple test for conversational tone. "As you revise, ask yourself if you would ever say to your reader what you are writing. Or imagine yourself speaking to the person instead of writing." And to help you write the way you talk, here are some tips for achieving a natural, conversational style:

- Use pronouns—I, we, you, they.
- Use colloquial expressions—"a sure thing," "turn on," "rip-off," "OK," "sick and tired."
- Use contractions—they're, you're, it's, here's, we've, I'm.
- Use simple words.

Don't be afraid to end your sentence with a preposition. Writers use a number of stylistic techniques to pack a lot of information in a few short paragraphs of smooth-flowing copy. One is to end sentences with a proposition.

Ending a sentence with a preposition adds to the conversational tone of the copy. And it's a perfectly acceptable technique endorsed by Zinsser, Flesch, Fowler, and most other authorities on modern writing. Some examples:

He's the kind of fellow with whom you love to have a chat.	He's the kind of fellow you love to have a chat with.
Air pollution is something of which we want to get rid.	Air pollution is something we want to get rid of.
For what are we fighting?	What are we fighting for?

Of course, use your judgment. If ending with a preposition sounds awkward, don't do it.

Begin sentences with conjunctions. Beginning a sentence with *and, or, but,* or *for* makes for a smooth, easy transition between thoughts.

Use simple conjunctions instead of more complex connectives. *But* is a shorter, better way of saying *nevertheless, notwithstanding,* and *conversely.* And don't use antiquated phrases such as *equally important, moreover,* and *furthermore* when *and* will do just as well.

The first lesson is free. But I can't call you. You have to take the first step.

The choice is simple. Be a pencil pusher. Or get the Messenger. And move ahead at the speed of sound.

ECS phones the first two numbers you've selected until someone answers. It announces the emergency. Gives your address. And repeats it.

Use graphics to emphasize words or phrases in copy and to separate thoughts. Using bullets, highlighting, underlining, italics, color, animation, and boldface can make words and phrases stand out in print advertising and promotion. Many readers skim copy without reading it carefully, so these techniques draw attention to key words, phrases, paragraphs, and selling points.

Of course, these devices should be used sparingly. If you underline every other word on your page, nothing stands out. On the other hand, if you underline only three words on a page, most prospects will at least read those words.

Here is a list of mechanical techniques you can use to call attention to key words and phrases online:

Bullets
Numbered lists
Underlining
Capital letters
Indented paragraphs
Boldface type
Italics
Change of type style or size
Borders and boxes
Color
Arrows and notes in margins
Yellow highlighting
Reverse type (white type on black background)
Marginal notes
Call-outs

P.S. (in e-mails)
Subheads
Flashing
Animation (movement)

Be credible. People instinctively mistrust marketing, even on the Web. Therefore you must work hard to convince the user that what you say is true.

One way to establish credibility is to include testimonials from satisfied customers. Another is to offer a demonstration or scientific evidence that proves your claim. An overlooked technique for getting people to believe you is to *tell the truth*. When you are sincere, it comes across to your readers and they believe your claims.

You can create strong credibility by including a negative or a disadvantage of your product in the copy, not just all the benefits or the advantages. But be selective. Inject one negative only. Do not list all the disadvantages of your product. Choose a flaw that is easily correctable or whose existence doesn't greatly matter to the customer.

Studies have shown that buyers want you to be honest about the limitations of your product as well as the advantages. An example is an ad for a pump company that begins with the headline, "Our pumps are only good for handling certain types of fluids. Know which ones?"

Other techniques for establishing your credibility:

- Talk about the benefits of your product.
- Show what features enable the product to deliver these benefits.
- Present test results.
- Show a list of satisfied users.
- Offer an unconditional money-back guarantee of satisfaction.
- Include ninety days of free service or support with the product.
- Use case histories showing how others benefited from the product.
- Show photographs of the product in use.
- Quote from favorable reviews or other positive articles.

Avoid Sexist Language on Your Site

There's an old saying, "you never get a second chance to make a first impression." And nowhere is this truer than on the Web. Your prospect forms an instant impression of you and your organization the second your home page downloads onto her screen. The last thing you want is to be offensive. And with so many women on the Web today, why turn them off with a sexist home page?

Sexist language offends a large portion of the population, and you don't sell things to people by getting them angry at you. The day of the advertising man, salesman, and Good Humor man are over. Now it's the advertising *professional, salesperson,* and *Good Humor vendor.*

Handling gender in writing is a sensitive and, as yet, unresolved issue. Do we change *manpower* to *personpower? His* to *his/her? Foreman* to *foreperson?*

Fortunately, there are a few techniques for handling the problem.

- **Use plurals.** Instead of "the doctor receives a report on his patients," write, "the doctors receive reports on their patients."

- **Rewrite to avoid reference to gender.** Instead of "the manager called a meeting of his staff," write, "the manager called a staff meeting."

- **Alternate gender references.** Five years ago, we used *his* and *he* throughout our copy. Now, we alternate *he* with *she* and *his* with *her.* Avoid the awkward constructions *he/she, his/her,* or *s/he.*

- **Create an imaginary person to establish gender.** For example: "Let's say Doris Franklin is working overtime. When she punches her timecard, she is automatically switched to her overtime pay rate."

- **Replace sexist terms with nonsexist substitutes.** Here is a list with some suggestions.

Sexist Term	*Nonsexist Substitute*
actress	actor
anchorman	anchor

advertising man	advertising professional
chairman	chairperson
cleaning woman	housekeeper
Englishmen	the English
fireman	firefighter
foreman	supervisor
a man who	someone who
man the exhibit	run the exhibit
man of letters	writer
mankind	humanity
manpower	personnel, staff
manmade	artificial, manufactured
man-hours	work hours
Mrs., Miss	Ms.
newsman	reporter
postman or mailman	mail carrier
policeman	police officer
salesman	salesperson
stewardess	flight attendant
self-made man	self-made person
waiter	server
weatherman	meteorologist, weather forecaster
workman	worker

7

Other Web Pages

WHILE THE HOME page sets the tone and style for your website, you will write many other pages for your site. In this chapter, we will look at some of these pages, their formats, and tips for making them more effective.

Welcome Visitors with a Guest Book

Like many houses of worship, our church has a guest book in the lobby which new visitors are encouraged to sign. Having them complete the guest book serves two purposes. First, it creates an immediate (if small) bond with the church. Second, and more important to the pastor, it builds a database of people who are looking for a house of worship and might be inclined to attend our church.

The church publishes a simple newsletter for its members. Potential members who complete the guest book also get this newsletter. A percentage of those come back again, and of those, some join as members. If we hadn't captured their personal information in a database and sent regular mailings to them, they might have gone somewhere else.

A guest book on your website serves the same purpose. It builds a database of Web prospects you can target with future marketing campaigns.

In offline marketing, experience shows that mailing to your database of existing customers yields five to ten times the response as mailing to a rented mailing list. This is because the customers know you and have done business with you, while the people on the rented list have no idea who you are.

The same principle is at work on the Internet. People who take time to fill out and submit a guest-book form have qualified themselves as being interested in what your site offers. Promotions to this group will yield higher results than marketing efforts targeting complete strangers.

The guest-book concept is nothing new in business, of course. Did you ever go to a store that asked you to fill out a card so they could notify you of specials and sales? They were doing on index cards what the guest book now does so much more efficiently and neatly on the Internet. But the idea is the same.

How a guest book should look is no mystery. Surf around on the Internet after you read this chapter. Within twenty minutes, you can review half-a-dozen guest books. Model your own after them and copy any features you like.

There is no need to spend time or money writing a program for your own guest book. Just visit scriptsearch.com. Prewritten Common Gateway Interface (CGI) scripts for guest books can be downloaded and put right on your site.

At minimum, a guest book asks the visitor to fill in his name and e-mail address. Most request complete contact information including company name (if the visitor is a business), street address, city, state, zip code, and phone and fax numbers.

One issue in guest-book design is how much information should be requested. For instance, how many employees do they have? Do they have children? Are they thinking of buying a new car? How soon? What magazines do they read? What websites do they visit? Do they own their own home? What is the annual household income?

You can think of the guest book on your website as the online equivalent of the reply card in a direct-mail package. As is the case with reply cards, there is a trade-off in guest books when asking questions. The more questions you ask, the better you qualify the prospect. But ask too many questions, and people will give up. They will stop halfway without completing or submitting the form, and your response rate will decline. I find that people will fill out a card or guest book with one to three simple questions. More than that and response rate drops. So limit your questions to three.

Your guest book should include an opt-in box. This is a box followed by text that reads, "Check here if you are willing to receive occasional e-mails about products and offers of interest to you." When the prospect clicks this box and submits the form, she has given you permission to send her promotional e-mails. These e-mail marketing messages can be from you or other companies to whom you rent your e-list. It is perfectly legal to send e-mails to these people, because they are said to have opted in by checking the opt-in box. If they have submitted the guest book without checking the opt-in box, it is illegal to send them unsolicited e-mail marketing messages. It is spam.

E-mail marketing messages sent to opt-in e-lists can generate response rates of 1 to 10 percent click-throughs. A 5 percent rate means that out of one hundred people on the list receiving the e-mail, five clicked to the sponsor's site for more information on the product or offer mentioned in the message.

If you build a substantial opt-in e-list through your guest book, you can rent the list to other Internet marketers for a fee. Opt-in lists rent for fairly high fees—$200 per thousand names or more—compared with e-lists that are compiled and not opt-in. The reasons? Opt-in lists generate better response. And compiled lists are illegal to use.

With a database of opt-in names from your guest book, you can market to your Web visitors much more effectively. You can segment your e-list in many ways and design promotions that target specific segments with relevant messages and offers. For instance, an online marketer of office products says he segments his opt-in list by recency—that is, by when they last visited the site.

Everyone who visited within the last seven days gets a message that says, in essence, "You were here but didn't buy. Please click on our

Monthly Specials page now so you don't miss our current hot products and big bargains." He reports that this strategy is very profitable.

Amazon.com sends highly customized e-mails to their customers based on recent purchases. If you buy a book, you may get a message saying, "We're glad you bought Book A. Based on this, we thought you might like Books B and C. And you can buy them right now at such and such discount off the list price."

Do you think it might be worthwhile to set up a guest book, capture prospects in a database, and do targeted marketing—online, offline, or both—to them? Some Web marketers require visitors to register in the guest book to gain access to specific content or features on their site. In a sense, you are "paying" the visitor to give you his information with free information or tools.

Of course not everyone will take you up on your offer. According to *Micro Software Marketing* newsletter (April 1997, p. 2), a survey by the Boston Consulting Group shows that 41 percent of visitors leave websites when asked to provide registration information. In addition, another 27 percent provide false personal information on website registration forms.

Therefore, you have to ask yourself: "How important is it for me to gather information on prospects through guest book registration? Am I willing to reduce the number of visitors and the time visitors spend on my site by requiring them to register to access advanced features or content?" Then, you can decide whether to use registration as an access control device.

Smooth Landing on Your Landing Page

A guest book is a general registration page for the website that is permanently a part of the site. A landing page—also known as a "jump" page—is a specialized registration page tied to a specific product or offer. It is called a landing page because the user "lands" there typically by clicking on a banner ad or an embedded URL in an e-mail message you have sent to her.

Here is a sample landing page for a subscription offer advertised via a banner:

Entertainment

TRY 2 ISSUES FREE!

Name: _____

Address: _____

City: _____

State/Province: _____ Zip/Postal: _____

E-mail: _____

GET 2 FREE CDs! Upon payment

RUSH my CD's! If I like my 2 RISK FREE issues, you'll charge my credit card for the next 25 issues (27 in all) at just $1.10 per copy. My FREE Music Collection will then be sent immediately! I will also be entitled to the benefits of the Automatic Renewal Program. *See details below.*

This site is secure for credit card transactions.

Card Type _____ Card # _____ Expires _____

OR

_____ Just send me 2 RISK FREE issues and if I like them, I'll be billed later for the next 25 issues (27 in all) at just $1.10 per copy. If not, I can cancel at any time by simply writing "cancel" on my bill and the two risk free issues are mine to keep. My FREE CDs will be sent after payment.

SEND MY ORDER NOW

☐ Yes, I would like to receive a weekly e-mail about future news, special offers, promotions and events from Entertainment Weekly's EW.com.

☐ Click here to try the ALL NEW AOL 6.0 for up to 700 hours FREE for a month. We'll send FREE software to the address above.

☐ Please do not contact me via e-mail with offers for Time Inc. products and services.

Offer Details

If after receiving your 2 RISK FREE issues you like our magazine and want to keep receiving it, do nothing. When your 2-week trial period runs out, we'll charge your credit card or bill you for your next 25 issues (a total of 27) at just $1.10 per copy. That's a total savings of 62% OFF the newsstand price! Also, your FREE Music will be shipped upon payment—which is immediate when using your credit card.

You are guaranteed the right to cancel at any time. Simply write "cancel" on your bill or call 1-800-828-6882. The 2 free trial issues are yours to keep, and you will receive a full refund on all unmailed issues. *Back To Order Form*

Automatic Renewal Program

Credit card users will continue to receive *Entertainment Weekly* with uninterrupted service until you tell us to stop. You may cancel at any time. After your initial subscription term, we'll simply charge your credit card every 6 months at the special guaranteed low rate then in effect. It's convenient, conserves natural resources by eliminating billing and renewal notices, and offers you great subscriber savings. If we are unable to charge your credit card, we'll simply bill you in time to lock in savings. *Back To Order Form*

Price is valid in US only. In Canada, *EW*'s cover price is $3.95. 27 issues = $28.50 (GST, QST, and HST not included). *Entertainment Weekly* is published weekly except for 4 issues combined into one and occasional extra, expanded or premium issues.

To learn more about practices, please read our *Privacy Policy*.

Most marketers design their landing pages to be single pages, but it doesn't have to be that way. Mark Joyner of Aesop.com pioneered the format of the multipage landing page. When you arrive at one of Mark's landing pages, you are given several consecutive pages of copy to read, which you get through by clicking the "next" button at the bottom of each.

Multipage landing pages work well for direct response offers requiring a lot of copy to make the sale. You can't fit all the selling copy in the e-mail that brought the prospect to the landing page, or even in a single landing page, so you use multiple pages in sequence to tell the story. The following example is a page from a successful site Mark used to sell the e-book *Hypnotic Writing*:

How to Hypnotize Anyone with Words

(And get them to buy, agree, follow, click—anything you want.)
—Mark Joyner, CEO, Aesop.com

There is **one forbidden word** in the language of marketers. At the mere utterance of this word, most marketers will cringe. You'll rarely hear a marketer use this word . . . not in public, at least.

That word, in case you were curious, is *admire*. Allow me to explain.

We're all trying to position ourselves as the "best in the universe." Just about every marketer pushing himself on the net claims that he is the best around and that no one else knows what they are doing. We erroneously assume that by admiring someone we are taking ourselves down a notch.

The fact is, I've never met a successful marketer who did not study the works of others constantly. I'll be the first to tell you that I'm constantly reading . . . learning . . . revising my tactics.

I'm going to break the code of silence, though. There is another marketer who, I am not ashamed to say, I truly admire.

This is a guy who, many years ago, taught me some things about copywriting that forever changed the way I advertise my products. The information he taught me is absolutely essential. The techniques he showed me work not only for copywriting, but can also be applied to just about any situation where **you need to persuade others**—to convince them to obey your commands.

This man's name is . . .

Next

Notice that the first screen deliberately breaks in the middle of a sentence rather than cleanly at the end of a sentence. This increases the probability of the user clicking "next" to go to the next screen and finish the sentence. And once he is there and still finds the text of interest, he will keep reading. Naturally, that screen also ends in the middle of a sentence, so he clicks to get to the next screen—and so on, and so on. That way—by breaking a document into multiple screens—long copy on the Web is made to work effectively.

A Shopping Cart Helps Visitors Purchase Online

A shopping cart is a specialized order form used on e-commerce sites. The most famous model is Amazon.com.

Here are some tips for creating effective shopping carts:

• **List all charges up front.** Sticker shock is a fast way to lose potential customers. Present product prices, shipping and handling, and taxes before you ask for billing and personal information. Drugstore.com does a great job on all those counts.

• **Let shoppers see what's in their carts.** Just as in a retail store, cybershoppers like to keep tabs on what they're buying. Give them a way to see a running tally of items and how much they've spent. Landsend.com's "shopping bag" is one solid example.

• **Allow customers to change orders.** Users like to be able to remove items and modify quantities, especially after seeing the bill. In addition to "buy lists," add "wish lists" that let customers put items on hold while they decide what they want to purchase. Make it simple for customers to transfer items from the wish list to the buying list and vice versa. Gap.com makes it easy to defer purchases.

• **Save contents for return visits.** Research shows that e-mail shoppers often put items in a cart and come back to the site later to make the purchase. Be sure to automatically save whatever was in the cart, even if there was no purchase. This is especially valuable at sites where the purchase is expensive. Travel site Expedia.com, for example, allows users to create and store priced-out itineraries.

• **Make special promotions easy to use.** It can be difficult for a shopper to figure out how to apply a special promotion to a purchase. Make this an obvious and simple step, and do it early in the checkout process.

• **Hold your customer's hand.** Let customers know when a purchase is on the way or held up. If it's the latter explain why, and keep the customer up to date via e-mail. Provide a way for the customer to return to the site and check order status. Nordstrom.com not only has online status information but also provides e-mail access to customer support and a toll-free number for live support.

• **Encourage shipping to multiple destinations.** If a shopper is buying gifts, make it easy to send them to a variety of addresses. Amazon.com does this well, in addition to offering personalized messages and wrapping-paper choices.

• **Keep forms as short as possible.** Ask only for the information you need to process an order. Also, if shoppers need to go back a screen to correct an error, do not clear all the fields on the page and force them to fill out the form again. Jcrew.com has a nearly painless registration process that asks only for the bare minimum of information.

• **State your guarantee and returns policy on the form.** "When it comes to warranties and guarantees, the Internet presents some excellent opportunities to assure your customers that your company stands by its products and that consumers won't get stuck with something they don't like," writes Barb Gomolski in *Infoworld* (March 12, 2001, p. 74).

Be clear about the length and conditions of the guarantee. Is the guarantee for ten, thirty, sixty, ninety days, or longer? Is it a lifetime guarantee? As a rule of thumb, the longer the guarantee, the better your sales results.

How and where to return defective or unsatisfactory merchandise is of particular concern to Internet buyers. A retail customer brings the product back to the store. A catalog buyer returns it to the address on the catalog. But you can't ship a product back to a URL. Give an address indicating where goods may be returned. Who pays the shipping—you or the customer? "A return-and-repair process that is easy on the customer and efficient for the business is essential," says Gomolski.

According to a survey by Esearch.com, the number one reason why consumers do not complete online transactions is that the Web page is too slow. Some other reasons include:

- The site does not accept credit cards
- The user can't find the checkout area
- Return policy is missing or unclear

Don't Miss a Links Page

To a golfer, the expression "hit the links" means going out and playing eighteen holes of golf. But to a Web surfer, links are one of the ways she finds her way around the World Wide Web.

Ilise Benun, a self-promotion and online marketing consultant, wrote an article called "Do's and Don'ts of Linking" for *The Art of Self Promotion* (Summer 2000, p. 4) in which she states, "The ability to utilize hyperlinks is what separates the Web from any other communication medium. Links allow you to abandon the linear path of the real world and be led instead by the muse of cyberspace. Links allow you to follow your train of thought, to easily get information about obscure topics, to jump into another community or conversation, far away or right around the corner, with a single click."

Links can take you from website to website. When you use a search engine, you are given a list of websites that match your interest. The names of the sites on the list are linked to the home pages of each one. You click on the name and go directly to the site. But what about using strategic hyperlinks not only to make your site easier to navigate, but to actually increase traffic and add value for your visitors?

Surf some sites as you read this chapter. You will find many that have a separate button on the home page labeled "links." When you click on it, you are given a list of sites. The names are highlighted because they are hot links. Click on the site name and you go directly to the site.

Why would you consider adding a links page to your site? There are several benefits. To begin with, your visitors will stay longer—

and come back to your site more frequently—the more they see it as a valuable Web source on your topic.

One way to make your site a more valuable information resource is through the addition of select links. As an example, take a look at espeakonline.com. The site is an online resource and forum for writers, editors, marketers, publishers, and others interested in communication in the Internet age. But to be useful, a site such as espeak has to be specific. It can't cover everything. If it did, it would be too cluttered, impossible to navigate, and it would lose the sharp focus that draws visitors in the first place.

Through a strategic links page, you can give your visitors access to content and resources that are relevant but that you don't want to (or can't) include on your site. Espeakonline.com deals with communication in a broad sense but does not focus specifically on Web design. So how does it provide more detailed information on Web design for visitors interested in that topic in-depth? By linking with sites that cover that topic in detail.

Another way to improve your website with links is to guide visitors to products and services that complement your own but are not in direct competition with you. For example, let's say you sell plants and bulbs through a website. Some of your plants probably require special grades of soil that are not always easy to find in nurseries and gardening stores. You want to help your customers but do not want to be in the soil or dirt business. What should you do? Add links to the websites of companies that sell the soil your customers will need. These links can appear on a separate links page. You can also have them appear on the product pages for the plants requiring these soils.

Customers will appreciate the convenience. And with the soil concern removed, you will sell more of these particular plants.

How do you establish a link from your site to others? Although there is some question as to whether you need permission to put up a link to someone else's site, most people will be glad to have you do it. I have never heard of someone telling another site operator, "Please do not link to my site"—although I suppose it could happen. (If it did, it's easy enough to remove the link.)

Add Web Profits with Affiliate Programs

Some websites link to other sites as a service to their visitors, with no financial arrangements. Often the agreement is reciprocal—if you link to my site, I want in exchange to be allowed to link to yours.

An increasingly popular arrangement is the "affiliate program." I put a link from my site to your site. If a Web visitor clicks from my site to your site and then makes a purchase, you pay me a percentage—typically 5 to 50 percent—of that sale. Amazon.com is probably the largest user of affiliate arrangements today. This is because many sites list recommended books on their topics or products as a service to readers. The plant site, for instance, might list recommended books on gardening.

An affiliate arrangement allows your visitors to click on those book titles and instantly order them online from Amazon.com. It's a value-added service on your site, and many websites have a separate button on the home page, "bookstore," just for this purpose.

Because most don't want to be in the book business, it's a lot easier and cheaper to link to Amazon.com than set up a book shopping cart and keep an inventory of books. They are happy instead to link to Amazon.com, not do any of the work, still provide visitors with a service, and take 15 percent of the sale.

An increasing number of marketers are offering affiliate programs. IBM recently began an affiliate program for Internet service providers (ISPs). The ISP puts a link on its website to IBM's e-commerce site. If a customer goes to the ISP site, clicks on the link, and buys a server on the IBM site, the ISP gets 3 percent of the sale—which, on a $300,000 server, is $9,000.

You may want to make an affiliate arrangement with other product sellers, especially if you think you're going to send more traffic to their website than they will send to yours. Think of your links page as a port of the overall content of your site. It's *not* a throwaway page. Treat the material within as you would the rest of your site.

Making the Links Page Work for You

If you plan on having more than just a few links (and there's no point in having a links page if you don't), some kind of structure is key to keeping visitors from being overwhelmed and clicking off. Arrange your links by industry or some other category, and put them in some kind of order.

People like to know where they're going, so tell them the company name, especially if it's not obvious from the Web address. Write one or two lines describing the link you're offering. Focus on what you like about the site and what it does well; offering your point of view enables you to become a guide for your prospect. This also increases your site's value and helps to position you as an expert. For examples of link descriptions, please see evendorsonline.com or visit artofselfpromotion.com.

Linking Techniques That Click with Visitors

Every link you add to your site is a doorway to another location, an escape hatch that moves the visitor out of your site and into another. And once visitors make that escape, they may not return to your site at all. So while you want to enhance your credibility and value by helping your visitors find related resources, you don't want to show them the exit to your site before you have a chance to show your own stuff. Try the following linking techniques.

Don't put links on your home page. Give visitors a chance to see what you're offering first. Put your links on pages that are nested at least one level below the home page of your website, so visitors will be exposed to some of your own information before they can head for the door.

Check out each resource yourself before linking to it. It's easy to grab a cool-sounding URL out of a magazine, an e-mail message, or a discussion group post. But you should always check out the resource yourself before linking to it. The URL may be wrong, gone, or the site may contain material that's detrimental to your own marketing efforts, even opposite to your point of view. Link to sites that augment, rather than compete with, the information you're offering.

Look for sites that offer more detail about a subject your site touches on. For example, the website of Melissa Galt's Atlanta-based interior design firm, Linea Interiors, (lineainteriors.com) offers a very comprehensive page of links that go more into depth about home furnishings than she does on her website. Her Resources page extends into categories such as Home Furnishing and Accessories Resources, Expertise on Home Improvement, Bed and Linen Sources, and Appraisers. The short, one-line descriptor of each link is also very helpful.

FAQ Page

Lists of frequently asked questions (FAQs) have long been a staple of online communication. A good FAQ helps the online audience by providing information while saving time. They don't have to submit a question and then wait for an answer.

However, a good FAQ also can directly benefit your customer or employer. It can save time that otherwise would be spent fielding and responding individually to the same questions over and over, and it can enhance relationships with customers and other online audiences by demonstrating that their perspectives and needs matter.

That said, FAQs often are missing from online venues that need them most. Also, many of the FAQs currently available online are outdated or poorly conceived, written, edited, or presented—making them an annoyance or barrier, rather than a resource.

What You Need to Know and Do Before Writing Your FAQ Page

Before you create your first FAQs spend time reviewing as many online FAQs as possible. Soon, you'll get a feel for what does (and does not) work well. Pay special attention to format and wording, length and organization, level of detail offered, how links or other references are used, obvious omissions, and anything that seems confusing. Keep a list of your favorite FAQs as guides.

Be sure to clarify your goals. Why does your client or organization want or need an FAQ? Are they spending too much time answering the same questions? Do people frequently misunderstand who they are, what they do, or what they're talking about? Do they need a quick way to summarize key points of a crucial topic?

For an FAQ to be truly useful, it shouldn't overwhelm people. Say only what you really need to say to accomplish the FAQ's main goal. Don't try to anticipate and answer every possible question—just address the most important or common questions. Also keep in mind that if your FAQ becomes too long or complicated, you should consider dropping some detail or breaking it up into separate pages.

When you create your FAQ page, you'll need to know the audience. What kind of people will probably be reading that FAQ and why? What knowledge, background, perspectives, biases, or concerns do they have regarding the topic or publisher of the site? What do they expect or want to accomplish?

Do your research. Talk to the people who currently field questions from the online audience, and develop a list of the most common questions that actually come in. Don't guess blindly about what people might be asking, and don't dictate what you think people should be asking. Obtain copies of as many questions as possible (in the form originally submitted), as well as responses offered for each question. This provides important clues about wording, context, relationships and relative priorities.

Keep your FAQ page up to date. Every six months or so, review it. Is the information still current? Have people been asking more or different questions? Are the topics you selected still important?

Formatting Your FAQ Page

Consider using a Q&A format. Many documents claiming to be FAQs are, in fact, outlines. Usually it's more reader-friendly to pose true questions that reflect how your audience thinks and the words they tend to use and to address readers directly by using second person when answering. Put those questions that the audience considers most important up top. If the list is long, divide it into sections containing about five Q&A pairs each.

People consult FAQs in order to save time and prevent confusion. Therefore, questions should be just a few words or a brief sentence. Answers should be just a sentence or two, or a brief paragraph or two, at most. If more detail is needed, create separate Web pages and link off to those.

If your FAQ list contains more than a handful of Q&A pairs, at the very top of your FAQ, list every question (in order) addressed on that page. This will be the Table of Contents (TOC) for your FAQ page. Also include titles of subsections, if any. Choose one key word or phrase within each question in the TOC, and designate that as a link down to the correct point in the FAQ. Do not designate complete questions as links in your TOC; when that much text appears underlined, it's very hard to read.

Let people ask questions. The point of an FAQ is to help the audience, not to thwart communication. Your FAQ page should offer an e-mail address, phone number, or other way for people to ask more questions.

Selling Your Wares with Product Pages

Although Chapter 3 outlines a process for converting existing printed product brochures to the Web, marketers are increasingly creating pages for new products for the Web first, then adapting them to print.

The principles of writing product copy for the Web are pretty similar to writing print brochures, catalogs, and sell sheets, with a few exceptions based on the Web user's shorter attention span and the interactivity of the medium.

Here are some guidelines to follow when writing online product pages.

Start Selling in the Page Headline

When someone opens a page about a product, it's usually the headline that makes your prospect either read further or click away. Yet the majority of online writers write throwaway headlines that are usually nothing more than the product name. The headline should contain a strong selling message. This message can identify the audience for the product or service, stress the usefulness of the product, or highlight other potential benefits.

A well-thought-out cover headline increases the selling power of any online document, from a Web page to an e-mail. Take, for example, this headline promoting a bank's Christmas club:

IMAGINE HAVING AN EXTRA $520 FOR THE HOLIDAYS.

It's easy.
It's painless.
It's automatic.
It's just $10 a week.

This headline is more likely to grab a depositor's attention than a banner or headline labeled, "Christmas Club Account."

Here are some other effective headlines:

Interactive multimedia in your broadband network products—now!

Lose 5 pounds in 9 days with the Internet Diet

Boosting melting productivity and efficiency with oxy-fuel combustion techniques

Seamlessly integrate telephony and computer technology

A headline isn't the only way to begin selling on the products page. Telling a story illustrated with dramatic photographs is another option. A site used in fund-raising for an animal welfare society might feature heartbreaking photos of mistreated animals. Usually, though, words and pictures together are stronger than images alone.

Make Your Story Flow

A website is in many ways like an online book, and, like a good book, a good brochure tells a story. That story should have a beginning, a middle, and an end, and it should flow smoothly from one point to the next.

Once you've written the first draft, sit back and read it as you would an article or short story. Does it progress logically? Or are there points where the transitions are awkward, where you are jarred by a phrase or sentence that doesn't seem to belong? If the transitions aren't smooth, perhaps the material needs to be rearranged a bit. Maybe adding a subhead, headline, or introductory paragraph will take care of the problem. Or, perhaps a transitional phrase can bridge the gap between one sentence and the next. Here are some of the transitional words and phrases that copywriters use to make a sensible connection between copy points:

Additionally	In other words
Also	In this way
And	Moreover
Another reason is	Most important
As a result	Obviously
As well as	Of course
As we've discussed	On the other hand
At the same time	Or
Best of all	Perhaps
But	Plus
But wait. There's more	The reason
By comparison	Remember
Chances are	Similarly
Even better	Since
Even worse	Still
First, . . . Second, . . . Third	That's where _____ can help
For example	The results
For instance	Then again
Here's how	Therefore
Here's why	There's more
However	Thus
If . . . then	To be sure
Imagine	What's more
Importantly	Why? Because
In addition	Yet

Strive for a Personal Tone

As discussed in Chapter 6, write your online copy in a natural, relaxed, friendly style. Strive for the easy, conversational tone of spoken language—short words, short sentences, the personal touch. If what you've written sounds stiff, unnatural, or dull, it's not conversational and you need to revise it. Your copy should make people want to do business with your organization.

Here are some examples:

> Today we live in the Age of Now . . . the nanosecond nineties. When customers order a product, they want it right away. You must deliver—fast. Or your customer might find someone else who can.

> An oxygen supplier who knows only oxygen is of limited value. But an oxygen supplier who knows oxygen and EAF steelmaking—like BOC Gases—can be the strategic partner who gives you a sustainable competitive advantage in today's metals marketplace.

> Losing your hair. It happens to millions of men. Yet unlike the millions of men who are actually walking around with bald heads, you have the power to do something about it. Now. Before it's too late.

Stress Benefits Not Features

Too many promotional websites stress the *features* of the product or service—the bare facts about how it works, what it looks like, how and where it is made, who designed it, and so on. Effective copy translates features into benefits—reasons why customers should buy the product. A benefit explains what the product can do for your customers.

After you identify the key features of your product, make a corresponding list of benefits. Here is a partial list for a familiar item—a clock radio:

Feature	Benefit
Large illuminated digital display	Time easy to see at a glance—even at night.
Snooze alarm switch	Tired? Just hit a button for 10 more minutes of sleep.
Digital alarm	Alarm wakes you at precisely the right time.

Wood veneer finish	Handsome design will complement your bedroom decor.
Felt pads on bottom	Won't scratch or smudge furniture.
Alarm/radio option	Wake to the sound that suits you—gentle strings, hard rock, or the buzz of an alarm.
AM/FM	Clear reception guaranteed. Gets all your favorite stations.

Be Specific

People visit websites because they want information. And they are quickly turned off by pages that are long on puffery and short on content. So be specific. Don't write, "saves you money" when you can say "reduces fuel consumption up to 50 percent." Don't say "we're reliable" if you can tell the customer, "The repairman arrives within 24 hours or we fix it free of charge." Don't be content to talk about "a lot of energy saved" if you know your insulation "reduces heating bills by 30 to 50 percent a month." Remember, specifics sell.

Give the prospect a reason to call or register on your guest book or e-mail now, rather than later. If you can only take on a limited number of assignments, and you take on new clients on a first come, first serve basis, say so.

Graphic artist Ted Kikoler writes in his self-promotion piece, "With my track record, you can understand that I'm busy and find it difficult to take on new assignments." Consultant Somers White formats his brochure in question and answer format. The first question is, "Why should I hire Somers White?" The unexpected—and challenging—answer is, "Perhaps you should not." He then tells what make his services exclusive and expensive, positioning himself as a top resource in his field.

Support Your Claims

Even if you stress benefits instead of features, even if you make specific claims, the customer still may not believe you. In his book *Direct*

Mail Copy That Sells! copywriter Herschell Gordon Lewis describes modern times as an Age of Skepticism:

> This is the Age in which nobody believes anybody, in which claims of superiority are challenged just because they're claims, in which consumers express surprise when something they buy actually performs the way it was advertised to perform.

How can you overcome skepticism and get people to believe you? Here are some things to include in your copy.

Track record. The most powerful copy for promoting a product or service is to say what it has done for other customers and the specific positive results. Ted Kikoler's promotion piece is packed with examples of how his direct-mail graphic design service increased response for numerous clients.

Guarantees. Offer a guarantee: money back, free replacement, free revisions and reworks, unlimited service, or work redone at no cost. Guarantees allow the customer to try your service at no risk, which will ensure satisfaction.

Testimonials. A testimonial is a statement of praise or endorsement from a satisfied client (or, in some cases, a celebrity). The testimonial is written in the customer's own words, appears in quotation marks, and is usually attributed to a specific person.

Client list. Include a list of your most prestigious, well-known clients. This impresses prospects by association. They figure if you are good enough for American Express or Lever Brothers, you're good enough for them too.

Case histories. These are success stories, which tell how a particular customer benefited by selecting, buying, and using your services or methods. They present the reasons why the customer selected your service over competitive offers and the results achieved through its application.

Demonstrate your reputation and stability. Talk about your track record and past successes. Cite number of years in the business, number of employees, the size of your operation, number of warehouses, number of plants, number of offices, annual sales, profits, reputation. This is usually done on a separate "about the company" page.

Use illustrations. Help customers visualize how your service works or is put together and why this makes it better. For example, a website claims a new four-step dental procedure to be quicker and easier than the conventional method. The site shows a Flash presentation to demonstrate the new procedure, step by step.

Show, don't tell. Don't just say your product or service saves money or improves life. Show that it does. Let's say you're selling an energy-efficient air-flow management system to building owners. Instead of just talking in a general sense about energy savings, provide sample calculations that show *exactly* how much money buyers can save based on their utility rates, building size, and thermostat setting. Put an interactive tool on your site that makes it easy for the visitor to perform the calculation and come up with money saved based on his specific situation.

Use comparisons. If your product or service clearly beats the competition, you can include comparisons, as long as they can be supported by documentation (i.e., specifications taken from competitors' brochures).

Keep the Copy Lively

Most copywriting texts tell you to keep sentences short because they are easier to read. But writing gets monotonous when all sentences are the same length. So, vary sentence length. Every so often, put in a fairly long sentence. Also use an occasional very short sentence or sentence fragment. Like this one.

Lively writing is personal, not impersonal. Personal pronouns (we, they, us, you) make the copy sound less lawyerlike, more like person-to-person conversation. Addressing the reader directly as *you* in the copy adds warmth and creates the illusion in the reader's mind that the copy was specifically written just for her or him.

Human beings have been telling and recording stories since the first cave dweller drew a crude picture of his latest hunting experience on the cave wall. Storytelling is an inherently powerful technique for getting your message across, much more so than a dry recitation of mere facts.

You can use storytelling to liven up your promotional copy. For example, instead of just stating that your bottle-coating process is superior, tell how, because of your better coating, one of your customers actually doubled his bottling business, got rich, and retired to Florida at age fifty-one. People have a great interest in other people.

Separate and highlight key information. If you need to include a detailed methodology outline, for example, put it in a separate table or sidebar, and keep your body copy lively. (A sidebar is a short section of copy separated from the main text and enclosed in a box or other graphic device.)

Make Sure the Information Is Relevant

All copy should be interesting to read, but not everything that's interesting to read belongs in your copy. It should be relevant to the message you're trying to communicate and to the people you want to reach—those who are most likely to buy your product, join your club, take your course, or donate to your cause.

If a site selling your website design services begins with an intellectual essay on the impact of the Internet, that may interest Web enthusiasts or techies. But the business owner looking for specific information on how to create a profitable website may not be willing to wade through this nonessential stuff to get to the part about how you can help them save time and make money.

Check for Accuracy

Then check it again. Then have three or four other people in your organization check it, too. Yes, mistakes on the Web are temporary and easily fixed. But by the time you notice your error, thousands may have seen it. So, even though proofreading is boring, it's well worth the time and effort.

In addition to accuracy, you should also check for consistency. Make sure you've used the same style of grammar, punctuation, capitalization, spelling, numerals, abbreviations, titles, and product names consistently from page to page, especially if pages were gathered from different sources (catalogs, ads, press releases) created by different authors. If you're inconsistent—if you write "GAF" in some places and "G.A.F." in" others—you're automatically wrong part of the time.

Contact Pages Put You in Touch

The contact page contains all your contact information in one place. It may also include trademark and other legal information. When putting together your contact page, make sure you include the following as needed:

- Company name
- Logo
- Physical mailing address
- Phone numbers and extensions, including toll-free numbers
- Fax number
- E-mail address
- Website
- Hours
- Map with driving directions
- Whether credit cards are accepted
- Branch offices
- Guarantee
- Disclaimers
- Other required legal wording
- Permissions and acknowledgments
- Trademarks and registrations marks
- Copyright notice
- Product codes and other official emblems (e.g., Good Housekeeping Seal, Underwriters Laboratory).

Information Pages Draw Visitors Like a Magnet

An information page contains content that is not directly related to selling a product, service, or organization. For instance, eng-software .com, a website designed to sell software to engineers who design piping systems, has several pages that contain how-to tips on engineering design. Although the tips can help readers use the software better, the how-to information in the articles can be applied even if you don't use the company's program. They promote the software indirectly but are not directly tied to it.

"There's a saying, 'an educated consumer is the best customer,' " writes David Ceolin in *DM News* (February 19, 2001). "Informative content begins the process that leads customers to make new purchases. Every day, consumers go online to find information to help them with pressing decisions."

Copywriter David Yale helped create a website for a firm selling novelty and gag fortune cookies as giveaways for corporate meetings and events. The site contains many pages that do not sell the product directly but instead help the visitor plan his meeting. Here is a sample information page from the site.

Meeting Message Profile, Page 3

Purpose & Main Messages

Click here to print your profile
Click here to save your profile
The information you save is confidential.

1. What is the **purpose** of this meeting, in 6 words or less?

_____

Is the **purpose** the same for all attendees? ☐ Yes ☐ No
(If "no" box is checked, the invitee type list from screen 2 comes up again with this message: List **purpose** of meeting for each type of attendee.)

2. What is your **main goal** for this meeting, in 6 words or less?

_____

Is the **main goal** the same for all attendees? ☐ Yes ☐ No

(If "no" box is checked, the invitee type list from screen 2 comes up again with this message: List **main goal** of meeting for each type of attendee.)

3. What **main message(s)** do you want to communicate, in 6 words or less? If you need different main messages for several types of attendees, enter them all here.

Your messages can be slogans, quotations, or even questions!

A. _____

B. _____

C. _____

D. _____

Keep in mind that that most people will remember only 3–4 main ideas. But if you really need more than 4 main messages, click below to add them. These are main messages—you'll get a chance later to develop variants for each main message, to make their presentation more interesting.
Button: Add more main messages (adds four more fill-in blanks to main messages field)

4. Do these messages reflect upper management's strategy?

☐ Yes ☐ No

Button: Continue
Logos: MPI, Indiana ASAE, BBB
MeetingPlanner.Com, a Division of FFC
6265 Coffman Road, Indianapolis IN 46268
(317) 299-8900
Email: MikeFry@MeetingPlanner.Com

Consider adding information pages to complement the product pages already on your website. If you sell light bulbs, have a guide that tells visitors the best type and wattage of bulb for their particular application (e.g., 80 watt tungsten bulb for a reading lamp).

"Offer vital information," advises Phillip Perry in *Smart Business Update* (First Quarter 2001, p. 8). "Content is the #1 element of success for a website. Information attracts surfers like a flower lures bees."

All About the "About Us" Page

Why do you need an "about us" page? Because people want to know who they're dealing with. If they come to your site for information, they want to know who stands behind it. If they come to buy a product, they want to know who's selling it to them. According to an article in *American Demographics* magazine (July 2000, p. 24), 51 percent of consumers and 59 percent of business executives say a company's reputation today is more important than it was five years ago. For that reason, your website should have an "about us" or "about the company" page.

"Don't assume that Web page visitors are familiar with your products, services, and your organization," writes David Yale. "The Web will bring you visitors from new market segments you haven't served in the past, and they will come from all over the world. So you can't assume they know anything about you. Make sure you introduce yourself and your products, and that your introduction focuses on the *benefits* (not features) your products offer."

The about-the-company page is a Webized version of your short-form corporate bio. If you have a corporate capabilities brochure, condense it down to a screen or two (or three at the maximum), and you have the makings of an about-the-company page.

The about-the-company page can be as simple and straightforward as a single html page of text, or it can be a sophisticated branching presentation that includes text, photos, video, and audio. You can have video clips of the launch of your telecommunications satellite, or an audio of the CEO's latest speech.

A helpful exercise is to ask yourself, "What's the page's purpose?" The overwhelming majority of "about us" pages have no visible purpose or mission. They simply present information and reproduce attractive photographs.

The key to success is to start with an objective. I recently worked on a site for a firm that offers civil engineering service to municipal clients. I asked the president why he needed such a corporate bio page in the first place, since the site has detailed pages on every service they offer.

He replied, "When an elected official has to decide which engineering firm should handle a municipal project, he needs to be confident that he is making the right decision and that the decision can be logically defended in case something goes wrong. The purpose of our 'about us' page . . . which we also have available as a printed color sell sheet . . . is to give that person a comfort level so he or she will not be criticized for selecting us and can defend that decision."

Another good question to ask when writing the "about us" copy is, "What information will show prospects how our company can solve their problems?" In another assignment, a chemical company asked me to write a site describing the capabilities of their glass coatings division. "We want this site and its companion brochure to be idea-stimulators," the client explained. "Anyone with an application that we might be able to handle should, after visiting the site, come away with the impression that we can solve their problem for them."

Problem solving is what 99 percent of all business products and services are about. As Bob Donath, editor of *Business Marketing*, points out, "Your readers are looking for solutions to their problems, not information on your people or your company." Yet too many "about us" pages talk only about the firm's excellent staff or reputation or years in business, never showing what the firm can do for the reader. That's a mistake.

Instead, find out what facts customers need to get to the point where they are comfortable doing business with you as a company. Then highlight this information on your "about us" page.

Your "about us" page can include:

- The business (or businesses) the company is engaged in
- The corporate structure (parent company, other members of the family; subsidiaries)
- Addresses and phone numbers of all offices, branches, and representatives
- Names and titles of major corporate officers
- History
- Plants and other facilities

- Geographical coverage
- Major markets
- Distribution systems
- Sales
- Ranking in its field relative to competition
- Extent of stock distribution
- Earnings record
- Dividends record
- Number of employees
- Employee benefits
- Noteworthy employees (e.g., scientists, inventors)
- Inventions
- Significant achievements
- Research and development
- Quality control practices
- Compliance with important standards, guidelines, and regulations (e.g., compliance with ISO 9000 quality standards, participation in Responsible Care environmental safety programs, and so forth)
- Actions with respect to the environment
- Contributions (to art, public welfare, and so forth)
- Awards
- Policies
- Plans

Can Long Copy Work on the Web?

In Chapter 1, we discussed the fact that, if everything else is equal, short copy seems preferable to long copy on the Web. But everything is usually not equal, and the exceptions to the always-use-short-copy-on-the-Web rule are proliferating daily.

Mark Joyner's three to five-page landing pages, discussed earlier on this chapter, are outperforming their one-page counterparts in conversions (orders). Bill Bonner, president of Agora Publishing, generates more than a million dollars in revenue a year with his free daily e-zine, *Daily Reckoning,* and finds that long promotional e-mails sent to his subscribers work very well.

Confused? Don't be. What we're seeing is the collision of two very different cultures—direct marketing and the Internet—and their convergence into a new medium, online direct response.

The Internet, for reasons discussed at length in Chapter 1, is a fast-paced medium where the audience has a short attention span. Therefore conventional online writing is concise and typically shorter than its print equivalent.

Direct marketing is perhaps the only advertising medium where long copy works better, for many audiences and offers (but not all), than short copy. When direct marketers initially tried to use the Internet as a marketing medium, they had poor results. Short copy, the favored mode of communication on the Internet, did not work for their long-copy offers. And this makes sense. If selling a product in direct mail requires long copy, there's no reason why simply switching from direct mail to the Internet would eliminate the need for that sales presentation.

Yet when direct marketers adapted their direct-mail packages "as is" to the Internet, it too failed. The long copy worked in print, but on the Internet, no one would read it. Now all that is slowly changing. The Internet is evolving along several paths from a short-copy only medium to one that allows a variety of lengths.

First, direct marketers are cultivating direct marketing audiences on the Web. *Daily Reckoning*, for example, goes to Agora Publishing's traditional market of print-newsletter subscribers. These folks are more likely than the average person to read long copy, and so Agora's long-copy e-mails work with this audience.

Second, marketers are discovering more palatable ways to present long copy in Internet formats. Instead of putting the entire sales argument from a direct-mail letter into an e-mail, we start the sales argument in the e-mail, then continue it on a landing page which in fact may be three or four pages or longer. It's not as long as the printed direct-mail package, but it's longer than traditional Internet copy— and it's working.

"Don't be afraid of long copy," writes David Yale. "While it may be OK to start a Web-based sales pitch with short blocks of copy, they should link to more information. This is especially true for complex buying decisions and high-priced products. People do read long copy on the Web if it's interesting and it has information they want to know."

If a product has a long story to tell, continue doing it in a single document. If the copy is too long to fit on one screen, break at a logical place, and have a "next" button for the user to click to go to the next page.

The idea is to present the complete selling argument—enough information for the visitor to make a purchase decision—on a single page, even if the page is several screens long.

"Whenever you come to the end of a page, you lose a high proportion of your readers," Nick Usborne explains. By presenting the entire selling argument to the visitor without requiring her to go to another page, you can increase your conversion rates (sales).

The Mark Joyner multiscreen landing page is the model on which Internet direct marketing is going to be based. It is popular on news sites, where the first paragraph of the story is shown, with a link stating "Click here for the complete article." It is used in printed direct mail, where the right-hand pages of a multipage sales letter always say "Over, please."

Here's a tip. When you break a multiscreen page, do so in the middle of a sentence rather than cleanly at the end of a sentence (this technique is always used by knowledgeable direct-mail copywriters and designers on purpose, and often in printed magazines by accident). The user will be more likely to click to the next screen to read the end of the sentence or thought. "If you end the page with the end of a sentence, the thought is complete, and the reader's inclination (to stop reading) is unopposed," says Usborne.

To Sum It All Up

Websites are modular and each page has its own purpose. Use familiar, standard page types (FAQs, "about us," contact) that the reader is familiar with. And don't forget to use links to connect related pages rather than try to cram it all on a single page.

8

Internet Direct Mail

A COMMON BUSINESS mistake is putting up a website and then sitting around waiting for people to come.

But you should heed the old saying, "Some people sit around and wait for things to happen, while others go out and make them happen." If you want people to visit your website, you've got to make it happen. And sending an e-mail invitation to visit has proven extremely effective in building website traffic.

According to an article in *Hotline* (March 5, 2001, p. 5), Jupiter Communications estimates that the average online user gets thirty e-mail messages per day. They predict that the number of unsolicited e-mail marketing messages sent by 2005 will be forty times greater than it is today, and the annual revenue generated by these e-mails will be $7.4 billion.

In a recent survey from the Winterberry Group, as reported in *The Newsletter on Newsletters* (September 15, 2000, p. 5), 74 percent of direct-marketing executives agreed that the marketing objective for e-mail should be direct sales and product and service awareness, as opposed to reinforcing brand and image, collecting data, or initiating a customer dialog.

E-mail marketing results are generally measured in click-throughs. A 5 percent click-through rate means for every one hundred people receiving the e-mail, five clicked through to the website whose URL was embedded in the message.

The biggest advantages of e-mail marketing over traditional paper direct mail is better response at lower costs. In her article called "Email Everywhere" written for *Business 2.0* magazine (June 27, 2000, p. 308), Cathleen Santosus states that the cost of a direct-mail package is 75¢ to $2 apiece versus only 25¢ per message for e-mail marketing to opt-in lists. Response rate to direct mail is 1 to 1.5 percent, versus up to 11.5 percent for e-mail marketing.

Although there are a variety of response options available for Internet direct mail, an embedded URL link in the text is by far the most popular. Not having an embedded hyperlink in your e-mail message cuts response rates by half or more, which is why e-mail results are lower when mailing to users of older versions of AOL.

Another response option is to encourage the recipient to pick up the phone and dial a toll-free number. This works well for customers who do not spend much time online, and for companies that do not have marketing-oriented websites.

A more recent option is to build an online response form directly into the e-mail marketing message. The recipient fills in his name, company, e-mail, phone number, address, and other information in blank fields, then clicks on a button to reply. In some cases, the form can be prepopulated from the e-list database, meaning it's already filled out and all the recipient has to do is click "Send." This is the equivalent of a paper direct mailing in which the recipient's name and address (on a mailing label) is already affixed to the business reply card. Early results show good response with online order forms built into e-mail messages.

Opting in Your Lists

There are two audiences you want to reach with your e-mail invitations to click onto your site: returning visitors and those who have never been to your website.

Returning Visitors

According to an article in *DM News* (September 25, 2000, p. 22), two-thirds of e-mail marketing is targeted at existing customers, while one-third is designed to generate new customers.

At this point, you should already have a check box on your guest page that states, "Check here if you are willing to receive periodic e-mails from us and other companies on offers that may be of interest to you." If you don't, put it up now. Visitors who check this box when registering are said to have "opted in," meaning they have given you permission to send commercial e-mail messages to them. Mailing to opt-in Internet users is perfectly legal and not considered spam under the law.

Some websites use the negative wording, "Check here if you don't want to receive e-mails." If someone doesn't check the box and then submits the completed guest page, the site owner considers this to be a granting of permission. Is this a legitimate opt-in? Certainly it's not as good as the positively phrased, "Check here to give permission."

You can e-mail past visitors to get them to come back to your site again. You can even rent your list to other online marketers, who will gladly pay $100 to $200 or more per thousand names for the privilege of sending their promotional e-mails to your Web-responsive list of visitors, prospects, and customers.

The New Website Visitor

You can rent lists of Internet users and e-mail them to get them to try your site. If they visit and register, you can add their names and Internet addresses to your "house" list of visitors.

When renting a list from an e-list broker (available at evendorson line. com), make sure it's an opt-in list. When in doubt, ask to see the opt-in language from the site on which the names and e-mail addresses were collected. Be wary about renting any e-list for which the broker or list owner will not show you the opt-in language or give you the URL so you can check it out for yourself.

Warning: Even mailing to a legitimate opt-in list does not ensure that your e-mail marketing won't annoy some of the recipients. According to a survey from the Wharton School of Business, 14 percent of those on opt-in lists considered some of the messages they received to be spam. What annoyed them most was too-frequent contact, so when renting an opt-in list, ask how often the list is mailed to.

Basic Format

Today the overwhelming majority of e-mail marketing messages transmitted are sent as straight text. Figure 8.1 shows the basic format for a typical e-mail marketing text message. Note the major components.

• **From line.** Shows who the e-mail is from. Possibly the most important line of the message. As an attendee at a lecture I gave on e-mail marketing put it, "If it's from someone I know I click on it and read it; if it's from someone I don't know, I delete it without opening it." In a minute I'll show you how to write a from line that gets recipients to read your message even if they don't know you.

• **Subject line.** Tells what the e-mail is about. Probably the second most important line of the message. Equivalent to the outer envelope teaser on a paper direct-mail package, the subject line plays a role in whether the e-mail gets read or deleted. Since the e-mail readers on most computers are limited in the length of subject line they will display, keep yours to forty to fifty characters or fewer to make sure the entire message is displayed.

• **The lead.** The first sentence or two of the e-mail is vital. It should immediately make clear what you are writing about and why the recipient should be interested in what you are offering.

• **Response mechanism in lead.** In a traditional direct-mail letter, you typically "ask for action" at the close. In e-mail, you ask for action both at the close and earlier—usually within the first or second paragraph. By embedding a URL link in the lead, you get clickthroughs from prospects who want to see what you are offering without reading the whole e-mail message.

• **Body.** The body of the e-mail, usually just a few paragraphs (but sometimes longer), gives evidence that supports the claims made in the lead. In Figure 8.1, bullets are used to get the key points across in a quick-reading, concise manner.

• **Response mechanism in close.** As in a paper direct mail, ask for response in the closing paragraph of the message. Again this is typically a link to a URL, but it can also be a toll-free number.

• **Opt-out language.** The two rules of e-mail marketing are always mail only to opt-in lists, and always give the recipient the option of "opting out," which means asking that no further e-mails be sent. You handle the former by e-mailing only to genuine opt-in lists, and the latter by including a paragraph in your e-mail that tells the recipient how to opt out. This opt-out paragraph usually appears at the end, although some marketers use it as the lead.

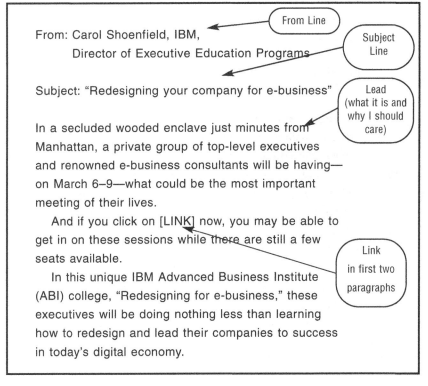

Figure 8.1 E-Mail Sent to a "House File" of Prospects and Customers (continued)

And when you join them, you too will learn—from some of the nation's top e-business experts and consultants—what it takes to compete and prosper in the new Internet era.

Including:

Bullets

- A framework for building your company's e-business strategy.
- The key components of e-business redesign.
- Adapting your corporate culture to satisfy today's Internet customer.
- How to gain a competitive edge with customer-valued Web solutions and services.
- Making accurate financial assessments of proposed new e-business projects.
- How to become a superior leader in the new digital economy.
- Opportunities and issues in global CRM (Customer Relationship Management).
- How to properly align IT with business plans.

If you agree that the Internet has irreversibly changed how business is done, and you want to successfully lead your company through these new electronic changes and challenges, I urge you to click on [LINK] for complete course details or to sign up now. Registration for this college will close out shortly, and once that happens, no further attendees can be accepted.

Close with link and offer

We respect your online time and privacy, and pledge not to abuse this medium. If you prefer not to receive further e-mails from us of this type, please reply to this e-mail and type "Remove" in the subject line.

Opt-out language

Figure 8.1 (continued)

What kind of response can you expect? Marketer William Davenport says, "Click-through rates on rented opt-in lists are 5 to 10 percent for business to business; 10 percent for consumers. E-mails to house files of customers have gotten click-through rates as high as 20 to 25 percent or more."

Davenport's e-mails follow the basic format used in Figure 8.1, but focus around the offer of a premium such as a CD-ROM or white paper, as shown in Figure 8.2.

Baiting the Hook

Sending an e-mail saying "come visit our site" isn't going to work very well. You have to give the recipient a reason to visit or he or she won't come. The most effective e-mails present a special offer that the recipient can accept only by coming to the site. As noted earlier, $10 off or a 10 percent discount have both been proven effective for consumer e-commerce sites.

Free-gift offers work well on the Internet. For example, Gazelle .com, an e-commerce site selling hosiery, offered a free sport bag for purchases of $40 or more. Free money is also effective. For instance, iwon.com has large cash prize drawings; all you have to do to qualify is use their portal. A job search site offered a $500 prize drawing open to participants who posted their resume on the site.

For business-to-business e-mail, a white paper or CD-ROM can work, as William Davenport suggests. You can also have a drawing with a nice prize, choosing from among people who register on the site within a certain time period.

What if you cannot think of a free offer? You probably can. If you're not an e-commerce site, you can still offer a free white paper, free report, or free access to an online tool. On studebaker.com, you can access a free online calculator to compute the monthly payment on a lease of any dollar amount. On edithroman.com, you can do a free database search to find mailing lists reaching particular audiences.

If there's truly no offer, then your e-mail should stress the benefit and utility of your site: great, informative product literature; a free library of articles; tips or news; links to useful resources.

Subject: **Free IDC White Paper on Software Management**

<body copy>
Are you struggling to deploy software to your users, keep it current and manage its use? The *free IDC white paper* "Application Management in the Era of Intranet Computing" explains just such a solution—one that is:

- Completely reliable (customers claim 100% success)
- Easy to install
- Easy to use
- Infinitely scalable
- Flexible and customizable to your unique environment
- Affordable

No doubt you'd like this solution to bring you other benefits like:

- Windows 2000 compatibility
- Works with Active Directory and Group Policy Editor
- Requires no proprietary server software
- Works in complex, heterogeneous environments
- Works across domains
- Extends beyond the firewall
- Handles remote offices and business-to-business users as simply as local users
- Doesn't drain CPU resources
- Frees IT staff to concentrate on other activities

This powerful solution, explained in the *free white paper*, is used by Fortune 500 companies to deliver and manage multiple applications at hundreds of offices across the globe while delivering fast ROI.

Order the *free IDC white paper* right now and get more information on this revolutionary solution. Make the time to read the white paper and you'll get the best answer to software management and distribution.

Figure 8.2 E-Mail Sent to a Rented List of Opt-In Names

Writing E-Mail Marketing Messages That Sell

By following these tips, you'll see an increased click-through rate to your website that will, in all likelihood, lead to increased sales.

The From and Subject Lines

At the beginning of the e-mail, put a from line and a subject line. The subject line should be constructed like a short attention-grabbing, curiosity-arousing outer envelope teaser, compelling recipients to read further—without being so blatantly promotional it turns them off. A good example would be "Come on back to Idea Forum!"

The from line identifies you as the sender if you're e-mailing to your house file. If you're e-mailing to a rented list, the from line might identify the list owner as the sender. This is especially effective with opt-in lists where the list owner (e.g., a website) has a good relationship with its users.

Some e-marketers think the from line is trivial and unimportant; others think it's critical. Internet copywriter Ivan Levison says, "I often use the word *Team* in the from line. It makes it sound as if there's a group of bright, energetic, enthusiastic people standing behind the product." For instance, if you are sending an e-mail to a rented list of computer people to promote a new software product, your subject and from lines might read as follows: "From: The Adobe PageMill Team / Subject: Adobe PageMill 3.0 limited-time offer!"

When choosing your own e-mail address, think about how people will react to it when seeing it in a from line. "Your name is a filtering device for many," observes copywriter Joel Heffner. "If they don't recognize it or feel that it isn't legitimate, they may never read your message." Heffner advises selecting a name that is easy to remember and respond to.

Despite the fact that the word *free* is a proven, powerful response-booster in traditional direct marketing, and that the Internet has a bias in favor of free offers rather than paid ones, some e-marketers avoid *free* in the subject line. The reason is the spam filter software some Internet users have installed to screen their e-mail. These filters eliminate incoming e-mail, and many identify any message with *free* in the subject line as promotional.

Short statements that tease the reader, similar to "fascinations" in printed direct mail (e.g., "What never to eat on an airplane" or "Win a digital camera"), work well as subject lines in Internet direct mail. Example: "Advice from Bill Gates" is better than "Bill Gates on Innovation."

The Headline and Body

Lead off the message copy with a powerful headline or lead-in sentence. You need to get a terrific benefit right up front.

In the first paragraph, deliver a miniversion of your complete message. State the offer and provide an immediate response mechanism, such as clicking on a link connected to a Web page. This appeals to Internet prospects with short attention spans.

After the first paragraph, present expanded copy that covers the features, benefits, proof, and other information the buyer needs to make a decision. This appeals to the prospect who needs more details than a short paragraph can provide.

The offer and response mechanism should be repeated in the close of the e-mail, as in a traditional direct-mail letter. But they should almost always appear at the very beginning, too. That way, busy Internet users who don't have time to read and give each e-mail only a second or two get the whole story.

John Wright, of the Internet marketing services firm MediaSynergy, reports that if you place multiple response links within your e-mail message, 95 percent of click-through responses will come from the first two. Therefore, you should probably limit the number of click-through links in your e-mail to three. An exception might be an e-newsletter or e-zine broken into five or six short items, where each item is on a different subject and therefore each has its own link.

Use wide margins. You don't want to have weird wraps or breaks. Limit yourself to about fifty-five to sixty characters per line. If you think a line is going to be too long, insert a character return. Internet copywriter Joe Vitale sets his margins at twenty and eighty, keeping sentence length to sixty characters, and ensuring the whole line gets displayed on the screen without odd text breaks.

Keep it short and conversational. Keep paragraphs short. It's hard to concentrate on long paragraphs, especially when you're staring at a computer monitor. Short paragraphs make your e-mail easier for the user to read. Take it easy on the all-caps key. You can use WORDS IN ALL CAPS but do so carefully. They can be a little hard to read—and in the world of e-mail, all caps give the impression that you're shouting.

Proofread carefully. "You may be judged by the quality of the messages you send," says Internet consultant Bill Ringle in his article "Email Able" (*Selling Power*, October 1999, p. 60). "To make sure yours are error-free, use your spell checker and reread your messages before you send them."

In general, short is better. This is not the case in classic mail-order selling where as a general principle, "the more you tell, the more you sell." E-mail is a unique environment. Readers are quickly sorting through a bunch of messages and aren't disposed to stick with you for a long time.

Regardless of length, get the important points across quickly. If you want to give a lot of product information, add it lower down in your e-mail message. People who need more information can always scroll down or click for it. The key benefits and deal should be communicated in the first screen, or very soon afterward.

The tone should be helpful, friendly, informative, and educational, not promotional or hard-sell. "Information is the gold in cyberspace," says Joe Vitale. Trying to sell readers with a traditional hyped-up sales letter won't work.

Stephanie Healy, cofounder of winfreestuff.com, wrote "5 Tips for Successful E-Mail Marketing," (*Business-to-Business Marketer*, April 2000, p. 7) in which she states "write copy that contains valuable information." People online want information and lots of it. You'll have to add solid material to your sales letter to make it work online. Refrain from saying your service is "the best" or that you offer "quality." Those are empty, meaningless phrases. Be specific. How are you the best? What exactly do you mean by quality? And who says it besides you? And even though information is the gold, readers don't want to be bored. They seek, like all of us, excitement. Give it to them.

Long copy often works best in certain segments of the direct-marketing industry, particularly in the marketing of newsletters, magazines, and other information products. But initial testing seems to indicate that short copy works best in e-mail marketing. One solution is to use the e-mail to get the recipient to accept a free trial rather than pay for a subscription up front. A series of conversion e-mails then gives compelling reasons for the recipient to convert to a paid subscription. Another solution: Put more sell copy on the response form.

One marketing manager makes this wise observation: "People don't hate Internet direct mail, but they are often bored, indifferent, or annoyed by it." One way to overcome this is through personalization: adding customized information based on the prospect's previous buying habits, preferences, Web surfing, or other data. For example, Amazon.com suggests books you should buy based on books you have ordered in the past.

Offer awards and incentives. As with printed direct mail, offers that contain a "bribe"—a discount, free gift, free shipping and handling, buy one and get one free—are extremely effective in e-mail marketing.

Free money is a powerful offer and, given the dynamics of online buying and the lifetime value of an Internet customer, it can often be profitable. For example, one marketer told potential registrants that one of them who signed up on the website during a specified period would win $500 in cash. A major national e-marketer offers an incredible $10 million drawing once a year as well as regular drawings with smaller cash prizes. When you have a strong offer, put it in the subject line and the lead of your e-mail. Do not bury it midway in the text.

Do not make the offer exclusive to the recipient, as is sometimes done in traditional direct mail. Encourage the recipient to forward the e-mail—and the offer—to friends and colleagues. Here's an example: "Give this special gift offer to your friends by forwarding them this e-mail now. They'll be glad you did!" E-marketers refer to this tactic as *viral marketing.*

Viral e-mail. This is any e-mail that encourages the recipient to pass the e-mail on to others. For example, when the Denver Nuggets basketball team used e-mail to sell season tickets, they gave recipients who passed on their e-mail to five friends the chance to win a signed jersey.

According to Bryan Heathman, president of I Promotion for 24/7 Media, an online direct-marketing company, 81 percent of all viral e-mail recipients will pass the e-mail on to at least one other person, and 49 percent will pass the e-mail on to at least two other people.

Why does viral marketing work so well? Because it uses the Internet to amplify the power of word of mouth, which has traditionally been one of the most effective marketing tools. An article in *American Demographics* magazine (July 2000, p. 22) notes that seven out of ten consumers consider their friends top sources of advice on new products.

Provide a link. People on opt-in e-lists overwhelmingly prefer to respond to Internet direct mail online versus calling a toll-free number or printing out a reply form that has to be faxed or mailed offline. That doesn't mean you shouldn't offer those other response options as an alternative. But you should always have a link to a Web-based response form embedded in your e-mail message. For example, a software marketer decided to offer an upgraded version only on CD-ROM with no option to download from their website. When they sent a direct mail with this offer, many recipients went to their website and downloaded the *old* version—that's how strong their preference was to conduct the entire transaction online.

Most people think of an e-mail marketing campaign as having only one part: the e-mail. But in reality it has two parts: the e-mail the prospect receives, plus the Web-based response form he goes to when he clicks on the link embedded in the message. The headline and copy at the top of the response page should carry the theme of the e-mail and motivate the reader to complete and submit the form.

The Opt-Out Statement

Always include an opt-out statement that makes it easy for recipients to prevent further promotional e-mails from being sent to them. Here's a sample: "We respect your online time and privacy, and pledge not to abuse this medium. If you prefer not to receive further e-mails from us of this type, please reply to this e-mail and type 'Remove' in the subject line." Most e-marketers put this at the end of the e-mail message; some place it at the top.

Before you begin e-mailing to your house file, send an e-mail notifying them of your intention and stating the benefits (e.g., they will get special discounts available only online). Tell them that if they'd rather not get these e-mails, they can click reply and type "Unsubscribe," and you will take them off the e-mail list. On subsequent e-mails to those who agree to be on the e-list, always include the opt-out statement. Never send *any* e-mail marketing message without including an opt-out option.

Frequency

When e-mailing to a house file, an ideal frequency seems to be twice a month. Make one of these e-mails an informative e-zine; the other can be a special offer or promotion. Space them two weeks apart. Your e-zines should be at least 80 percent news and useful information, with perhaps 20 percent of the content promotional.

Enhance Your E-Mail Marketing with Graphics and Animation

Although most e-mail marketing messages are plain text, the use of html format, which offers enhanced graphics—including fonts, typefaces, colors, illustrations, and photos—is growing.

Michelle Feit, president of ePostDirect, an e-mail marketing firm, says that html can increase response up to 20 percent, but doesn't always.

"Testing helps," says Hollis Thomases of WebAdvantage, Inc., an Internet marketing consulting firm. "Test your response rate to html versus text versions before making any conclusions and switching from one format to another."

My feeling is that html in e-mail is similar to the issue of whether to go with a plain-looking, typed sales letter in direct mail instead of a more elaborately designed package.

- If the selling proposition is communicated effectively in words without pictures, straight text should do the job nicely.
- If the selling proposition needs to be illustrated, a graphic format allows the necessary pictures to be included. For instance, if you are selling music CDs, show pictures of the CD packages.
- Make your mailing stand out from the crowd. If everyone else in the field is doing straight text e-mails, make yours an html. If everyone else is doing colorful html e-mails, make yours straight text.

In addition to straight text and html e-mail, a third category—rich media—is emerging. These are graphic e-mails that include either video or audio or both. According to an estimate from eMarketer.com, spending on rich media e-mail may be as high as $300 million a year by 2002.

Does rich media e-mail work? Experience is limited, but there are already success stories. Bacardi sent a rich media e-mail to 150,000 young men who enjoy nightlife and follow music and entertainment. The click-through rate was an incredible 52 percent.

The creative and production costs for rich media e-mail are much higher than straight text or html—anywhere from $5,000 to $10,000 or even higher to produce a thirty- to sixty-second streaming video or audio message.

To Sum It All Up

E-mail marketing typically delivers twice the response rate of paper direct mail at about half the cost. Increasingly, tests are finding that html e-mail often pulls better than straight text. To enjoy this success, keep in mind that the two most important parts of your e-mail are the from and subject lines.

9

Advertising on the Internet: Banner and E-Zine Ads

THERE ARE TWO main ways to advertise your products and services on the Internet. One is to run banner ads. These are small html messages that pop up on other people's websites (not for free; you pay them to run your banner). The second is to put a small text ad, usually fifty to one hundred words, in someone else's e-zine—and again, you pay them to run it.

Writing attention-getting ads is a craft with a century or more of tested experience resulting in proven principles, almost all of which were developed offline. Yet many of these ad-writing rules seem to apply with equal effectiveness to online writing. In this chapter, we'll take a look at how to write effective ad copy, as well as specific tips for both banners and e-zine ads.

Banner Ads Versus E-Mail Marketing

As the money devoted to online marketing grows, so does knowledge about what's working and what's not. The latest question: is the Internet a better tool for building awareness or for direct marketing?

The key awareness tool on the Internet—which is also used for direct response—is banner advertising. A banner ad is a small banner or box that contains your message and appears periodically on someone else's website.

An article in *B2B Direct* newsletter estimates that spending on banner advertising exceeded $5 billion in 2000. One Web-marketing consultant says that banner ads generate a 40 percent recollection rate, which is comparable to TV commercials.

Many Internet marketing agencies now seem to be scoffing at banner advertising, the most common method of building visibility on the Web. The oft-cited statistic of doom is the click-through rates on banner ads averaging 0.5 percent, which means that for every two hundred prospects who see the banner ad, only one clicks on the Web link embedded in the message.

According to an article in *DM News* (September 20, 1999, p. 26), Estée Lauder gets a 1 percent click-through rate to its banner ads. Of these, 2 percent become customers. The cost per new customer acquired through banner advertising is $175—much more than the $25 to $50 it costs the company to acquire a customer through traditional media.

Another negative statistic is that people who claim they don't look at banners rose from 38 percent to 48 percent in 1999, according to Market Facts. That same year, the number of people who said they often looked at banner ads dropped from 16 percent to 9 percent. Of two thousand people surveyed by Jupiter Communications, 71.4 percent said banner ads need to be more informative, and 33 percent said they need to be more creative.

A separate survey of 403 Internet users found that 52 percent had not clicked on any banner ad in the past week. Of those who had clicked on a banner ad during that week, four out of ten could not remember any online ad.

Paul Baudisch, president of NetMarquce (a marketing agency based in Needham, Massachusetts), says Internet users are visually discounting the presence of banner ads.

Increasingly, companies are testing the direct-marketing model, sending complex e-mails to highly targeted lists of prospects. This technique works much the same way as offline direct-marketing campaigns. Companies build databases of e-mail addresses by enticing customers to register on a site in exchange for information or access to a special offer.

CATeLOG has built an extensive database by posting registration forms on a variety of popular consumer sites. The agency then puts together e-mail campaigns for different clients, and sends them to appropriate consumers mined from that database.

For instance, when A&E Television Networks wanted to advertise its "Live by Request" program, they sent their customers an entertaining e-mail that contained music and other audio enhancements. "I don't think there is a better, more concise, less expensive way to get people one-on-one," says Mike Mohamed, A&E's vice president of marketing.

When companies use their own homegrown lists, online direct marketing works even better. That's the tactic that New England Business Service (NEBS) employs. This manufacturer of forms and supplies (based in Groton, Massachusetts) started an e-mail newsletter last year. Customers register to receive the newsletter, which includes tips for business owners and special offers. Circulation is at six thousand and growing, says Janie Marshall, NEBS's manager for marketing communications.

But NEBS has also experimented with banner advertising on different sites that small-business owners frequent. "Some did very well," Marshall says. "We continued the ones that worked, we're working on the ones that didn't."

This is a wise strategy according to Michele Slack, an analyst in the online advertising group of Jupiter Communications, who warns that rumors of the death of banner advertising have been greatly exaggerated. "The novelty factor is wearing off," Slack says. "When an ad is targeted well, and the creative is good, click-through rates are much higher."

And in time, fancy e-mailed messages might not be opened either. "It's a novelty right now," Slack says. "When people's in-boxes get flooded, you'll see a fall-off there too." So, what is her advice? Incorporate both philosophies into a marketing plan. "The Web is one of the few places where you can combine the two (branding and direct marketing)," she says. "To see it as an either/or, you're missing out on what the Web can do."

Other companies report more positive banner results. Start sampling.com acquires members for its free product sample site at $1 a member, a rate ten times more efficient than through print ads and radio commercials.

Pros and cons of banner advertising are listed in Table 9.1. As online technology gets faster, many of the negatives are disappearing.

Table 9.1 Banner Advertising Weaknesses and Strengths

Cons	Pros
Not all target audiences are wired to the same degree	The Internet continues to attract new users, approaching a "mass media" makeup
The online audience is highly fragmented	Vertical sites are treating markets of Web surfers with common interests
Branding on the Web is highly questionable	Marketers are beginning to redefine brands in ways that take advantage of the interactive nature of the Internet
Bandwidth problems limit creative options	DSL, cable, and convergent technologies are progressing, although slower than many expected
Internet users find ads intrusive	Web marketers are getting better at communicating with online consumers, thus making ads less intrusive
Advertisers have not integrated online and offline efforts	Some advertisers are beginning to combine the two efforts effectively
Personalization technology raises questions about privacy	Guidelines are being developed to quell consumers' fears

Source: Business2.com, March 20, 2001, p. 82

Nine Common Banner-Ad Mistakes to Avoid

"Never underestimate the selling power of a well-positioned banner ad," writes copywriter Joe McAllister in *Target Marketing* magazine. He says the banner copy should feature a benefit, and that bright colors, borders, and animation are all effective techniques.

Banner-advertising expert Rob Frankel advises e-marketers to avoid the following mistakes when creating their banner ads:

- **The ad is overloaded.** If there are too many colors, it'll be too slow to load and too hard to read. Nobody wants to grow old waiting for your banner ad to load. Frankel advises designing banner ads that will load and be viewed easily with last year's technology. "Personally, I design pages for people running no more than Netscape 2.0 on the equivalent of a 486 running at 66 MHz and 256 colors," says Frankel. "That means your art should still be no deeper than eight bits, unless you're a true minimalist and can bring it in at no more than four."

Today's technology enables the transmission bureau to determine bandwidth and send a different banner based on download capability. Susan Bratton, a vice president at Excite@home, recommends preparing banner ads in four different sizes: 5, 10, 15, and 20K.

- **It's unattractive.** People like good-looking stuff. What works for Cindy Crawford can work for you, too. (Her site, by the way, is cindy.com.) So if you're not a digital Leonardo da Vinci, find someone who is and pay him a few bucks to make your banner look great.

- **It's got too many bells and whistles.** Just because technology offers you bells and whistles doesn't mean you have to use every one of them. Chances are that the average Web surfer has been through several sites before he gets to your banner. Give him a break. Don't overdo motion, movement, or message changes. Give the reader some time to digest what you're displaying.

- **The ad is illiterate and illegible.** These are the ads that make you squitch up your face and twist your head trying to make some sense out of the illegible scrawl that some knucklehead thinks is cool. But prospects don't care how cool you think it looks. If they can't read it, you've lost any chance of them clicking on it.

• **There's a missing link.** Your banner looks great, but isn't linked to anything, That's a mistake that anyone should be able to detect and prevent with a simple check.

• **It has link errors.** Your banner looks great. The link works . . . directly to a 404 message (meaning the requested Web page was not found). Maybe this one isn't your fault. Maybe your Web master inadvertently forgot to tell you he switched servers. But even if it was his fault, who do you think he's going to blame? Keep checking those banner links every few days.

• **The message is weak.** The same things that make good ads make good banners. Unfortunately, the same things that make bad ads make horrible banners. If you don't know how to write and design a clever, compelling message, hire someone who does. Nothing turns off potential prospects more than a really stupid attempt at being clever, an offense usually committed with the aid of a bad pun. Remember that your ad is a representative of you, containing a smattering of your personality and ability. If it looks dopey to a viewer, guess what they're going to think about you? It's better to be clear than clever.

• **The message is confusing.** Your banner looks pretty, but nobody understands what the heck you're talking about. This is the number one mistake made by do-it-yourselfers. See previous point.

• **The banner is boring.** One common mistake is that your banner doesn't compel your recipients to respond within a certain time frame. Without a deadline, there is no immediacy to act, which means they scroll away.

Since banner ads are written in html, you have flexibility in color and font. Experiment. Mina Lux, a vice president with Doubleday Interactive, found that indenting a banner ad five spaces and using a larger headline increased click-through 184 percent.

Here are some additional banner ad tips from an Infoseek presentation at the Web Advertising conference and from Digiware Interactive Multimedia:

- Use the words *click here* to make it clear to the viewer that she is supposed to click on the ad. Link the banner to a page specifically related to the offer, not to the home page.
- Use animation to capture attention. However, if animation is located on a page where the user would dwell for an extended period of time, it can be more annoying than beneficial.
- Vary the banner ad. Infoseek finds that on their site, the same ad wears out after 200,000 to 400,000 impressions. Yahoo! says banner response drops off dramatically after two weeks. So switch frequently to a new ad.
- Contests don't work in banner advertising.
- Intrigue and sex sell.
- Bigger is better. Wide banner ads, typically sixty-eight or five hundred pixels across, get more click-throughs than smaller ones.
- Create urgency. Phrases like "last chance" prompt users to click now.
- Use the word *free* and have the ad click through to a free offer.

Placing Banner Ads

The basic options for banner advertising are a site buy, category buy, or run of network.

A site buy refers to placing a banner ad on a specific website. A category buy places your banner ad on a selection of websites all in a specific category—for example, a group of sites all related to sports, TV, computer programming, or whatever. A run of network buy places your banner ad on a bunch of unrelated sites all managed by the same hosting service.

In banner advertising, the best media buy is not obvious and is contrary to what works in traditional direct marketing, where targeted media work best. So you want to place your ad in publications where you know the readers are interested in your type of offer. If you are selling fishing lures, for instance, you run in the fishing magazines.

If you are selling accounting software for small businesses, run in small business magazines.

Why does this work best? You are targeting a large group of readers you know have an interest in your offer. So your response is high.

Specialized magazines, with limited circulations, are usually less expensive to advertise in than large-circulation general publications. Also, when you run a specialized offer in a generalized magazine, you are in essence paying to reach a lot of people who are not your prospects. So the cost per order is most favorable in the more targeted magazine.

On the Web, the cost difference between a site buy and a run of network buy is not as great as in print. And, although a lot of the people who browse your ad on a run of network buy are not your prospects, enough *are* so that it still pays off. Some early testing suggests that run of network buys are actually more profitable than site or category buys. But it's too early to call this a definitive rule.

E-Zine Advertising

An e-zine—short for electronic magazine—is a newsletter distributed over the Internet. Chapter 10 shows you how to write effective e-zine copy. But in addition to publishing your own e-zine, you can advertise in other marketers' e-zines. And this medium has proven extremely effective.

According to Jaffer Ali, CEO of PennMedia Network—a network of more than six hundred e-zines—e-newsletter ads generate up to twenty times higher response than banner ads, based on conversion rates.

Markus Allen, a direct-marketing expert, says, "It's much harder to spread the word from paper than from the Internet." He says his own e-zine was mentioned in both the print version and the electronic version of the same newsletter. "I had twenty-five times more registrations from the electronic version."

Many e-zines will now accept advertising in their publications. For a fee, you can run a one-hundred-word product ad, similar to a classified ad, in someone else's e-zine. The ad includes a hyperlink to your website.

A good example was the e-zine published by Egghead.com. With the Egghead.com E-Mail Newsletter Program, you could prominently display your personalized text message in their daily e-mail newsletter with a hyperlink to your web page or order form.

If you get good results advertising in a company's e-newsletter, you may want to test an e-mail to their e-list as well. Foofoo.com, a website that bills itself as "the definitive authority on the Internet for fun and the finer things in life," sent a separate e-mail to one million people receiving the Egghead.com e-zine. They received twenty thousand replies, which is a decent 2 percent response rate.

A big advantage of advertising in other e-zines is reach. Some of them reach millions of Internet users. Another is the relatively low cost. Running an ad in an e-zine costs $40 per thousand versus $150 to $400 per thousand cost of renting and transmitting an e-mail message to an opt-in e-list.

Today, advertising in e-mail newsletters is becoming one of the most popular forms of online marketing. Why? Because it is inexpensive, highly targeted, and produces results.

Most e-zines accept only one or two ads per issue, so ad clutter is not a problem. And, the e-zine ads get an implied endorsement from the editors by being positioned inside with the rest of the content.

With e-zines, you get incredibly cost-effective marketing. For example, there are e-zines where you can reach a targeted audience of thousands of readers at 1.5¢ to 3¢ per reader or less, all of whom have opted in to receive the publication that carries your advertisement. This is permission marketing at its very best.

Why use newsletter advertising? Many Internet marketing strategies depend on visitors voluntarily coming back to a website. By itself, this strategy will not work. No Internet marketing plan is complete unless it incorporates both an inbound and outbound strategy. Drawing customers to your website is an inbound tactic. Sending messages out includes the use of e-mail and newsletter advertising. A Web marketer must use both strategies to have an effective website.

What are the advantages of newsletter advertising? One advantage is a better response rate as compared to banner ads, which makes it a more cost-effective medium. Another is transferability, a fairly unique e-commerce concept. When people receive a newsletter of high interest, they often send it to a friend or coworker. This pass-along readership is free advertising and is highly encouraged.

Like all other advertising, you must select the newsletter with the right audience. You must also choose one with good content, i.e., one that people will read and has few ads. Most newsletters are fun, enjoyable, readable, and contain about three ads.

Most newsletter ads are currently text only. They consist of about fifty words and compare to a short e-mail message ad. Each ad contains a URL that directs the reader to your website where your marketing action takes place. Make sure that the URL does not wrap and works well prior to ad placement.

Newsletter Ad Components

Newsletter ads contain some basic parts just like any other ad and can be changed to fit your needs. But primarily the ad will contain a headline, fifty to one hundred words of body copy, and a URL to let readers respond. You can also change and test the length of the message and the creative style.

In addition to format and copy tests, you should be constantly testing offers. As in traditional marketing, event marketing is an extremely effective tool in e-commerce. Special offers for Father's Day, Mother's Day, and other holidays can be put together quickly and inexpensively to maximize your website's return on investment.

"Have something of perceived value to give away," writes Michael Pendleton in *DM News* (December 25, 2000, p. 23). "People want something for nothing, so offer them specific and tangible information." His suggestions include a white paper, CD-ROM, or case study. "Better still, package your offer as an information kit and give it a compelling name, like 'The Busy Executive's Guide to IT Recruiting.'"

The most effective call to action for e-zine ads is an embedded link to your website, preferably to a page specifically related to the offer in the ad. The second-best response option is to call a toll-free number.

Format for your e-zine ad will vary with the publisher. For Egghead.com, for example, the format was as follows.

Headline in caps:

GET 5 CDs FREE—JOIN THE CBA MUSIC CLUB

Three lines of advertising copy (sixty characters per line including spaces)

Select 5 FREE CDs from our huge inventory of
Classical, R&B, Country, Rap, and popular artist
CDs. Click here to order your favorite CDs online!

One line optional hyperlink

www.cdbmusic.com/egghead1.html

This ad in the Egghead e-zine cost $40 per thousand, including the transmission fee.

Each e-zine will have its own advertising requirements and rates. Typically the sponsored ads range from a few words and a link to a URL to around a hundred words plus a headline and link.

Figure 9.1 shows an ad that ran in the free e-zine distributed by Boardroom, publishers of *Bottom Line Personal* newsletter. William Davenport says the e-zine ad in Figure 9.2 was successful but did not give me specific results.

** SPECIAL OFFER! NATURE'S HEALING MIRACLES *******
The more you learn about your own body, the more you find
that today's most potent cures come straight from nature.
Discover the absolute best ways to reverse arthritis, lose
weight, halt osteoporosis, combat Alzheimer's, heart
disease and more in The Complete Encyclopedia of Natural
Healing. Over 1,900 life-saving, money-saving, anti-aging
techniques from award-winning scientist Gary Null, PhD.
Click here for your free trial . . .

Figure 9.1 E-Zine Ad for Boardroom

FREE IDC WHITE PAPER gives you the story on the easiest way to manage software. Over the Web—NO PROBLEM! Through the firewall—NO PROBLEM! Mixed environments; Windows 2000—NO PROBLEM! Deploy and manage any software, to any users, anywhere, anytime! Get your FREE report right now
www.osa.com/cmp

Figure 9.2 Ad in a Third-Party E-Zine

How to Write Headlines That Sell

In today's environment of "information overload," you must work harder than ever to get your ad or commercial noticed. Wherever you turn—magazines, television, radio, the World Wide Web, today's paper, or the in-basket of a busy executive—too many things are competing for your audience's attention. In all forms of advertising, the first impression—the first thing that is seen, read, or heard—can mean the difference between success and failure. If the first impression is boredom or irrelevance, the ad will not attract your prospect. But if the copy offers news or helpful information or promises a reward for paying attention, it is well on its way toward persuading the reader to buy your product.

What, specifically, is this first impression? In a banner or e-zine ad, it's the headline. Here are some tips for making your headlines more effective and compelling.

Appeal to Your Audience's Self-Interest

When we shop, we want products that satisfy our needs—and our budgets. Good copywriters recognize this fact, and put *sales appeals*—not cute, irrelevant gimmicks and wordplay—in their headlines.

They know that when readers browse ad headlines, they want to know "what's in it for *me*?" The effective headline tells the reader, "hey, stop a minute! This is something you want!"

A classic appeal to self-interest is the headline "How to Win Friends and Influence People," from an ad for the Dale Carnegie book of the same name. The headline promises that you will make friends and be able to persuade others if you read the ad and order the book.

A recent ad for Kraft Foods appeals to the homemaker with the headline "How to Eat Well for Nickels and Dimes." If you are interested in good nutrition for your family but must watch your budget carefully, this ad speaks directly to your needs.

The headline for a Hellmann's Real Mayonnaise ad hooks us with the question, "Know the Secret to Moister, Richer Cake?" We are promised a reward—the secret to great cake—in return for reading the copy.

Each of these headlines offers a benefit to the consumer, a reward for reading the copy. And each promises specific, helpful information in return for the time invested in reading the ad and the money spent to buy the product.

Get Your Audience's Attention

We've already seen how headlines get attention by appealing to the consumer's self-interest. Here are a few more examples of this type of headline:

Give Your Kids a Fighting Chance	(Crest)
Why Swelter Through Another Hot Summer?	(GE air conditioners)
For Deep-Clean, Oil-Free Skin, Noxzema Has the Solution.	(Noxzema moisturizer)

Another effective attention-getting gambit is to alert the reader to something new. These headlines often use words such as *new, discover, introducing, announcing, now, it's here, at last,* and *just arrived.*

New Sensational Video Can Give You Thin Thighs Starting Now!	(exercise video tape)
Discover Our New Rich-Roasted Taste	(Brim decaffeinated coffee)

Introducing New Come 'N Get It Bursting   (Come 'N Get It dog food)
With New Exciting 4-Flavor Taste.

If you can legitimately use the word *free* in your headline, do so. *Free* is the most powerful word in the copywriter's vocabulary. Everybody wants to get something for free.

For example, the headline of a *TV Guide* insert for Silhouette Romance novels reads, "Take 4 Silhouette Romance Novels FREE (A $9.80 Value) . . . And Experience The Love You've Always Dreamed Of." In addition, the word *free* is used a total of twenty-three times in the body copy and on the reply card.

Other powerful attention-getting words include *how to*, *why*, *sale*, *quick*, *easy*, *bargain*, *last chance*, *guarantee*, *results*, *proven*, and *save*. Do not avoid these words because other copywriters use them with such frequency. Other copywriters use these words because *they work*.

Headlines that offer the consumer guidance are also attention-getters. The information promised in the headline can be given in the copy or in a free report the reader can download. The following are some examples.

Free New Report on 67 Emerging Growth Stocks   (Merrill Lynch)

Three Easy Steps to Fine Wood Finishing   (Minwax Wood Finish)

Use Appropriate Appeals

Many advertisers try to get attention with headlines and gimmicks that don't promise a benefit or are not related to the product. One industrial manufacturer featured a photo of a bikini-clad woman in several of their ads, along with an offer of a reprint of the photo to readers who clipped the coupon and requested a brochure on the manufacturer's equipment.

Does this sort of approach get attention? Yes, but not attention that leads to a sale or to real interest in the product. Attention-getting for attention-getting's sake attracts the curious—but precious few serious customers.

When you write a headline, get noticed by picking out an important customer benefit and presenting it in a clear, bold, dramatic fashion. Avoid headlines and concepts that are cute, clever, and titillating but irrelevant. They may generate some interest, but they do not sell.

Here are some headlines that lure the prospect in an appropriate, relevant fashion designed to generate interest and response:

Now save thousands of dollars on stationery printing costs . . . With Instant Stationery, you'll never buy costly printed stationery again!

WALT DISNEY'S *MAID* built a $9 million stock portfolio using the simple technique inside this envelope!

Now get business and accounting software equivalent to the systems run by *multi-billion dollar conglomerates* . . . at a tiny *fraction* of the cost Fortune 500 companies have paid.

Speak Directly to Your Audience

Use your headline to define your audience and appeal to your target market. This will increase readership and response while cutting down on "tire-kicker" type inquiries.

For instance, if you are selling life insurance to people older than sixty-five, there is no point in writing an ad that generates inquiries from younger people. In the same way, an ad for a $55,000 sports car should make it obvious that "This is for rich folks only!" You don't want to waste time answering inquiries from people who can't afford the product.

The headline can narrow in on the ideal audience for your ad and screen out those readers who are not potential customers. A good headline for the life insurance ad might read, "To Men and Women Over 65 Who Need Affordable Life Insurance Coverage." One possible headline for the sports car ad is, "If You Have to Ask How Many Miles to the Gallon It Gets, You Can't Afford to Buy One."

Here are a few more headlines that do a good job of selecting the right audience for the product:

Is Your Electric Bill Too High?	(utility ad)
We're Looking for People to Write Children's Books.	(The Institute of Children's Literature)
A Message to All Charter Security Life Policyholders of SinglePremium Deferred Annuities	(Charter Security life insurance)

Do not explicitly identify the audience in the headline if the nature of the product or service makes it unnecessary or redundant. A recent ad in the New York *Daily News*, "Penile Enlargement for Men Only," would have been stronger with the simpler and more direct headline "Penile Enlargement." Another ad offered "Maternity Clothes for Pregnant Women." Who else would wear the stuff?

Deliver a Meaningful Message

According to David Ogilvy, author of *Ogilvy on Advertising*, four out of five readers will read the headline and skip the rest of the ad.

If this is the case, it pays to make a complete statement in your headline. That way, the ad can do some selling to the 80 percent of readers who read headlines only. Here are a few headlines that deliver complete messages:

Caught Soon Enough, Early Tooth Decay Can Actually Be Repaired by Colgate!	(Colgate toothpaste)
Gas Energy, Inc. Cuts Cooling and Heating Costs Up to 50%	(Hitachi chiller-heaters)
You Can Make Big Money in Real Estate Right Now	(Century 21)

Ogilvy recommends you include the selling promise and the brand name in the headline, although many effective headlines don't do so. But if you suspect most of your prospects won't bother to read the copy underneath, then include the product name in the headline.

Draw the Reader into Your Body Copy

A few product categories—liquor, soft drinks, and fashion, for example—can be sold with an attractive photo, a powerful headline, and a minimum of words. But most items—automobiles, computers, books, CDs, telephones—require that the reader be given a lot of information. That information appears in the body copy, and for the ad to be effective, the headline must compel the reader to read this copy.

To draw the reader into the body copy, you must arouse his or her curiosity. You can do this with humor or by being provocative or mysterious. You can ask a question, promise a reward, give news, or offer useful information.

A sales letter promoting motivational pamphlets was mailed to business managers. The headline of the letter was, "What Do Japanese Managers Have That American Managers Sometimes Lack?" Naturally, American managers wanted to read on and find out about the techniques the Japanese use to manage effectively.

The headline of an ad for a facial lotion reads "The $5 Alternative to Costly Plastic Surgery." The reader is lured into the ad to satisfy her curiosity about what this inexpensive alternative might be. The headline would not have been as successful if it had said, "$5 Bottle of Lotion is an Inexpensive Alternative to Costly Plastic Surgery."

PFS Software begins its ad with the headline, "If You're Confused About Buying a Personal Computer, Here's Some Help." If you *are* confused about computers, you will want to read the ad to get the advice offered in the headline.

Use Direct Headlines for Straightforward Offers and High-Interest Products

Direct headlines state the selling proposition in straightforward terms, without wordplay, hidden meanings, or puns. "Pure Silk Blouses—30 Percent Off" is a headline that's about as direct as you can get. Most retailers use newspaper ads with direct headlines to announce sales and bring customers into the stores.

Direct headlines work best when the offer is simple and attractive and the product is in demand. For example, people know what silk blouses are, and 30 percent off is a clear, understandable offer.

Here's another example. A pet store in New York City was losing business because of the manager's disagreeable personality. The owner found out and fired him. The next day, employees put up a sign in the store window that read, "The Nasty Old Man Is Gone." The new manager reported an immediate increase in business.

Inject News into Your Headline

If you have news about your product, announce it in the headline. This news can be the introduction of a new product, an improvement of an existing product ("new, *improved* Bounty"), or a new application for an old product. Some examples of headlines that contain news:

The First Transportable Computer Worth   (Apple IIc)
Taking Anywhere

Finally, a Caribbean Cruise as Good as   (Norwegian American Line)
Its Brochure

The Norwegian American headline, in addition to containing news, has added appeal because it empathizes with the reader's situation. We've all been disappointed by fancy travel brochures that promise better than they deliver. Norwegian American gains credibility in our eyes by calling attention to this well-known fact.

Offer to Teach the Reader Something Useful

The words *how to* are pure magic in advertising headlines, magazine articles, and book titles. (There are more than seven thousand books in print with the words *how to* in their titles.) Some copywriters claim if you begin with the words *how to*, you can't write a bad headline. They may be right.

How-to headlines offer the promise of solid information, sound advice, and solutions to problems: "How to Turn a Simple Party Into a Royal Ball." "How to Write Better and Faster." "How to Stop Smoking in 30 Days . . . Or Your Money Back."

Whenever I'm stuck for a headline, I type "How to" on my keyboard, and what follows is always a decent, hard-working headline—good enough to use until something better comes along.

Ask a Provocative Question

To be effective, the headline must ask a question that the reader can relate to or would like to have answered. Some examples:

When an Employee Gets Sick, How Long Does It Take Your Company to Recover?	(Pilot Life Insurance)
Is Your Pump Costing You More to Operate Than It Should?	(Gorman-Rupp pumps)
Do You Close the Bathroom Door Even When You're the Only One Home?	(from a letter selling subscriptions to *Psychology Today*)
Have You Any of These Decorating Problems?	(Bigelow carpets)

Question headlines should focus on the reader's self-interest, curiosity, and needs—and *not* on the advertiser's. A typical self-serving question headline used by many companies reads something like, "Do You Know What the XYZ Company Is Up to These Days?" The reader's response is "Who cares?" and a turn of the page.

Tell Customers What You Want Them to Do

Headlines that directly tell prospects to buy a product, visit a dealer, or take other action are called "command headlines." Command headlines generate sales by calling for immediate action. Here are a few command headlines:

Make Your Most Valuable Information Worthless.	(Destroyit paper shredders)

Microwave Your Pain Away.   (Megamooch)

Aim High. Reach for New Horizons.   (Air Force recruitment)

The first word in the command headline is a strong verb demanding action on the part of the reader.

Use the "Reason Why" Approach

One easy and effective way of writing body copy is to list the sales features of your product in simple 1–2–3 fashion. If you write your ad this way, you can use a reason-why headline to introduce the list. Examples of reason-why headlines include "Seven Reasons Why You Should Join the American Institute of Aeronautics and Astronautics," "120 to 4,000 Reasons Why You Should Buy Your Fur During the Next Four Days," and "11 Reasons Why ProtoTech Should Make Your Next Prototype."

Reason-why headlines need not actually contain the phrase "reasons why." Other introductory phrases such as "6 ways," "7 steps," and "here's how" work just as well.

Put the Headline in Quotation Marks

In a testimonial advertisement, your customers do your selling for you. An example of a testimonial is the Publishers Clearing House commercial in which past winners tell us how they won big prize money in the sweepstakes.

Testimonials work because they offer *proof* that a business satisfies its customers. In print-ad testimonials, the copy is written as a direct quote from the customer, who is often pictured in the ad.

When writing testimonial copy, allow the customer's own words to make the point. A natural, conversational tone adds believability to the testimonial, so try not to edit the quote too much.

The most important part of the testimonial ad is the headline. Headlines in quotation marks attract more attention than those without. In fact, quotation marks increase readership so sharply that it is desirable to use them even if the headline is not a direct quotation and the ad is not a testimonial ad. Simply put quotations around the headline. For example, instead of:

Get all the money you need for your business—guaranteed

use:

"Get all the money you need for your business— guaranteed."

Placing headlines and body copy in quotation marks when they are not actual quotes is a technique known as the "unattributed testimonial." It is the *advertisers*, not their clients, who are saying the phrases in quotation marks . . . and they are, in effect, quoting themselves in their own copy. It's tricky, but perfectly ethical and perfectly legal.

Avoid Being Clever for the Sake of Being Clever

Creativity should be used to gain attention and interest in a manner that promotes the product. Your goal is to sell something. If you entertain while doing it, fine, but entertainment is a means to an end, not the end itself.

Showmanship, clever phrases, and ballyhoo do not, by themselves, make for a good headline and can actually end up obscuring your point. Creating headlines that are wonderfully clever is worthwhile only if the cleverness enhances the selling message and makes it more memorable.

If you have to choose between being clever and obscure or simple and straightforward, we advise you to pick the latter. You may not win any advertising awards, but at least you'll sell some merchandise.

Be careful of wording that can give an unintended meaning to your headline. A recent newspaper ad headline proclaimed, "Supreme Adult Organ." Only after a closer reading did it become clear the ad was for keyboard instruments.

Jim Alexander, founder of Alexander Marketing Services, a Michigan-based ad agency, is a firm believer that headlines should sell.

> We believe in dramatizing a product's selling message with flair and excitement. Those are important ingredients of good salesmanship

in print. But simple statements and plain-jane graphics often make powerful ads.

For example, the headline "Handling Sulfuric Acid" might sound dull or uncreative to you. To a chemical engineer who's forever battling costly corrosion, that simple headline implies volumes. And makes him want to read every word of the problem-solving copy that follows.

So before we let our clients pronounce an ad dull, we first ask them, "Dull to whom?" Dull to you, the advertiser? Or dull to the reader, our potential customer? It's easy to forget that the real purpose of an ad is to communicate ideas and information about a product. Too many ads are approved because of their entertainment value. That's a waste of money.

10

Electronic Newsletters: E-Zines

IN TODAY'S AGE of specialized information, newsletters—both off- and online—are popular. Sources estimate that there are more than ten thousand print newsletters and at least five hundred e-zines published in the United States—and probably several thousand.

In the online world, many e-marketers publish electronic newsletters that they distribute via e-mail free to their customers and prospects. The main purpose of such an e-zine is to:

- Keep your customers and prospects informed about new products, services, and offers
- Contact your customers and prospects more frequently than you can affordably do by other methods (mail, visits, phone calls)
- Build your credibility with a select audience (the people who receive the newsletter) over an extended period of time

Instinctively, most marketers recognize that they should be in touch with their customers and prospects far more often than they actually are. You know, for instance, that there are many people in your life—business and social—whom you don't think about, see, or talk to for long periods of time simply because you are busy and not thinking of them.

Well, your customers and prospects are busy too. And while you may be agonizing over why Joe hasn't placed an order from you recently or called your firm to handle a project, Joe isn't even thinking about you . . . because he has so much else on his mind.

You know you should be doing something to keep your name in front of Joe and remind him of your existence. But how? You may want to call or send a letter, but you think this is too pushy . . . and besides, there's no real *reason* to call, and you don't want to seem like you're begging for business.

An e-zine solves this problem. It regularly places your name and activities in front of your customers and prospects, reminding them of your existence, products, and services on an ongoing basis. And you don't need an "excuse" to make this contact because the prospect *expects* to receive an e-zine on a regular basis. The e-zine increases the frequency of message repetition, and it supplements other forms of communication such as catalogs, print ads, and sales letters.

Size and Frequency

How long should your e-zine be? How often should it be published? In my opinion, your e-zine should feature five to ten short items, each only a paragraph or two in length. You can also add one or two longer features, but these should be no more than one or two screens.

There are already too many e-zines, and yours won't be read unless it's a reasonable length. In this regard, the fact that the e-zine is electronic instead of print works against you. Readers will put a print newsletter in their briefcase to read later if they don't have time now. But with an e-zine, it's too tempting for them to click the delete button.

As for frequency, e-zines can be daily, weekly, monthly, semi-monthly, or even less frequent. Although with their low production and distribution cost (virtually zero), most marketers opt for at least once a month. (The ability to contact the prospect cheaply and often is why they are doing an e-zine in the first place).

As discussed in Chapter 8, the optimum schedule for contacting your customers and prospects via e-mail is twice a month with weekly being the maximum recommended frequency. There are very few organizations, including yours, whose members or customers need to hear from them more often than once a week. That's only one of the reasons why I advise against a daily e-zine for most marketers.

The other rationale for avoiding a daily e-zine is that most companies don't have enough news to fill 250 issues each year. If your schedule is too frequent, you may find yourself putting unnecessary fluff and filler in the newsletter just to get something in the mail. Your readers will be turned off by the lack of quality and poor content, so this would hurt you rather than help. Not to mention it's a big burden that you really don't need to take on.

Building Your E-Zine Subscriber List

Who should get your e-zine? Basically, it should go to anyone with whom you want to establish a regular relationship. These people can include:

- Current customers
- Past customers
- Current prospects
- Past prospects
- Expired accounts (past subscribers, "expires," and so on)
- Employees
- Vendors
- Colleagues
- Consultants, gurus, and other prominent members of your industry
- Referral sources (influential people who can refer business to you)
- Trade publication editors, business columnists, and other members of the press who might possibly use material in your newsletter in their own writings

"All your current clients should receive your client newsletter," says Steve Klinghoffer, president of WPI Communications. "The newsletter is an important vehicle for keeping in touch on a regular and predictable basis. It confers automatic high visibility and does so in the best possible way: by reflecting you as professional, knowledgeable, and competent. This not only builds your image, but also helps to ensure that your current clients will remain responsive to your recommendations."

Klinghoffer adds, "Do not neglect to send the newsletter to clients who use your services or products in a very limited manner, or whom you have not visited with recently. You may not think of them as current clients, but of course, they are. What's more, rather than drifting away from you, the newsletter offers the kind of visibility that prompts many 'limited clients' to expand their use of your products and services."

Here is how you build the subscriber list.

1. **Put all current and past prospects and customers on the list.** But don't use names that are too old. For past prospects and customers, for example, you might go back two or three years—but no more than that.

2. **Get your salespeople to give you all the names of the people they call on regularly.** Salespeople have their own favorite prospects, and these people may not be in the advertising inquiry files. So get them to give you names of people who should get the newsletter. You essentially want to convert the dozens of individual Rolodex™ files kept by various salespeople and sales reps into a single, integrated subscriber list for your newsletter.

3. **Go to your PR department or agency and add its media list.** Get the names of all editors who should receive the newsletter.

4. **Make sure all new inquiries and new customers are automatically added to the subscription list.** This includes every response, every sales lead generated by your company's banner advertising, e-mail marketing, and other promotions.

5. **Network at trade shows.** Create a subscription application form and offer a free one-year subscription to anyone who stops by your booth and completes the form.

6. **Don't forget your own company.** Make sure the subscriber list contains the names of your immediate supervisors, your product and brand managers, your sales and marketing managers, your CEO, and any other key personnel whose support you need to run an effective advertising department. Company managers enjoy getting the newsletter and will often offer ideas for articles and stories you can use. You might also approach your most important colleague and ask him or her to contribute a regular column.

7. **Offer free subscriptions to your e-zine on your home page to anyone who gives you their e-mail address.** Because the e-zine is a type of e-mail, you cannot send it to anyone unless they have opted in and agreed to receive promotional e-mail from you. Therefore, you can't send your e-zine to strangers unless they have opted in at your website or by some other method. If you send it to customers and prospects who have not opted in, you should add this message to the top of their first issue: "You are getting this e-zine because you are a customer or prospect of XYZ Corporation. If you do not want to receive future issues, click reply and type "Unsubscribe" in the subject line."

To see an online e-zine subscription form, look on the home page of my website bly.com.

Promoting the E-Zine

In addition to compiling the list in this manner, you can do a number of things to promote the electronic newsletter (and to use the newsletter offer as a promotion):

• **Use your e-zine as an incentive in your direct mail.** You can offer the newsletter to people who respond to your e-mail or direct mail. In direct mail, this can be as simple as adding a line to your reply cards with a box that says, "☐ Check here if you would like a free 1-year subscription to our monthly electronic newsletter, [title of newsletter]." You could also stress the newsletter offer in the P.S. of your sales letter.

• **You can offer the electronic newsletter as an extra incentive for responding to your space ads.** Again, add an option to the response coupon that says "☐ Check here for a free 1-year subscription to our e-zine, [title of newsletter]."

• **Use your e-zine as a springboard.** At speeches, seminars, and presentations, your company representatives can use the newsletter offer to get listeners involved in conversations with them. At the end of the talk, the presenter says, "Our monthly electronic newsletter, [title of newsletter], will give you more information on this topic. Just give me your business card and e-mail address, and I'll see to it you get a free one-year subscription." This way, the presenter will collect more business cards for follow-up than he or she would get if there were no newsletter offer.

• **Tap into a rented e-list.** You could rent an e-list (see Chapter 8) and send them an e-mail offering a free subscription to your e-zine.

• **Use a press release.** Send out a press release offering a free sample copy of the newsletter to people in your industry who e-mail you.

Designing Your E-Zine

E-zines do not have to be elaborate. Many are straight text. The masthead simply gives the name of the newsletter, the issue date or volume, and number. It may also have a descriptor under the newsletter name, such as "Weekly Process Design Ideas from XYZ Consulting."

Each story has a headline followed by a couple of paragraphs of text. It also has a link to a location on your website for more detailed information on the product, application, or service discussed in the story.

Figure 10.1 shows the beginning of a weekly e-zine I get from the Sovereign Society, which advises its members on offshore investment opportunities.

Subject: BAHAMAS TURMOIL GROWS. A-LETTER. 04.20.01

Date: Fri, 20 Apr 2001 11:39:51 -0400

From: "Sovereign Society's Offshore A-Letter"

<sovsoc@agoramail.net>

Reply-To: A-Letter@sovereignsociety.com

To: <rwbly@bly.com>

===

THE SOVEREIGN SOCIETY OFFSHORE A-LETTER

Your Link to Freedom, Prosperity & Privacy in the Offshore

World

Friday, April 20, 2001 - Vol. 3 No. 32

===

In This Issue:

* OFFSHORE: More Bahamas Turmoil. Bermuda Clamps

Down. Channel Islands. Security Problems. Chile Wants

Investors. Peruvian Cash Hunt. Texans on Offshore Trusts.

OECD News: Tax Notes, Int. Herald Tribune, US Senate

Critic. Gibraltar Sellout? Canada Passports . . .

Figure 10.1 Sovereign Society E-Zine

If you want to dress up your e-zine, you can use html to add type-faces, fonts, and colors. An html newsletter can stand out in a field if all the other e-zines from your competitors are straight text. And html makes sense if your e-zine needs to be illustrated. For instance, an airplane manufacturer might want to show a photo of its new test plane breaking the sound barrier. Figure 10.2 shows an html e-zine.

E-Zine Content

The material in your promotional electronic newsletter does not have to be original, nor must it be created solely for the newsletter. In fact, an e-zine is an ideal medium for recycling other promotional and pub-

HTML Messages

Subject: e-PostDirect Newsletter - May 17, 1999
   Date: Monday, 17 Mar 1999 18:40:42 -0800 (PST)
   From: staff@epostdirect.com
      To: michelle.feit@epostdirect.com

e-POSTDIRECT   Email Newsletter

The Best Way to Get Your Email Noticed
Many people have been laboring under the idea that email copy adheres to the same principles as traditional direct mail copy. Our staff brings you 10 new ideas to separate your email copy from traditional copy..

Appending Your House File With Email Addresses
Sure, you have a highly organized and responsive list of your clients and prospects. But, do you have their email addresses? We can help you append your house DM files, and help you obtain a whole new marketing tool!.

Internet Economy

May 17, 1999:
Marketing on The Net

Some of the Internet's biggest marketers walk on the wild side.

Read more in the weekly report.

confidential

Figure 10.2 E-PostDirect E-Zine

licity material created by your company, including speeches, articles, press releases, annual reports, presentations, and so on. Keeping this in mind helps you get maximum use out of material you've already created while minimizing the time and expense of writing and producing the newsletter.

Decide what stories you want to run in the next issue. If you are unsure as to how much room you have, it's better to select one or two extra ideas than one or two too few. You can always use the extra material in a future edition.

The third step is to create a file folder for each article and collect the information that will serve as background material for the person who writes the story. This background material typically includes sales brochures (for product stories), press releases (which are edited into short news stories), and reprints of published trade journal articles on a particular topic (which are often combined and compiled into a new article on a similar topic).

The fourth step is to write each story based on this material. Many companies write their own e-zines. Others hire freelance online content writers to write and edit their company newsletters. A few hire their ad agency to do it. Using freelancers can usually be more cost-effective. Besides, while most freelancers relish such assignments, most ad agencies don't like doing company newsletters, because they find them unprofitable.

Some articles may require more information than is contained in the background material. In this case, supply the writer with the names and phone numbers of people within your company whom he or she can interview to gather the additional information. Notify these people ahead of time that a freelance writer will be calling them to do an interview for the newsletter. If they object, find substitutes. Once you get the copy, the fifth step is to edit it, send it through for review, and make any final changes.

Twenty-Nine Article Ideas for Your E-Zine

If you create an e-zine monthly or more frequently, you'll be working on at least twelve or more issues a year. How are you going to fill all that space? Here are twenty-nine ideas for stories you can run in your e-zine:

1. **Product stories:** Offer information on new products, improvements to existing products, new models, new accessories, new options, and new applications.

2. **News:** Write about joint ventures, mergers and acquisitions, new divisions formed, new departments, other company news. Also, industry news and analyses of events and trends may interest your reader.

3. **Tips:** Offer tips on product selection, installation, maintenance, repair, and troubleshooting.

4. **How-to articles:** These are similar to tips, but have more detailed instructions, for examples, how to use the

product, how to design a system, or how to select the right type or model.

5. **Previews and reports:** Write about special events such as trade shows, conferences, sales meetings, seminars, presentations, and press conferences.

6. **Case histories:** Either in-depth or brief, report on product applications, customer success stories, or examples of outstanding service or support.

7. **People:** Inform the subscriber about company promotions, new hires, transfers, awards, anniversaries, employee profiles, or human interest stories (unusual jobs, hobbies, and so on).

8. **Milestones:** Make important announcements, such as "1,000th unit shipped," "sales reach $1 million mark," "division celebrates 10th anniversary," and so on.

9. **Sales news:** Fill in the subscriber on new customers who are on board, bids that have been accepted, contracts that were renewed, or the receipt of satisfied customer reports.

10. **Research and development:** Describe new products, technologies, or patents; technology awards; inventions; innovations; and breakthroughs.

11. **Publications:** Inform the subscriber about new brochures that are available, new ad campaigns that are underway, technical papers that were presented, which reprints have become available, which manuals are new or updated, and any announcements pertaining to recently published literature or audiovisual materials.

12. **Explanatory articles:** Discuss how a product works, industry overviews, or background information on applications and technologies.

13. **Customer stories:** Present interviews with customers, photos, or customer news and profiles. Include guest articles by customers about their industries, applications,

and positive experiences with the vendor's product or service.

14. **Financial news:** Offer the quarterly and annual report highlights, presentations to financial analysts, earnings and dividend news, or reported sales and profits.

15. **Photos with captions:** Show people, facilities, products, and events.

16. **Columns:** Include a president's letter, letters to the editor, guest columns, or regular features such as "Q&A" or "Tech Talk."

17. **Excerpts, reprints, or condensed versions:** Include excerpts from press releases, executive speeches, journal articles, technical papers, or company seminars.

18. **Quality control stories:** Write about quality circles, employee suggestion programs, new quality assurance methods, success rates, or case histories.

19. **Productivity stories:** Describe new programs or methods and systems to cut waste and boost efficiency.

20. **Manufacturing stories:** Include statistical process control/statistical quality control (SPC/SQC) stories, computer integrated manufacturing (CIM) stories, new techniques, new equipment, raw materials, production line successes, or detailed explanations of manufacturing processes.

21. **Community affairs:** Write about fund-raisers, special events, the company's support for the arts, scholarship programs, social responsibility programs, environmental programs, or employee and corporate participation in local/regional/national events.

22. **Data processing stories:** Describe new computer hardware and software systems, improved data processing and its benefits to customers, new applications, or explanations of how IT systems serve customers.

23. **Overseas activities:** Report on the company's international activities, including profiles of facilities, subsidiaries, branches, people, and markets.

24. **Service:** Write about the background of company service facilities, case histories of outstanding service activities, new services for customers, or customer support hotlines.

25. **History:** Include articles about the company's, industry's, product's, or community's history.

26. **Human resources:** Describe the company benefit programs. Announce new benefits and training and how they improve service to customers. Explain the company's policies.

27. **Interviews:** Include interviews with company key employees, engineers, service personnel, and so on; customers; or suppliers (to illustrate the quality of materials going into your company's products).

28. **Forums:** The top managers may answer customer complaints and concerns; service managers may discuss customer needs; or customers may share their favorable experiences with company products and services.

29. **Gimmicks:** Include contests, quizzes, trivia, puzzles, games, cartoons, recipes, or computer programs.

"Make sure your newsletters contain timely, provocative information and advice that will be of specific interest to your targeted audience," recommends Klinghoffer. "The writing in your newsletters can make or break your newsletter marketing program. So make sure your newsletters feature solid information and advice framed in easy-to-read, action-oriented copy."

E-Zine Writing Tips

Of course, the basics of online writing discussed throughout this book apply to e-zines as well as Web pages, e-mails, and other forms. But there are a few additional pointers that I want to pass along on writing e-zine copy.

The closest print analogy to an e-zine article is an article in a print newsletter. But e-zine articles are usually half the length—and often a quarter or less in length—of a typical print newsletter article. Therefore, they are more like abstracts or summaries than actual articles.

For this compressed form, the journalistic style known as the "inverse pyramid" works well. Every student who has ever taken journalism 101 has learned it—but many programmers and designers have never heard of it.

In a pyramid, the foundation, or bottom, is the strongest part. Everything stands on the foundation. The higher-up portions are not vital to the structure. If the top of a pyramid is removed, the pyramid still stands. But if the foundation is taken away, the whole thing falls.

A newsletter article is like an inverted pyramid. Instead of putting the vital foundation at the bottom, you put it at the top in the lead. Then, as you proceed in the story, everything below amplifies or expands on the lead but is not vital to the story. That way, if the subscriber reads only a paragraph or two, and ignores the rest of the article, she gets the gist of the story. You can see this in front-page news stories in major daily newspapers such as the *Boston Globe* or the *New York Times*.

An e-zine is written in this style, except that the first paragraph or two is usually the entire e-zine article. There's no room for optional material; you tell the vital part and then end with a link to a page on your website where the reader can click for more detail. If your article is about a product winning an award, the link would go to the page for that product on your site.

Journalism school also teaches the "5 W + 1 H" technique for writing article leads, and this too works well with the e-zine article format. The 5 Ws and 1 H stand for *who, what, when, where, why,* and *how*. Your article should at least cover these basic questions about the topic.

Let's say your product wins Best Product of the Year award. Your story should answer these questions:

- Who gave you the award?
- What product was it for?
- When was the award given?
- Where was it presented?
- Why was the product chosen to receive the award?
- How did it come to be chosen? (Did they find out about you on their own or did you enter a competition?)

Statistics work very well in e-zines. The Internet is a medium conducive to picking up tidbits of information on various topics. Drop short articles into your e-zines that highlight the findings from survey results or other industry statistics. Attribute the statistics to the original source, if it's not you.

Stories also get attention and make your e-zine stand out from the clutter of similar newsletters the user is receiving. They're even more effective than statistics. Earlier, I referred to the famous *The Cluetrain Manifesto* quote, "Markets are conversations." Well, when people talk, they tell stories; they don't cite statistics.

"If a newspaper reports the sad story of a youngster dying of cancer and how the family is planning an early Christmas for him, letters, money, and gifts will come to them from perfect strangers. People sympathize with and are saddened by the plight of an individual," writes Joseph Kelley in his book *Speechwriting: The Master Touch.* "A few columns away from the story, an item may report the deaths of ten thousand in a flood in India; it will be scanned and passed over."

I send a monthly e-zine to my copywriting and consulting clients; here is a story I featured as the lead in a recent issue:

> An off-Broadway play got a terrible review from the *New York Times* theater critic—usually signaling the death of the production. But, the smart theater publicist fought back. He sent out a press release saying, "Even the *New York Times* Makes Mistakes!" The offer: Anyone who found a typo in the *New York Times* and sent it in would get a free ticket to the play. Sales picked up and the production continued successfully.

Another piece of advice from Kelley that can also be profitably applied to e-zines is, "Everything God created has a kernel of excitement in it, as has everything civilization invented or discovered." Internet users are interested in the offbeat, the quirky—odd little bits of interesting information on a variety of subjects.

If you can provide a good fact, statistic, or anecdote with an unusual twist, readership will pick up, and people will even forward your e-zine to their colleagues and friends. David Yale was interviewing a former janitor turned millionaire for an article he was writing on the commodities trading system the man had invented. At one point, the ex-janitor said, "When I was cleaning toilets, the only decision I had to make was whether to swirl the water clockwise or counterclockwise," a gem that David quite correctly used in his article.

Oddball how-to tips are also appreciated by e-zine readers. For instance, I remember former boxing champion Muhammad Ali in an interview many years ago giving this summertime grooming tip: wear a shirt that is one size too big and lightly starched to make it stand away from your body. That's the kind of thing that would work well in an e-zine for an apparel site.

Veteran newsletter editor Ed Coburn gives these tips for article writing that apply equally to both off- and online newsletters:

• **Help subscribers solve problems, act on opportunities, or avoid expense.** Whether the information you present to customers is interesting or fun, they won't continue to pay your prices for your e-zine if it doesn't help them. Make sure you know what concerns your readers as well as what challenges they face.

• **Don't just deliver helpful information—sell it to your reader.** As in advertising or direct mail, the headline is critical for capturing the reader's interest in the story. Numerals attract attention, as well as verbs. *You* is always powerful. Humor and puns can be used effectively, but be careful. It shouldn't distract from the topic and it must be understandable and inoffensive to all readers. When in doubt about using humor, avoid it altogether.

The lead should grab the reader's interest. A brief anecdote is often effective and can immediately develop emotional involvement. A startling statistic or research result may work just as well. Starting with a brief summary of the article and the lessons to be learned is also effective in many cases.

Make the article follow some sort of natural progression. It's a good idea to start with a story outline, particularly for longer articles. Have someone else review the outline for clarity. It's easier to make changes to an outline rather than shifting long passages after they're written.

• **Write for all possible readers.** Your readers are industry veterans as well as newcomers. They're geographically dispersed, and they have many different titles. They are at many levels in their separate organizations, and their organizations are of many sizes. The greatest risk is assuming too much knowledge on the part of the reader, although assuming too little knowledge can be just as bad. You don't want to leave readers behind, yet at the same time you don't want the experts to think you're low-level.

• **Get real success and failure stories.** People love to know what others have done. But be sure to get adequate detail and explicitly list lessons to be learned. In other words, don't make readers guess. If you're looking for a specific expert analysis, contact experts in the same field but of different backgrounds, for example, an investor, a customer, a competitor, or an industry analyst.

• **Look for action-oriented tips and advice to provide to your readers.** Active verbs, particularly in the imperative, can make an article more hands-on.

"Do not accept the first price offered by your current long distance supplier . . ."

"Make a reference copy of each form before submitting it . . ."

"Take 10% of all profit generated and create a . . ."

Do not leave the reader to guess about the conclusion. Explicitly state what the reader should do with this information. If there isn't an immediate lesson or action for the individual to take, should it be in the newsletter? There may be times when it should be, but make sure this is the exception and not the rule. Certainly, don't have a major article without explicit action items.

11

Web Documents

THE AVERAGE SOFTWARE engineer or html programmer cannot write clear, lucid prose. He or she may know the basics—sentence structure, grammar, punctuation, exposition. But most techies have just a few poor stylistic habits that mar their writing, making it dull and difficult to read.

This becomes a problem in the online world where, as Nick Usborne noted in Chapter 1, the attitude is "anyone can write words." Often, to save time and money, a Web designer or programmer is pressed into service to "provide the copy." Not having the time or desire to write, and being more focused on graphics or functionality, the techie makes a quick, half-hearted effort at "throwing some content together"—and the lack of care usually shows through in the finished product.

Why do so many computer people write so poorly? Many feel that writing is time consuming, unimportant, and unpleasant. Others lack confidence in their ability to communicate, or they simply don't know how to get started. A third group has the desire to write well but lacks the proper training.

Often, documents prepared by professional writers for print media can be adapted—using the techniques outlined in Chapter 3—to the Internet without great agony or rework. In such cases, you benefit from a professionally written document without having to create it from scratch.

But there is not always a print document you can Webize, adapt, or copy. Sometimes the Internet is the first (or only) medium in which a document will appear. How do you create effective documents for online publication and distribution?

Guidelines for Writing Copy for the Internet

As we have discussed throughout this book, the principles of effective writing remain consistent both on- and offline, yet online communication has special considerations—interactivity, animation, and technological—that do not apply to print.

Having said that, I offer the following collection of writing guidelines to help you create effective, original documents for the Internet.

Select an Appropriate Organizational Scheme

According to a survey, poor organization is the number-one problem in writing. As technical writer Jerry Bacchetti points out, "If the reader believes the content has some importance to him, he can plow through a document even if it is dull or has lengthy sentences and big words. But if it's poorly organized—forget it. There's no way to make sense of what is written."

Poor organization stems from poor planning. While a computer programmer would never think of writing a complex program without first drawing a flow chart, he'd probably knock out a draft of a user's manual without making notes or an outline. In the same way, a builder who requires detailed blueprints before he lays the first brick will write a letter without really considering his message, audience, or purpose.

Before you write, plan. Create a rough outline that spells out the contents and organization of your paper or report. The outline does not need to be formal. A simple list or rough notes will do—use whatever form suits you.

By the time you finish writing, some things in the final draft might be different from the outline. That's OK. The outline is a tool to aid in organization, not a commandment cast in stone. If you want to change it as you go along—fine.

The outline helps you divide the writing project into many smaller, easy-to-handle pieces and parts. The organization of these parts depends on the type of document you're writing.

In general, it's best to stick with standard formats. A laboratory report, for example, has an abstract, a table of contents, a summary, an introduction, a main body (theory, apparatus and procedures, results, and discussions), conclusions and recommendations, nomenclature, references, and appendices. An online operating manual includes a summary; an introduction; a description of the equipment; instructions for routine operation, troubleshooting, maintenance, and emergency operation; and an appendix containing a parts list, spare-parts list, drawings, figures, and manufacturer's literature.

If the format isn't strictly defined by the type of document you are writing, select the organizational scheme that best fits the material. Some common formats include:

- **Order of location.** An article on the planets of the solar system might begin with Mercury (the planet nearest the sun) and end with Pluto (the planet farthest out).

- **Order of increasing difficulty.** Computer manuals often start with the easiest material and, as the user masters basic principles, move on to more complex operations.

- **Alphabetical order.** This is a logical way to arrange a website on vitamins (A, B_3, B_{12}, C, D, E, and so on) or a directory of company employees.

- **Chronological order.** Here you present the facts in the order in which they happened. History books are written this way. So are many case histories, feature stories, and corporate biographies.

- **Problem/solution.** Another format appropriate to case histories and many types of reports, the problem/solution organizational scheme begins with "here's what the problem was" and ends with "here's how we solved it." This format is particularly appropriate for user stories.

- **Inverted pyramid.** This is the newspaper style of news reporting where the lead paragraph summarizes the story, and the following paragraphs present the facts in order of decreasing importance. You can use this format in journal articles, letters, memos, reports, home pages, and corporate overviews.

- **Deductive order.** Start with a generalization, then support it with particulars. Scientists use this format in research papers that begin with the findings and then state the supporting evidence.

- **Inductive order.** Begin with specific instances, and then lead the reader to the idea or general principles the instances suggest. This is an excellent way to approach trade journal feature stories.

- **List.** The section you're now reading is a list article because it describes, in list form, the most useful tips for online writing. A technical-list Web page might be titled "Six Tips for Designing Wet Scrubbers" or "Seven Ways to Reduce Your Plant's Electric Bill."

Write for the Online Reader

When I admit to doing some direct-mail copywriting as part of my consulting work, people turn up their noses. "I always throw that junk in the garbage," they say. "Who would ever buy something from a letter addressed to 'Dear Occupant'?"

They're right, of course. Written communications (and online writing is still writing, even though it appears on a computer screen and not as ink on paper) are most effective when they are targeted and *personal*. Your writing should be built around the needs, interests, and desires of the reader.

With most technical documents—websites, online pdf documents, articles, papers, manuals, reports, brochures—you are writing for many readers, not an individual. Even though we don't know the names of our readers, we need to develop a picture of who they are—their job title, education, industry, and interests.

• **Job title.** Engineers are interested in your compressor's reliability and performance, while the purchasing agent is more concerned with cost. A person's job influences his perspective of your product, service, or idea. Are you writing for plant engineers? Office managers? CEOs? Machinists? Make the tone and content of your writing compatible with the professional interests of your readers.

• **Education.** Is your reader a Ph.D. or a high-school dropout? Is she a chemical engineer? Does she understand computer programming, thermodynamics, physical chemistry, and the calculus of variations? Write simply enough so that even the least technical of your readers can understand what you are saying.

• **Industry.** When engineers buy a reverse-osmosis water purification system for a chemical plant, they want to know every technical detail down to the last pipe, pump, fan, and filter. Marine buyers, on the other hand, have only two basic questions: "What does it cost?" and "How reliable is it?" Especially in promotional writing, know what features of your product appeal to the various markets.

• **Level of interest.** An engineer who has responded to your banner ad is more likely to be receptive to a sales call than someone who is called on "cold turkey." Is your reader interested or disinterested? Friendly or hostile? Receptive or resistant? Understanding his state of mind helps you tailor your message to meet his needs.

• **Internet savvy.** Are you writing for power PC users? Newbies (new Internet users)? People who use computers reluctantly or eagerly? Find out as much as you can about the comfort level of your target prospects with computers and the Internet. For instance, if you are writing to doctors, do they embrace the Internet? I am told that doctors are too busy to spend time noodling around online, and if that's true, anything you write for them must be brief, clear, and to the point.

If you don't know enough about your reader, there are ways to find out. If you are writing an article for a trade journal, for example, get several copies of the magazine and study it before you write. If you are presenting a paper at a conference, look at the conference brochure to get a feel for the audience who will be attending your session. If you are contributing text to product descriptions, ask the marketing or publications department about the format in which the material will be published, how it will be distributed, and who will be reading it. If you are writing pages for an existing website, look at existing pages in the same sections and model yours after their format and style.

Writing in "Technicalese"

Anyone who reads technical documents knows the danger of "technicalese"—the pompous, overblown style that leaves your writing sounding as if it were written by a computer or a corporation instead of a human being.

Technicalese, by my definition, is language more complex than the concepts it serves to communicate. By loading up their writings with jargon, clichés, antiquated phrases, passive sentences, and an excess of adjectives, technicians and bureaucrats hide behind a jumble of incomprehensible memos and reports.

To help you recognize technicalese (also known as "corporitis"), I've assembled a few samples from diverse sources. Note how the authors seem to be writing to impress rather than to express. All of these excerpts are real.

> Will you please advise me at your earliest convenience of the correct status of this product?
>
> —Memo from an advertising manager

> All of the bonds in the above described account having been heretofore disposed of, we are this day terminating same. We accordingly enclose herein check in the amount of $30,050 same being your share realized therein, as per statement attached.
>
> —Letter from a stockbroker

> This procedure enables users to document data fields described in master files that were parsed and analyzed by the program dictionary.
>
> —Software user's manual

This article presents some findings from surveys conducted in Haiti in 1977 that provide retrospective data on the age at menarche of women between the ages of 15 and 49 years. It considers the demographic and nutritional situation in Haiti, the cultural meaning of menarche, and the source of data.

—Article abstract

How do you eliminate technicalese from your writing? Start by avoiding jargon. Don't use a technical term unless it communicates your meaning precisely. Never write "mobile dentition" when "loose teeth" will do just as well. Legal scholar Tamar Frankel notes that when you avoid jargon, your writing can be easily read by novices and experienced professionals alike.

Use contractions. Avoid clichés and antiquated phrases. Write simply. Use the active voice where action is expressed directly: "John performed the experiment." In the passive voice, the action is indirect: "The experiment was performed by John." The Internet allows, even encourages, a very conversational style, probably because of the conversational nature of its most prevalent application—e-mail. When you use the active voice, your writing will be more direct and vigorous; your sentences more concise. As you can see in the samples below, the passive voice seems puny and stiff by comparison:

Passive voice	*Active voice*
Control of the bearing-oil supply is provided by the shutoff valves.	Shutoff valves control the bearing-oil supply.
Leaking of the seals is prevented by the use of O-rings.	O-rings prevent the seals from leaking.
Fuel-cost savings were realized through the installation of thermal insulation	The installation of thermal insulation cut fuel costs.

E-mail is closer to conversation than formal letter writing. Obviously, online marketing documents should not have typos, grammatical errors, and other sins common to everyday e-mail. But, they can and should benefit from the informal, almost casual style e-mail users have become accustomed to.

Use Short Sentences

Lengthy sentences tire the reader and make your writing hard to read. A survey by Harvard professor D. H. Menzel indicates that in technical papers, the sentences become difficult to understand when they exceed thirty-four words.

One measure of writing clarity, the Fog Index, takes into account sentence length and word length. Here's how it works.

First, determine the average sentence length in a short (one hundred to two hundred words) writing sample. To do this, divide the number of words in the sample by the number of sentences. If parts of a sentence are separated by a semicolon (;), count each part as a separate sentence.

Second, calculate the number of big words (words with three or more syllables) per one hundred words of sample. Do not include capitalized words, combinations of short words (butterfly, moreover), or verbs made three syllables by adding *ed* or *es* (accepted, responses).

Finally, add the average sentence length to the number of big words per hundred words and multiply by 0.4. This gives you the Fog Index for the sample.

The Fog Index corresponds to the years of schooling you need to read and understand the sample. A score of 8 or 9 indicates high school level; 13, a college freshman; 17, a college graduate.

Popular magazines have Fog Indexes ranging from 8 to 13. Technical journals should rate no higher than 17.

Obviously, the higher the Fog Index, the more difficult the writing is to read. In his book *Gene Control in the Living Cell* (Basic Books), J. A. V. Butler leads off with a single seventy-nine-word sentence.

> In this book I have attempted an accurate but at the same time readable account of recent work on the subject of how gene controls operate, a large subject which is rapidly acquiring a central position in the biology of today and which will inevitably become even more prominent in the future, in the efforts of scientists of numerous different specialties to explain how a single organism can contain cells of many different kinds developed from a common origin.

With seventeen big words, this sample has a Fog Index of 40—equivalent to a reading level of twenty-eight years of college education! Obviously, this sentence is way too long. Here's a rewrite I came up with:

"This book is about how gene controls operate—a subject of growing importance in modern biology."

This gets the message across with a Fog Index of only 14.

Give your online writing the Fog Index test. If you score in the upper teens or higher, it's time to trim sentence length. Go over your text, and break long sentences into two or more separate sentences. To further reduce average sentence length and add variety to your writing, you can occasionally use an extremely short sentence or sentence fragments of only three to four words or so. Like this one.

Short sentences are easier to grasp than long ones. A good guide for keeping sentence length under control is to write sentences that can be spoken aloud without losing your breath (do *not* take a deep breath before doing this test).

Avoid Big Words

Business executives and techies alike sometimes prefer to use big, important-sounding words instead of short, simple words. This is a mistake; fancy language just frustrates the reader. Write in plain, ordinary English and your readers will love you for it.

Here are a few big words that occur frequently in technical literature; the column on the right presents a shorter—and preferable—substitution:

Big word	Substitution
terminate	end
utilize	use
incombustible	fireproof
substantiate	prove
eliminate	get rid of

Every discipline and specialty has a special language all its own. Technical terms are a useful shorthand when you're communicating within the profession, but they may confuse readers who do not have your special background.

Take the word *yield*, for example. To a chemical engineer, yield is a measure of how much product a reaction produces. But to car drivers, yield means slowing down (and stopping, if necessary) at an intersection.

Other words that have special meaning to chemical engineers but have a different definition in everyday use include *vacuum, pressure, batch, bypass, recycle, concentration, mole, purge, saturation,* and *catalyst.*

Use legitimate technical terms when they communicate your ideas precisely, but avoid using jargon just because the words sound impressive. Do not write that material is "gravimetrically conveyed" when it is simply dumped.

Tips for Handling Writer's Block

Writer's block isn't just for professional writers; it can afflict executives and entrepreneurs, too. Writer's block is the inability to start putting words on paper or PC, and it stems from anxiety and fear of writing.

When nonwriters write, they're afraid to make mistakes, and so they edit themselves word by word, inhibiting the natural flow of ideas and sentences. But, professional writers know that writing is a process consisting of numerous drafts, rewrites, deletions, and revisions. Rarely does a writer produce a perfect manuscript on the first try.

Here are a few tips to help you overcome writer's block:

• **Break the writing up into short sections, and write one section at a time.** Tackling many little writing assignments seems like a less formidable task than taking on a large project all at once. This also benefits the reader. Writing is most readable when it deals with one simple idea rather than multiple complex ones. Your entire document can't be simple or restricted to one idea, but each section can.

• **Write the easy sections first.** If you can't get a handle on the main argument of your report or paper, begin with something routine, such as the sections on your guarantee or methods of payment. This will get you started and help build momentum.

- **Write abstracts, introductions, and summaries last.** Although they come first in the final document, it doesn't make sense to try to sum up a paper that hasn't been written yet.

- **Avoid grammar-book rules that inhibit writers.** One such rule says every paragraph must begin with a topic sentence (a first sentence that states the central idea of the paragraph). By insisting on having topic sentences, teachers and editors throw up a block that prevents students and engineers from putting their thoughts on paper. Professional writers don't worry about topic sentences (or sentence diagrams or ending a sentence with a preposition). Neither should you.

- **Sleep on it.** Close your file and come back to it the next morning—or even several days later. Refreshed, you'll be able to edit and rewrite effectively and easily.

Narrow the Topic

Effective writing begins with a clear definition of the specific topic you want to write about. The big mistake many online writers make is to tackle a topic that's too broad. For example, the title ''Project Management'' is too all encompassing for a white paper or perhaps even an entire website. You could write a whole book on the subject. But by narrowing the scope, say, with the title "Managing Chemical Plant Construction Projects with Budgets Under $500,000," you get a clearer definition and a more manageable topic.

It's also important to know the purpose of the document. You may say, "That's easy; the purpose is to communicate content." But think again. Do you want the reader to buy a product? Change methods of working? Look for the hidden agenda beyond the mere transmission of facts.

Genuine prospects for your product or service—those who are seriously considering a purchase—are often interested in detailed technical information about the product, including facts, figures, conclusions, recommendations. Do not be content to say something is good, bad, fast, or slow when you can say *how* good, *how* bad, *how* fast, or *how* slow. Be specific whenever possible.

General	Specific
a tall spray dryer	a forty-foot-tall spray dryer
plant	oil refinery
unit	evaporator
unfavorable weather conditions	rain
structural degradation	a leaky roof
high performance	95 percent efficiency

The key to success in online writing is to *keep it simple*. Write to express—not to impress. A relaxed, conversational style can add vigor and clarity to your work.

Formal technical style	Informal conversational style
The data provided by direct examination of samples under the lens of the microscope are insufficient for the purpose of making a proper identification of the components of the substance.	We can't tell what it is made of by looking at it under the microscope.
We have found during conversations with customers that even the most experienced of extruder specialists have a tendency to avoid the extrusion of silicone profiles or hoses.	Our customers tell us that experienced extruder specialists avoid extruding silicone profiles or hoses.
The corporation terminated the employment of Mr. Joseph Smith.	Joe was fired.

Add Strong Content

OK. You've defined your topic, audience, and purpose. The next step is to do some homework, and gather information on the topic at hand. Most subject-matter experts I know don't do this. When they're writing a Web page or white paper, for example, their attitude is, "I'm the expert here. So I'll just rely on my own experience and know-how."

That's a mistake. Even though you're an expert, your knowledge may be limited and your viewpoint lopsided. Gathering information from other sources rounds out your knowledge or, at the very least, verifies your thinking. And there's another benefit: backing up your claims with facts is a real credibility builder.

Once you've crammed a file folder full of reprints and clippings, take notes on index cards or a PC. Not only does note taking put the key facts at your fingertips in condensed form, but reprocessing the research information through your fingers and brain puts you in closer touch with your material.

Get a Rough, First Draft Together

Once you gather facts and decide how to organize the piece, the next step is to sit down and write. When you do, keep in mind that the secret to successful writing is rewriting. You don't have to get it right on the first draft. The pros rarely do. E. B. White, essayist and coauthor of the writer's resource book *The Elements of Style*, was said to have rewritten every piece nine times.

Maybe you don't need nine drafts, but you probably need more than one. Use a simple three-step procedure that I call SPP—Spit, Prune, and Polish.

1. **When you sit down to write, just spit it out.** Don't worry about how it sounds, whether the grammar's right, or if it fits your outline. Just let the words flow. If you make a mistake, leave it. You can always go back and fix it later. Some executives find it helpful to talk into a tape recorder or dictate to an assistant. If you can type and have a personal computer, great. Some old-fashioned folks even use typewriters or pen and paper. Probably not you, if you're reading this book.

2. **Prune by printing out your first draft (double-spaced, for easy editing) and giving it major surgery.** Print a hard copy, take a red pen to the draft, and slash out all unnecessary words and phrases. Rewrite any awkward passages to make them smoother, but if you get stuck, leave it and go on; come back to it later. Use your word processing program's cut and paste feature to cut the draft apart. Reorganize it to fit into and improve upon your outline. Then print out a clean draft. Repeat the pruning step as many times as necessary to get it right. Remember, in the online world, shorter is better. Be concise. Omit needless words.

3. **Polish your manuscript.** Check equations, units of measure, references, grammar, spelling, and punctuation. Again use the red pen and print out a fresh copy with corrections.

Be Consistent in Usage and Style

"A foolish consistency," wrote Ralph Waldo Emerson, "is the hobgoblin of little minds." This may be so. But, on the other hand, inconsistencies in online documents will confuse your readers and convince them that your work and reasoning are as disorganized as your prose.

Good online writers strive for consistency in the use of numbers, hyphens, units of measure, punctuation, equations, grammar, symbols, capitalization, technical terms and abbreviations, fonts, heads, and subheads.

For example, many writers are inconsistent in the use of hyphens. The rule is two words that form an adjective are hyphenated. Thus, write: first-order reaction, fluidized-bed combustion, high-sulfur coal, space-time continuum.

The U.S. Government Printing Office Style Manual, Strunk and White's *The Elements of Style*, and your organization's writing manual—if you have one—can guide you in the basics of grammar, punctuation, abbreviation, and capitalization.

Be Concise

Internet users, especially those in the business world, are busy people. Make your writing less time-consuming for them to read by telling the whole story in the fewest possible words.

We often say "Internet copy must be brief," but actually it should always be concise. *Brief* and *concise* are not the same thing, though they are related. *Brief* simply means short. *Concise* means "expressing much in few words." Or, getting across your message in the fewest words possible.

How can you make your writing more concise? One way is to avoid redundancies—a needless form of wordiness in which a modifier repeats an idea already contained within the word being modified. For example, a recent trade ad described a product as a "new innovation." Could there be such a thing as an *old* innovation? The ad also said the product was "very unique." Unique means "one of a kind," so it is impossible for anything to be *very* unique.

By now, you probably get the picture. Some other redundancies that have come up in copy are listed below, along with the correct way to rewrite them:

Redundancy	Rewrite as
Advance plan	Plan
Actual experience	Experience
Two cubic feet in volume	Two cubic feet
Cylindrical in shape	Cylindrical
Uniformly homogeneous	Homogeneous

Many writers are fond of overblown expressions such as "the fact that," "it is well known that," and "it is the purpose of this writer to show that." These take up space but add little to meaning or clarity.

The following list includes some of the wordy phrases that appear frequently in technical literature. The column on the right offers suggested substitute words:

Wordy phrase	Suggested substitute
During the course of	During
In the form of	As

In many cases	Often
In the event of	If
Exhibits the ability to	Can

Use Page Layouts That Make Online Documents Scannable

To enhance readability, break your writing up into short sections. Long, unbroken chunks of text are stumbling blocks that intimidate and bore readers. Breaking your writing up into short sections and short paragraphs—as in this section—makes it easier to read.

Use visuals. Drawings, graphs, and other visuals can reinforce your text. In fact, pictures often communicate better than words; we remember 10 percent of what we read but 30 percent of what we see.

Visuals can make your technical communications more effective. The different types of visuals and what they can show are listed in the following chart:

Type of visual	*This shows*
Photograph or illustration	What something looks like
Map	Where it is located
Exploded view	How it is put together
Schematic diagram	How it works or is organized
Graph	How much there is (quantity); how one thing varies as a function of another
Pie chart	Proportions and percentages
Bar chart	Comparisons between quantities
Table	A body of related data

These tips should help eliminate some of the fear and anxiety you may have about writing original documents for the Internet from scratch, as well as make the whole task easier and more productive.

Keep in mind that success in writing—or any form of communication—is largely a matter of attitude. If you don't think writing is important enough to take the time to do it right, and you don't really care about improving, you probably won't. But, if you believe that writing is important and you want to improve, you will.

Special Considerations for High-Tech Marketers

When I was the advertising manager for a process equipment manufacturer, one of my responsibilities was to serve as liaison between the advertising agency we hired to write our product literature and our staff engineers. The engineers, because of their technical expertise in the subject matter, were responsible for reviewing the agency's work. As is often the case in our industry, the engineers complained that those "ad types" at the agency didn't understand the product or the audience—and that their copy was way off base.

The agency countered that engineers may know technology but don't know writing, marketing, design, or selling—and that they wanted to cram the product documents with too much unnecessary detail that would dilute the sales message.

Who was right? The fact is both arguments have some merit.

On the agency side, ad agency and Web marketing folk often have a flair for creative, colorful communication, which can help a website or html document gain attention and be noticed. On the other hand, clients—especially the engineers who review the agency's brochure copy—often complain, sometimes correctly, that the agency's copy is superficial.

Laziness is often the cause. The writer did not do sufficient research to understand both the technology and the needs, concerns, and interests of the target audience. The copy he writes reflects this lack of understanding. When you read it, you immediately think, "This person doesn't know what he is talking about"—and you are probably right.

Another problem with professional or agency-written product literature is a tendency toward cleverness for the sake of being clever. "Be creative!" the client instructs the agency. But the reader often doesn't get the joke, pun, or reference in the headline; the creativity goes over her head; and she is turned off rather than engaged.

Engineers who write their own product documents are rarely superficial; they usually have a solid understanding of the product and its technology. However, engineers tend to assume that the reader knows as much as the writer, speaks the same jargon, and has the same level of interest in the technology. And often, this is not the case.

Take jargon. Today, people frequently use the term "open systems architecture" in sales literature. But do they really know what this means? Write down your own definition, ask five colleagues to do the same, and compare. I guarantee they will not be the same. Engineers who write often aren't striving for clarity. So they fall back on buzzwords and clichés that, unfortunately, don't get across the messages they wish to convey.

Given these conditions, how can you—as an entrepeneur or manager who either writes, edits, or approves Web copy or provides input for ad agencies or freelance online writers—do your job better so the finished website is the best one possible?

Here are some simple guidelines to follow.

Define the Topic

Is your online document about a solution? A system? A product line? A product? A specific model of that product? A specific industry use or application of that product? The support services you offer for that product? The accessories?

Define what the document is about. The narrower the topic, the more focused, specific, and effective your Web page can be within the limited space available.

Here's a tip. Your online document doesn't have to cover everything. You can always provide links to other documents that go into more depth on certain aspects. For instance, you can talk about satisfied users in case histories. You can expand on specifications on another page. Some marketers use application briefs to focus on a specific application or industry. Others develop separate pages on each key feature, allowing more in-depth technical discussion than is possible in a one or two-screen overview page.

Know Your Audience

Are you writing to engineers or managers? The former may be interested in technical and performance specifications. The latter may want to know about support, service, ease of use, scalability, user benefits, or return on investment.

If you are writing to engineers, are they well-versed in this particular technology? Or do you have to bring them up to speed? Someone being a chemical engineer does not guarantee that she'll know as much about industrial knives, turbine blades, corrosion-resistant metals, ball valves, or your particular specialty as you do. Indeed, she probably won't.

When in doubt, explain and don't assume that they already understand. No engineer has ever complained to me that a print brochure or Word document I wrote was too clear.

Write with Your Objective in Mind

Unlike a Victoria's Secret catalog, which gives the buyer all the information she needs to place an order, many business-to-business websites support the selling process but are not designed to complete it on their own.

Is the objective of the online document to convince the prospect that your technical design is superior to your competition's? Or is it to show that you have more features at a better price? Or do you want to demonstrate that your system will pay back its cost in less than six months? (The latter might be a good opportunity for an interactive online Excel spreadsheet.)

Establish a communication objective for your document, and write with that goal in mind. For instance, if the objective is to get a meeting for you to sell consulting services to the client, you only need to include enough information to convince them that the meeting is worth their time. Anything more is probably overkill.

Include the Two Things Every Web Document Should Contain

As discussed, these simply are

1. What your prospects need and want to know about your product to make their buying decision

2. What you think you should say to persuade them that your product is the best choice—and your company is the best vendor

The weight, dimensions, power requirements, operating temperature, and whether it can perform certain functions are what a prospect may want to know about an industrial product.

You might want to tell them how your product's performance compares with competitive systems in benchmark tests (if you were the winner, of course), that your product was cited as "Best Product" by an industry publication, that it won an award from a trade association, or that it is the most popular product in its category with an installed base of more than 10,000 units.

Be Selective

While ad agency copy is sometimes too light and tells the reader too little, engineer copy often makes the opposite error, attempting to cram every last technical fact and feature into a four- or eight-page brochure.

Keep in mind that your prospect is bombarded by more information than he can handle on a daily basis. Everyone has too much to read and not enough time to read it.

Be selective in your presentation. Copywriter Herschell Gordon Lewis has a formula, $E^2 = 0$. Or as Lewis says, "When you emphasize everything, you emphasize nothing." If every fact about your product is given equal weight, the key facts that make the most persuasive case for buying it will not stand out.

Understand the Selling Environment

There are three basic selling situations for product selling. You must know what situation your product falls into, so you can market it effectively.

1. **The prospect is not acutely aware of the problem he has that your product can solve.** Or he is aware of it but does not consider it a priority. In this situation, to get your prospect's attention, your home page and related online marketing efforts must dramatize the problem and its severity, then position your product as the solution.

For example, mainframe computer operators did not realize that certain operations accidentally overrode and erased files stored on magnetic tapes. An e-mail marketing message sent to IT managers, promoting a utility that prevented this operation from occurring, began, "Did you know that your storage devices may be accidentally wiping out important files even as you read this sentence?" It alerted them to the problem in a dramatic way.

Once alerted to a problem they didn't know existed, the readers were eager to find a solution, which the utility handily provided. Sales were brisk.

2. **The prospect is aware of the problem or need your product addresses, but is not at all convinced that your type of product is the best solution.** For example, a chemical manufacturer warned wastewater treatment plants that their current activated charcoal bed systems were too costly.

The plant managers believed that, but didn't believe that the manufacturer's alternative filter technology was a viable solution. A white paper reprinting lab test results plus the offer of a free trial overcame the disbelief and got firms to use the new filter system.

3. **The prospect knows what his problem is, believes your type of product is the right solution, but needs to be convinced that your product is the best choice in the category, and better than similar products offered by your competitors.** One way to demonstrate superiority is with a table comparing your product with the others on a feature-by-feature basis. If you have a more complete feature set than they do, such a table makes you look like the best choice.

Another technique is to give specifications that prove your performance is superior. If this cannot be quantitatively measured, talk about any unique functionality, technology, or design feature that might create an impression of superiority in the prospect's mind.

There are many copywriting techniques available to produce superior online marketing documents in any of these three situations; this is why I've devoted the past twenty years—my entire professional life—to practicing and studying copywriting—and the last five or so devoted specifically to online copywriting.

But, if you follow these basic guidelines and do nothing else, I guarantee an improvement in your online marketing that you, your sales reps, and your customers will appreciate. You might even some day receive that rare compliment: "You know, I went to your website, and it told me what I needed to know!"

12

Web Promotions

ALTHOUGH THE NUMBER of hits received by a website is not the most important measure of its marketing effectiveness, hits are the easiest result to measure. Therefore, nearly every Web marketer seems interested in increasing hits to their site. (Perhaps the desire to increase hits is partially due to the counter so many sites have that publicly displays the number of hits received; the marketer responsible for the site is afraid senior management will think less of him if the hit counter registers a low number.)

This chapter presents methods—both on- and offline—for driving traffic to your site.

Bookmark

Direct-marketing guru Denny Hatch, author of *Method Marketing*, observes that you can increase repeat visits to your site if you can get people to bookmark your site. "Is there any site to which you frequently return again and again that you have *not* bookmarked?" he asked me in a recent e-mail to make his point about the importance of bookmarking. Of course people bookmark sites that they like and want to return to, but are there any techniques for driving them to do it? Hatch says you can get more people to bookmark your site by making it "indispensable and addictive."

"In terms of getting people to bookmark your site, you have to create a sense of, 'I've got to have this thing at my fingertips,' " says Hatch. "Make your site so overpoweringly interesting at first hit, and so current on every succeeding hit, that people want to come back and back and back."

Marketers know that often, you can get people to take an action either by asking them to do it or telling them to do it. So a banner on a home page that says "Bookmark this site now!" seems a logical start.

Taking it one step further, you can remind them why it makes good sense to bookmark the site. For instance, "Bookmark this site and visit frequently for our weekly specials!" or "Bookmark this site to quickly check current precious metals prices online."

Beyond reminding them of an existing incentive, you can create an added incentive for them to bookmark and frequently visit your site—for instance, to take advantage of special one-day sales and discounts you offer on the Web only.

In Search of . . . Search Engines

Of 360 Internet users surveyed by IMT Strategies, 45.8 percent said they found out about new websites through search engines—more than any other method of finding sites. (Banner ads, by comparison, result in only 1 percent of the traffic on sites from first-time visitors.) The conclusion? If you want more people to find your site, get it registered with the important search engines.

There are a number of online services promoting that they'll register your site with one hundred search engines for $99 or a similar fee. But to ensure registration with the important search engines, keep in mind the old adage, "If you want something done right, do it yourself." By registering your site manually with each search engine, you ensure that more Web surfers searching the World Wide Web by topic are likely to come up with your site.

Contact each, and follow their procedures. They will most likely ask you to submit a list of key words which, when entered into the engine, will result in your site being recommended. For instance, if your site is about collectible antique duck stamp plates, your key words might include *plates*, *collectibles*, *duck stamps*, and *antiques*.

When shoppers are looking for goods and services like yours, you want your site to show up at the very top of a search engine's list, not on the tenth (or even the third) page. How can you accomplish this?

To begin with, not all search engines are alike, and the difference boils down to the various ways that they acquire, store, categorize, and search through data. Some send automated robots (sometimes called "spiders" or "crawlers") out to scour the Web, then take the information back to index it. Others wait for you to submit your site to them. And still others do a little bit of both.

So if you want to be included in the search engines, you have to do two things. First, design your website so that it can be easily found by the search engines that scour the Web. And second, submit your site to the major search engines and directories.

As soon as your site goes up, companies may e-mail you and say "just pay us $99 and we'll get you top search engine rankings!" It would be nice if that were true, but if it were true then everyone would do it, and everyone can't get onto the first page of a popular search, right? So, you're better off learning how to make sure your site is ready for search engines, and submitting your site yourself.

If you want the robots and spiders to find you, your website needs a relevant title for your home page. The title of a Web page appears in two very important places: at the top of the browser window when someone visits your site and as the name of the bookmark when a visitor bookmarks your site. Search engines also often display your title when your website appears in their search results.

Sometimes the title is the only thing a person will see. That may be what they base their decision to click or not to click on, so make sure your title is a phrase or sentence that clearly describes your website. For example, if your site is about a sewing service, you might title it, "Sewing services, custom design and production on curtains, pillows, slipcovers, and clothing alterations." That way you've not only said what your service is, but you've also included key words that people might search for.

A word that appears in your title is considered more important by most search engines than words that appear in the body of your page. So try to include specific words you think people looking for your products or services would search for.

Most search engines *don't* have a limit on how long a title can be. But only seventy or so characters will actually appear in the results.

Choosing Keywords

You need keywords for your site. These are all the words related to your product or service that your customers will use to search for your site. Your keywords should be included in the computer code of your website. You should also include your keywords in an introduction to visitors on your home page.

For example, Everyday Gaiters is a small business run by Sarah Tyree and her husband. Their site, boothuggers.com, sells gaiters and boothuggers, and their first page includes keywords that relate to their product, such as gaiters, boots, gloves, mittens, winter, snow, skiing, snowboard, snowmobiling, ice fishing, children, kids, sliding, clothing, and hunting. So when someone performs a search using one of these keywords, boothuggers.com should appear in the results.

More and more, the number of links to and from a website is being used as a ranking device. The idea is that the more links you have, the more popular your site must be, so it deserves a higher ranking. That's why, in addition to submitting your site to the search engines, it's essential to spend time trading links with sites of similar topics. And, be sure to have a Links page of your own with lots of connections to sites of similar interests.

As Ilise Benun points out in "Getting Realistic About Search Engines" on her website artofselfpromotion.com, it's essential to submit your site to the search engines. Because there are so many search engines, there are search engine submission services, such as selfpromotion.com and submitit.com, available to help you. Some are free, and others charge a fee. To make sure it's done correctly, submit your site yourself to the major search engines.

Yahoo! is a special case. It is a directory, rather than a traditional search engine, and you are required to submit your site manually by filling out an application on the site. Then, they send a real person (not a robot) to visit your site, evaluate it, and place it in the hierarchy of the directory, which can take several months, so be patient.

For those in a hurry, Yahoo! offers a service where, for approximately $100, your site gets a priority viewing, but that doesn't guarantee that you get listed any faster. Although Yahoo! requires a lot of extra effort, it is one of the most popular directories on the Web, so listing your site here is well worth the extra effort.

There are also search engines, like GoTo.com, where you can buy your way to the results. They offer an inexpensive pay-for-placement arrangement that can provide a fast jump start. You select the search terms or keywords that you think people will use to find a site like yours, then you decide how much you are willing to pay on a per-click basis for each of those search terms. The higher your "bid," the higher in the search results your site appears.

Creative webmasters are using websites like eBay.com as a search engine. An eBay listing costs as little as $2 and can generate lots of leads from people who are in the market for your product. So it's a fast, effective way to reach a targeted group. (This works best for people with products, rather than services.)

According to an article in *The Industry Standard*, the trend for the future is away from the currently popular general search engines and toward topic-specific search engines that specialize in particular industries, such as music or graphic design.

You don't have to sign up for every search engine on the planet— just the major ones, and the ones that specialize in your particular field (if they exist). In some fields, there are no search engines, but there are popular sites that contain a lot of lists. If you find a site like this, contact the webmaster to see if you can trade links.

Search engines are important when it comes to online marketing, but there's still no guarantee that if you follow these steps, your site will be listed in the top rankings. So, don't make the mistake of depending solely on search engines to drive traffic to your website.

Promote Your Website in All Your Marketing

Be proactive, and use the other forms of marketing outlined in this chapter to spread the word. First and foremost, put your Web address everywhere you can think of. Spend time networking—online and offline.

Go to the websites where people are already researching and discussing your topic. Participate in the discussion forums on those sites. Get a link to and from those sites. Do whatever you can to get your name out there in cyberspace, because it's the accumulation of references and links to your site that will turn surfers into visitors and visitors into buyers.

Off- and online marketing do not compete with one another; they are complementary. You can effectively use traditional offline promotions—advertising, direct mail, TV commercials, radio spots, or billboards—to build awareness and traffic to your website.

How? Here are some ideas that can work for you:

• Include your URL in every single printed piece you mail or hand out—letterhead, business cards, sales brochures, catalogs, trade show panels, signage.

• Make the URL prominent. Put a box around the URL, or print it in bold large type. Draw attention to it with highlighting, such as a burst.

• Have special offers that are available only on your website and not through dealers, brick-and-mortar retailers, or print catalogs. One nutritional supplement seller offers an extra ten-day supply with the purchase of a thirty-day supply but only for Internet orders—not at health stores. For consumer e-commerce sites, a 10/10 offer seems to work well.

• Encourage prospects to register with you to build your e-mail database. Offer a resource and document center, free demos, catalogs, samples, white papers, or an e-mail newsletter.

• Consider testing banner ads. Try offering some of your content in exchange for a free banner ad.

• Link your site to others. Set a goal of submitting a certain number of link requests per week. Search on your keywords to identify the top-ranking sites and then submit to those. Consider associations, magazines, consultants, and complementary sites.

- Build strategic partnerships and alliances. List your products on another company's site in exchange for a small royalty on any sales. Consider submitting articles for an e-mail newsletter in exchange for a Web link and additional promotion.

- Make it "sticky." Offer your prospects a reason to keep coming back. Good content, free resources and tools, and contests or drawings work well.

Power-Packed Direct Mail

Direct mail is an extremely effective medium for driving traffic and sales on websites. Dozens of e-businesses use direct mail in addition to other promotions, including opt-in e-mail.

A mailing can have many different formats—a direct-mail "package" (letter, reply form, and brochure in an envelope), a folded self-mailer, or even a postcard. Postcards are particularly effective for promoting response to websites because the recipient doesn't have to open an envelope to find the URL. It's right there in front of her.

You can also make mailings three-dimensional. For example, New York–based online wedding resource company, The Knot, recently mailed a box of goodies to 400,000 brides-to-be.

The Knot Box contains, among other items, a pocket calculator from PointPathBank.com and a ring sizer from jeweler Mondara.com. The box also contains a binder with inserts that help couples plan all aspects of their wedding from vows to the reception.

Each insert has a link to a specific page on The Knot's website. Mailing costs were completely underwritten by advertisers, and the campaign was so successful that The Knot plans to distribute more boxes next year.

Using Direct Mail to Drive Business-to-Business Leads to Your Website

A reliable model has emerged for obtaining qualified business leads at modest cost. It requires a website, a white paper or similar document of value to prospects, a telemarketing capability, and a reliable list. Actually a reliable list is key. If there's any doubt about the accuracy of your list, wait until you're sure—and you'll want to have phone numbers with that list.

How does the model work? First, review your website. If it isn't up to snuff, you'll need to take care of that before you launch this project. Your website, for better or for worse, tells prospects more about you than you can do in a direct-mail piece or even in person. It may, in fact, be telling them more than you'd like if your material has become stale, links are broken, or the date indicated for the most recent update is more than a few months ago.

Review the look and feel of your site and determine what kind of image it's sending out to visitors who you hope will become prospects. Check the navigation again and see if it's intuitive and if the visitor is able to come away with something of value, including a reason to come back. You needn't be overly concerned with having the latest rich media bells and whistles. They may be big with kids who want to swap music files and watch rock stars, but few business-to-business users have the time or interest to mess with them.

If visiting your website is an insurmountable problem (some prospects are not Internet savvy), you can offer to mail the white paper rather than have the prospect visit your site and download it. That should be an available option in any case.

The second step is to create a document that you can offer, as a premium, that communicates your expertise in your specialized business sector. This is normally done with a white paper, but there are a few alternatives. A white paper is a written document dealing with a technical or business aspect of the application or problem your product solves. It may include charts and graphs, formulae and other technical data, but it should be eminently readable. It should be substantial but not oppressive; the typical length is five to fifteen pages.

There is a quality of instant gratification to a free premium such as this, and the prospect wants to feel that he or she can digest it in about thirty minutes. Naturally, the more detailed the material, the higher the perceived value of the document. The title needs to be carefully chosen to target one or more key interests, and it should be clear that the paper is altruistic in nature—valuable in and of itself—requiring no further contact with you in order to implement its recommendations, strategies, or techniques (but obviously, you could help).

The free white paper is your offer. In lead generation, the offer—not you or your world-class services—is what you sell. It's the essential first step in getting your prospect's attention, establishing credibility, and making him or her available—and, you hope, positively oriented—to your sales pitch.

Interactive marketing works best with people who, by virtue of their personal experiences, previous buying patterns, or company responsibilities can reasonably be expected to be predisposed to your product or service. If you have to sell them first on your product or service category, then again on why they should obtain it from you, you're probably dead in the water.

For example, if you have to convince a company that they need a customer relationship management (CRM) program before you can sell them on your particular flavor, you will be less successful. Ideally, you want to contact companies who may be already evaluating CRM providers or about to begin that search, in this example.

An alternative to the type of white paper described above could be a detailed case study that provides a useful blueprint for the process you plan to offer. You needn't identify the company by name, only by size and category. Most prospects appreciate the need for confidentiality.

A variation would be a collection of ten to twelve one-page case studies carefully titled to project value: "How Three Fortune 500 Companies Reduced Costs and Increased Sales with Sales Automation," for example, assuming Fortune 500 companies are your target. If your target were small business, you might try, "How Sales Automation is Boosting Profits for Small Business." Another possibility is an industry survey or study, so long as the data are significant and the analysis sound and meaningful.

Case studies are powerful marketing tools because they provide the decision influence of a positive experience with your company described by objective third parties. They also offer prospects a snapshot of what it might be like to work with your firm and to go through the product selection and installation or deployment process. Further, they act as triggers to give a decision-maker permission to contact you, since another peer or colleague—perhaps even someone or some company the prospect knows—has attested to their own good decision to do so.

Direct Mail Offers

Direct mail used to drive Web traffic to your site should have two offers: a soft offer and a hard offer. The soft offer is the white paper, downloadable from the site or mailed as a hard copy. The hard offer is you, either face-to-face or over the telephone. It's your free on-site needs assessment, free demo, or free consultation and analysis. It requires you to get an appointment to visit the company, to interact with the prospect, and so forth. And the resulting report is actually a thinly disguised proposal, but probably without the numbers. The report is also your foot in the door, so if at all possible, you want to deliver it in person to explain key points and answer questions (and not incidentally, show your prospect how you would apply it to his particular situation). You'll want to be sure the prospect's decision-makers are at that meeting.

The white paper, as noted, is your soft offer. It is soft because it's an arm's-length transaction. It promises minimal exposure and no commitment on the part of the prospect. It is available via mail or online.

As you've no doubt discovered, not everyone is ready to have you pop in for a face-to-face appointment at any given point in time. That suggests some level of commitment on their part, even if you make it clear that there is none. That's one reason we have the soft offer—to make it easier for interested prospects to respond at arm's length and at least capture their contact information for follow-up.

The promotional vehicle for this offer is a lead-generating sales letter. It can be one or two pages. You can print on the front and back of a single sheet if your prospect is middle management, but you'll want to consider two sheets of quality stationery if you're writing to top executives.

Writing Direct-Mail Copy

Your opening for the letter should build around an abbreviated version of a successful case study. Tell the story and make the point in no more than three paragraphs. The more compelling the imagery the better. Write as you would talk if you were sitting across the desk from your prospect and don't be afraid to be direct, and reasonably casual, as if you were talking to a colleague.

Write in second person—using the word *you.* Use one-syllable words as much as possible. Sentences and paragraphs should be short. Avoid "corp-speak," except for light use of "insider" jargon that will help demonstrate your familiarity with the prospect's business. Show at the outset of your case study that this story contains a valuable benefit for the reader: "XYZ corporation slashed inventory costs 39 percent in five months—and you can, too!" Note the specifics of 39 percent and five months. They lend credibility.

In the letter, you want to demonstrate your knowledge of the field and lead the reader to the white paper which will greatly expand on your points and provide (or at least point to) solutions (which you will be happy to implement). The letter must sell the offer (the white paper) not the product, tempting as it may be to launch into your sales pitch.

In addition to selling the white paper or other premium documents in the letter, you may want to add greater involvement to the package overall and further dramatize the premium through the use of an insert.

Other Direct-Mail Package Elements

The insert is a folded piece of paper, usually in some lightly colored stock to help it stand out from the letter. It can be a simple "buckslip," so-called because it's about the size of a dollar bill, roughly 8″ by 3½″, or it can be a larger piece, folded so it fits a #10 envelope. (All documents being machine inserted into an envelope require ½″ clearance left to right and ¼″ top to bottom. If the piece is folded, it must be inserted with the folded side down.)

The buckslip has text and graphics on one side, so the message is immediately accessible to the reader. Folded pieces are printed two sides with a teaser-type intro on the front and promotional text on the inside.

In addition to more dramatically promoting the premium, the insert provides an opportunity to project a visual look and feel for the firm, especially because there is no product brochure. If you insist on enclosing a trifold company brochure, let that be it and skip the buckslip. Again, including a company brochure will shift the nature of the communication slightly from editorial to commercial, or from objectively valuable "content" to self-serving "advertising."

Cool and wired, down home and friendly, button-down business or casually personal—whatever business "persona" you wish to communicate, you can do it with the insert. Naturally, the look and feel here should be consistent with the company's culture and visual image. Four-color design and printing is recommended for the insert.

The primary response mechanism is for the prospect to go to a specific URL where he can read and download the white paper being offered. You should give this URL in your letter. You can also feature it prominently on the buckslip.

If you are using direct mail to drive prospects to a Web URL, do you even need the traditional business reply card? Maybe not. But many marketers feel it is good strategy to have a snail mail reply card available for those who don't wish to go on the Web at that moment or who may be less comfortable (or more likely fed up) with the Web.

You must decide whether someone like that is a good prospect for your business. In addition, there's a school of thought that says a reply card, even if it isn't used, projects the idea of response.

On both the registration form on the website, and the reply card, you can further qualify your respondent by asking three to five questions beyond pure contact information, relating to the prospect and his company. Annual sales, number of employees, use of any competing products or services, or assigned budget and decision timeline are all valid questions to ask about.

One dynamic you'll want to consider in framing your offer is the universal truth that you can't have it both ways. The higher the quantity (volume) of response, the lower the quality (interest level) of the respondents will be. The more questions asked (and answered) therefore, the higher the level of qualification, but your gross response will be lower.

Direct Mail Costs

In a recent estimate for a similar model, costs were 90¢ per piece in the mail at 10,000 pieces, 75¢ each for 20,000, plus a one-time creative fee between $5,000 and $6,000.

Using these numbers, a 1 percent gross response on a mailing of 10,000 pieces delivers 100 prospects at $90 cost per inquiry. On a mailing of 20,000 pieces with a 1 percent response, the cost per inquiry is $75. If we assume a 20 percent conversion rate, you get a new customer for $450 if mailing 10,000 pieces.

These numbers do not include creative costs which are a one-time charge. Once you have a successful model, you can continue to mail it with comparable results, give or take the effects of list quality, timing, and other factors.

The conversion rate, or how many prospects eventually become customers, depends on your ability to promptly and effectively follow up leads and close sales. Response rates are notoriously fickle, depending first on the quality of the list, second on the perceived value and timing of the offer, and finally on the creative. The response range for an effort of this type can run anywhere from 0.25 percent to 4.0 percent.

The question you have to answer is "how much is a qualified lead worth?" Or more important, "How much is a customer worth?" Then plan accordingly. For another recent campaign, the budget was $30,000 to mail and telephone 3,500 names. The number of qualified leads was projected at 20± for a cost-per-lead of $1,500. However, the product/service being promoted (enterprise-wide ERP system) starts at $500,000 and can easily run into the millions.

Print Ads That Drive URL Visits

Your print advertising should feature your URL—prominently. Make it bold, and highlight it with a graphic.

Have a paragraph in your body copy or a brief sidebar that explains all of the benefits and features your site offers: downloads of software demos or evaluation copies, free white papers, a useful glossary, tech briefings, product data sheets, product reviews, press releases, and so forth.

You can mention them all, but highlight the most appealing feature as the primary motivation to visit your site, for example, "Click on www.netsaver.com/freetool.html to run a free, no-obligation online optimization of your network design and see how NetSaver can reduce your leased-line costs today."

"Don't be wacky," advises an article in *Business2.com* magazine (April 3, 2001, p. 62). "Get away from loopy advertising. It has to be focused on the value that has been delivered—the tangible benefits."

Should you spend the money to run print ads solely dedicated to driving traffic to your site? Only if you are a pure dot-com or if your site offers a powerful advantage in buying your type of product that your competitors and their sites do not. Otherwise, it's probably more sensible just to run your regular ads with an increased emphasis on your URL.

Match the Response Form with the Promotional Offer

In the example from the previous section, we didn't just send the reader to NetSaver's home page netsaver.com. Instead, we sent her to the specific page on the site—netsaver.com/freetool.html—that we advertised in our copy. This is sometimes called a "landing page," because the user lands on the page after clicking on the URL.

If you are using your website as a response mechanism for your print ads, direct-mail campaigns, and other offline promotions, it's usually a good idea to send the respondents to a specific page on your site for the particular offer you are making in the promotion. If you send them just to the home page, they may lose interest when they can't easily navigate to the tool, form, or document you promised them in your copy.

Think of it this way. If a prospect at a trade show asked for your phone number, which would you hand him—your business card or the telephone book? If the Web page speaks directly to the offer that brought the prospect to it in the first place, more click-throughs will be converted to leads and sales.

Another advantage of having a customized Web page for each ad or direct mail is that you can track response more efficiently. In the previous example, you know that any click-throughs to freetool.html must have come from the ad in which this URL was featured.

Henry Haugland, of WebReply.com Inc., has pioneered sending promotions to recipients with personalized response URLs incorporating the contact name. For example, if they sent me a promotion driving me to their site, the URL would be http://bob-bly.webreply .com. (The general URL is www.webreply.com.)

"What we have found is that if we use e-mail to invite a contact to visit their personal message portal, we average click-through rates of 52 percent," says Haugland. "When a postcard is used to invite a contact to visit their personal message portal, click-through rates have varied between 3 and 16 percent."

Make Your Website Famous with the Power of PR

To paraphrase a famous saying, "Just because you build a better website doesn't mean Internet users will beat a path to your URL." In fact, with more than ten million domain names registered with Network Solutions, it's a wonder people even get to a fraction of them.

An increasing number of entrepreneurs are finding that public relations—once considered the second string of marketing beneath advertising—has emerged as the preferred offline promotional vehicle for generating buzz and website traffic. For instance, one of the most successful e-commerce sites, Allherb.com (an online store for vitamins) was built entirely on PR—no paid advertising.

Fortunately, you don't need a big budget to conduct a PR campaign for your website, and you can easily do it yourself. Every website owner should send out a press release announcing the site when it is up. Summarize the site's intended audience, purpose, and benefits in a pithy, one-page press release.

Here is the beginning of a press release for espeakonline.com, a site dedicated to communications. It isn't rocket science:

From: Bob Bly, Center for Technical Communication
     For immediate release
     Phone: 201-385-1220

Is Reading Dead?
New website, www.espeakonline.com, provides online forum
for evaluating "the state of the printed word in a
cyberspace society"

Does the rise of the Internet spell the end of the printed word? Will downloadable e-books make paperbacks obsolete? Do people today prefer to get their news from a portal instead of a newspaper? Now you can get some answers—or at least ask these questions—at a new Website, **www.espeakonline.com.** Site founder Bob Bly, a copywriter and the author of more than 50 books, describes espeakonline.com as "an online forum and resource for people concerned about the Internet and its impact on writing, publishing, information marketing, and communication —in print and on the Web."

The rest of the release goes on to describe the features of the site, such as the library of free information available. It also encourages people to visit, participate in an online community of interest, and sign up for a free e-zine subscription.

Send the press release to any and all media likely to be read, seen, or watched by your potential audience. For instance, if your site is for PC users, send the release to magazines like *Byte* and *PC World*. *Bacon's Information* will, for a very reasonable fee, distribute your press release to magazines, newspapers, and TV and radio stations. They can be reached toll free at 800-621-0561.

Always include your URL in your press release. Interestingly, offline direct marketers, whose response mechanism is an 800 number, sometimes have difficulty getting the number included when their PR materials are used, since editors and producers view it as too promotional. Online marketers have no such problems getting their URLs included when their releases run, because websites are perceived by the media as informational rather than promotional.

The media love news. Whenever there is a new development on your website, send out a press release announcing the news.

When you add new features to your website—e-commerce capability, a chat room, a message board, free downloadable software or information, or access to an online database—send a release. Changing the background color on your home page from yellow to blue, on the other hand, is not sufficient news to warrant a press release.

The media are always looking for new information. Espeakonline has a poll that surveys visitors on communications issues, such as whether they read fewer books since going online. The site periodically sends out press releases announcing the survey results, which are of great interest to editors looking for interesting tidbits for their readers.

Let's say you have a website linking consumers with dentists and information on dental care. Do an online survey to determine how many people hate going to the dentist. Or, have people on a message board swap horror stories about dentists. Then send out press releases detailing the results. When there's no news to announce, create news with a clever promotion you can publicize in the media.

Here's an example. A few years back, when virtual pets were the hot fad, schools began prohibiting children from bringing their Tamagotchis to class—which was a problem, because virtual pets that weren't frequently "fed" (virtually, that is) would "die" (again, virtually). One consumer products company garnered a lot of press by opening a day care center for virtual pets!

Allherb.com did a Valentine's Day PR campaign based on a survey of which foods people found to be the best aphrodisiacs. This tied in with their site objective of providing an online resource for people to learn about alternative medicine and nutrition.

SxSportsMed.com, a website featuring sports medicine products and information, sent out a release inviting Web surfers to come to its site and get free advice from professional sports trainers. Here is the copy from their press release:

Ask the Certified Athletic Trainer

Ever try and ask your pharmacist how to tape a sore ankle? How about asking the clerk at the sporting goods store about tendinitis? A major frustration for consumers isn't knowing what to ask, but rather who to ask. SxSportsMed.com offers free, personalized information from experts in the sports medicine industry—the same pros that keep top collegiate and professional athletes in the game.

Willy Gissen, an account supervisor with the public relations firm Levin Public Relations in White Plains, New York, offers the following additional tips for publicizing your website:

• Distribute press releases and other publicity materials to online journalists. Consider online distribution sources such as intenetwire .com. Create an electronic press kit for distribution to the press.

• Update your website frequently with the latest press releases and other publicity materials, giving journalists a reason to come back. Obtain the capability to do so within hours, as a precaution if necessary for crisis communication.

• Go to deja.com, a search engine for news groups, and locate groups in your market categories. Before participating in any given discussion group or forum, monitor it for a few days to get an idea of the content and tone of discussions.

• Avoid overt promotion in the above news groups and forums, as many participants zealously guard against commercialism in these areas and will trash your company if you appear to be selling something. However, there are indirect methods that can be used such as giving something away, offering expert advice, announcing an event, and referring people to your website for information on a topic being discussed.

• Have a contest on your website with a free and unusual giveaway to create buzz. For instance, if you have a website lawyers.com that refers people to lawyers, ask them to submit lawyer jokes and give a prize for the funniest one.

Another idea, this one from consultant Joel Heffner, is to write and contribute articles to other e-zines produced by websites that don't compete with you directly but reach the same audience that you want to reach. Instead of payment, you can request a link from the article to your website.

Thousands of websites today are desperately trying to create or find relevant content they can use to fill their pages and entice visitors. If you already own a large body of content, you may be able to license it for a fee to these sites.

An alternative is to simply give the content away. Allow sites to use your material on a nonexclusive basis. That means you can continue to use it, and anyone else you wish to grant permission to can use it too. Almost no website will object to this; exclusivity seems not to be a factor on the Web as it is with print media.

Make it clear that you are the copyright owner and retain all rights. Your material, when used on other websites, should include a copyright notice. Also require any website using your content to include attribution crediting you as the author, as well as contact information, which is typically a link from the byline to your website.

Should you give away content free or charge for it? If your primary source of income is content itself, you should probably charge for it . . . although you might create some freebies to give away as lures to your paid-content site. If you are selling products or services that the content supports, giving content away in exchange for links that drive traffic to your site is the cheapest promotion you can do—and one of the most effective.

Resources

This APPENDIX LISTS resources for implementing some of the concepts discussed in this book. Updates may be found by visiting evendorsonline.com:

Affiliate Programs for Your Website

LinkProfits
14913 Braemer Crescent
Gaithersburg, MD 20878
Phone: 301-990-1450
linkprofits.com
Service: Consulting firm that helps e-businesses set up affiliate marketing programs.

Autoresponders

With an autoresponder, you can automatically answer e-mails and website requests, without human intervention, using prewritten standard messages.

Aweber Systems
4547 Old Oak Road, Suite B
Doylestown, PA 18901
Phone: 800-938-6220
aweber.com

Crown Industries
1630 N. Main Street, #10
Walnut Creek, CA 94596
Phone: 925-938-0770
E-mail: info@moneyfun.com
moneyfun.com

General Interactive
66 Church Street
Cambridge, MA 02138
Phone: 617-354-8585
E-mail: info@interactive.com
echomail.com

Bulk E-Mail Programs

Email King
1040 S. Mt. Vernon Avenue,
#G146
Colton, CA 92324
Phone: 909-797-5424
netbillions.com

Exactis
707 17th Street, #2850
Denver, CO 80202
Phone: 800-699-7006
E-mail: ExpressSales@exactis.com
exactis.com

Collaborative Filtering

Collaborative filtering enables you to send prospects personalized e-mail based on their buying habits, preferences, demographics, and other characteristics.

Andromedia
818 Mission Street
San Francisco, CA 94103
Phone: 800-700-3282
andromedia.com

Macromedia, Inc.
600 Townsend Street
San Francisco, CA 94103
Phone: 800-326-2128 or
415-252-2000
macromedia.com

Net Perceptions
7901 Flying Cloud Drive
Eden Prairie, MN 55344-7905
Phone: 800-466-0711
netperceptions.com
E-mail: sales@netperceptions.com

E-Mail Broadcasting and Management Software

Frontier Productions
310 Wesley Drive
Chapel Hill, NC 27516
Phone: 919-942-1386
frontierproductions.com

E-List Brokers

Act One
165 Pleasant Street, Suite 19
Village Plaza 1
Marblehead, MA 01945-2308
Phone: 800-228-5478
E-mail: actlist@maultranet.com
actonelists.com

Direct Media, Inc.
200 Pemberwick Road
Greenwich, CT 06830
Phone: 203-532-1000
directmedia.com
Services: E-lists, transmission,
merge/purge

Admail.net
DM Group
Aurora, Ohio 44202
Phone 330-995-0864
http://dm1.com
Services: E-list brokerage, management, hygiene, merge/purge, database management, bulk e-mailing

ALCi Interactive
2 Stamford Landing, Suite 100
Stamford, CT 06902
Phone: 203-921-0375
E-mail: Buildemail@ALCinteractive
.com
amlist.com

Services: Transmission, database marketing, e-list rentals, e-list management,

Applied Information Group
100 Market Street
Kenilworth, NJ 07033
Phone: 908-241-7007
E-mail: daveb@appliedinfogroup.com
appliedinfogroup.com
Services: HTML and visual e-mail, online campaign tracking, e-mail transmission, database management

Bigfoot Interactive
1841 Broadway, Suite 609
New York, NY 10023
Phone 212-262-1118
bigfootinteractive.com
Services: E-lists, transmission, Internet database management, consulting

Digital Impact
digitalimpact.com
Service: Personalized e-campaigns

DoubleClick
450 West 33rd Street, 16th floor
New York, NY 10276
Phone: 212-381-5705
E-mail: info@doubleclick.com
doubleclick.com
Services: Closed-loop banner ad and e-marketing

EClass Direct
625 Miramontes Street
Half Moon Bay, CA 94019
Phone: 650-712-6700
E-mail: info@eclassdirect.com
eclassdirect.com

Services: E-mail marketing and transmission bureau

Egain Communications
455 W. Maude Avenue
Sunnyvale, CA 94086
Phone: 888-603-4246
E-mail: sales@egain.com
egain.com
Services: Software and services for e-commerce sites

E-Post Direct
1 Blue Hill Plaza
Pearl River, NY 10965
Phone: 800-409-4443
Fax: 914-620-9035
E-mail
michelle.feit@edithroman.com
epostdirect.com
Services: Opt-in e-mail list management; e-mail list brokerage; I-marketing consultation; personalized Internet campaign creation, execution, and tracking; html and Visual Mail© transmission; e-mail address appending; merge/purge; website design; banner ad placement; e-commerce

Iq.com
12950 Saratoga Avenue, Suite B
Saratoga, CA 95070
Phone: 408-777-4000
E-mail: info@iq.com
iq.com
Services: Online e-mail and Web-based promotions for e-marketers

Merchant Mail Network
Phone: 650-286-7300
digital-impact.com

Service: Specialized in transmitting targeted rich media e-mail to existing customers

Millard Group
10 Vose Farm Road
P.O. Box 890
Peterborough, NH 03458-0890
Phone: 603-924-9262
Fax: 603-924-7810

Net Masters
Phone: 800-242-0363, ext. 2082
E-mail: Netmasters@grabmail.com
Services: Bulk mailing, URL submission, search engine ranking, e-lists, website design

OakNet Publishing
2630B NW 41st Street
Gainesville, FL 32606
Phone: 352-376-5822
E-mail: editor@oaknetpub.com
oaknetpub.com
Service: Transmission of e-zines

Pinpoint Media
1400 East Hill Boulevard
Deerfield Beach, FL 33441
Phone: 954-725-6455
E-mail: info@pinpointmedia.com
pinpointmedia.com
Service: Opt-in e-lists

Postmaster.com
6601 Park of Commerce Boulevard
Boca Raton, FL 33487
Phone: 888-239-3831
E-mail: success@postmaster.com
postmaster.com
Service: Opt-in e-list broker

PostMasterDirect.com
A NetCreations Company
379 West Broadway, #202
New York, NY 10012
Phone: 212-625-1370
E-mail sales@postmasterdirect.com
postmasterdirect.com
Services: Opt-in e-lists, merge/purge, transmission

ROI Direct.com
100 Bush Street
San Francisco, CA 94104
Phone: 800-420-4224
E-mail: info@roidirect.com
roidirect.com
Services: E-commerce site development and hosting, e-mail marketing programs, e-list and database services, inbound e-mail customer service

SparkList
1800 W. Mason Street
Green Bay, WI 54303
Phone: 920-490-5901
E-mail: info@sparklist.com
sparklist.com
Services: E-list hosting and management services, online discussion hosting

24/7 Media
1250 Broadway, 28th floor
New York, NY 10001
Phone: 212-231-7284
E-mail: mtuohy@247media.com
Service: Opt-in e-lists

Walter Karl
1 Blue Hill Plaza

Pearl River, NY 10965
Phone: 914-620-0700
E-mail: kathye@walterkarl.com

Internet Sales Tax

Vertex Inc.
1041 Old Cassatt Road
Berwyn, PA 19312
Phone: 800-355-3500
vertexinc.com
Services: EQuantum software for
calculating sales and use tax on
e-commerce transactions

Online Customer Service

LivePerson
665 Broadway, Suite 1200
New York, NY 10012
Phone: 212-277-8950
liveperson.com
Service: Software that enables your
visitors to chat online with live customer service reps while viewing
your website

Periodicals

Adweek
IQ Interactive Report
1515 Broadway
New York, NY 10036
Phone: 212-536-5336

CIO Web Business
492 Old Connecticut Path
P.O. Box 9208
Framingham, MA 01701-9208
Phone: 800-788-4605
cio.com

*E-ZineZ: The E-Zine About
E-Zines!*
1112 First Street, Suite 167
Coronado, CA 92118
Phone: 800-305-8266
E-mail: kate@e-zinez.com
e-zinez.com

I-Marketing News
100 Avenue of the Americas
New York, NY 10013
Phone 212-925-7300

Industry Standard
315 Pacific Avenue
San Francisco, CA 94111
Phone: 415-733-5401

Interactive Week
Quentin Roosevelt Boulevard,
Suite 400
Garden City, NY 11530
Phone: 516-229-3700

Internet Marketing Report
Progressive Business Publications
370 Technology Drive
Malvern, PA 19355
Phone: 800-220-5000

Internet World News
50 E. 42nd Street, 9th floor
New York, NY 10017
Phone: 212-547-1811

Marketing With Technology
370 Central Park West, #210
New York, NY 10025
Phone 212-222-1713
E-mail: sarah@mwt.com

Silicon Alley Reporter
Rising Tide Studios

101 East 15th Street, 3rd floor
New York, NY 10003
Phone: 212-475-8000

Wall Street & Technology
Miller Freeman
P.O. Box 1054
Skokie, IL 60076-8054
Phone 800-682-8297
wstonline.com

Web Techniques
600 Harrison Street
San Francisco, CA 94107
Phone 415-908-6643

What's Working Online
Georgetown Publishing
1101 30th Street NW
Washington, DC 20007
Phone 800-915-0022

Search Engines

Search Directories
Yahoo!
yahoo.com

LookSmart
looksmart.com

Excite
excite.com

Lycos
lycos.com

Search Services
These two are the quickest way
to index site selections (usually
within days).

AltaVista
altavista.com

Infoseek
infoseek.com

Fee-Based Services
Will submit your site to as many
as four hundred search engines
and directories.

SubmitIt!
submitit.com

Register-It!
registerit.com

Taking Credit Cards Online

CyberCash
2100 Reston Parkway, 3rd floor
Reston, VA 20191
Phone: 703-620-4200
cybercash.com
Service: Provider of secure Internet
credit card processing services

1ClickCharge
1clickcharge.com
Service: Specializes in low-dollar-
amount credit card purchases

Tracking Internet Marketing Results

Etracks.com
A division of Learn2.com
516 El Camino Real
Belmont, CA 94002
Phone: 650-232-1000
etracks.com
Services: Adaptive Proxy Tracking
tracks e-mail recipients who

respond to a particular URL in reply to an e-mail broadcast. Measures click-throughs to the site as well as online purchases.

Website Design Firms

Network Creative
Kent Martin
104 Mountain Avenue
Gilette, NJ 07930
Phone 908-903-9090

Quadrix
Susan Mintzer
255 Old New Brunswick Road,
Suite South 220
Piscataway, NJ 08854
Phone: 732-235-2600
quadrix.com
Service: E-commerce websites

Silver Star Productions
Mr. Jason Petefish
2300 West Ina Road, #2201
Tucson, AZ 85741

Phone: 520-229-9283
E-mail: jason@silverstar-online.com

Website Incentives

e-centives
6903 Rockledge Drive, Suite 1200
Bethesda, MD 20817
Phone: 877-323-6848
e-centives.com
Services: Personalized digital coupons, printed coupons, and other special offers delivered to Web surfers based on their unique shopping profiles and interests

MyPoints.com
565 Commercial Street, 4th floor
San Francisco, CA 94111-3031
Phone: 415-676-3700
E-mail:
steve.markowitz@mypoints.com
mypoints.com
Service: Internet bonus-point rewards programs

Glossary

Ad clicks—Number of times users click on an ad banner.

Ad click rate—Sometimes referred to as "click-through," this is the percentage of ad views that resulted in an ad click.

Address—A unique identifier for a computer or site online, usually a URL for a website or marked with an @ for an e-mail address. Literally, it is how your computer finds a location on the information highway.

Affiliate program—An arrangement in which a company pays you a percentage of the sale for every online customer they get through a link from your website to theirs.

Banner ad—A banner is the small, boxed message that appears atop commercial websites (usually the home page or on the first page of an e-zine) that are usually linked to the advertiser's site.

Buttons—Objects that, when clicked once, will cause something to happen.

CGI (common gateway interface)—An interface-creation scripting program that allows Web pages to be made on the fly based on information from buttons, checkboxes, text input, and so forth.

Chat room—An area online where you can chat with other members in real time.

Click—The opportunity for a visitor to be transferred to a location by clicking on an ad, as recorded by the server.

Click-through rate—Percentage of times a user responded to an advertisement by clicking on the ad button/banner. At one time the granddaddy of Web-marketing measurements, click-through is based on the idea that online promotions that do what they're intended to do will elicit a click. Also, the percentage of people receiving an e-mail who will click on a URL embedded in the message to reach a specific Web page.

Cookie—A file on your computer that records information such as where you have been on the World Wide Web. The browser stores this information which allows a site to remember the browser in future transactions or requests. Since the Web's protocol has no way to remember requests, cookies read and record a user's browser type and IP address, and store this information on the computer. The cookie can be read only by a server in the domain that stored it. Visitors can accept or deny cookies, by changing a setting in their browser preferences.

Domain—Part of the DNS (domain naming system) name that specifies details about the host. A domain is the main subdivision of Internet addresses, the last three letters after the final dot, and it tells you what kind of organization you are dealing with. There are six top-level domains widely used in the United States: .com (commercial) .edu (educational), .net (network operations), .gov (U.S. government), .mil (U.S. military), and .org (organization). Other two-letter domains represent countries: .uk for the United Kingdom and so on.

Drill down—A term used to express what a surfer does as he or she goes further into a website—deeper into the back pages, deeper into data. Make certain that when someone takes the time to drill down into your site that he or she comes back with information worth digging for.

E-commerce—Using electronic information technologies on the Internet to allow direct selling and automatic processing of purchases between parties.

E-list—A direct-mail list containing Internet addresses and used to distribute promotional messages over the Internet.

E-mail—An abbreviation for electronic mail, which is a network service that allows users to send and receive messages via computer. Once confined to a closed group within a particular network, the Internet and common message protocols make it possible to send and receive messages worldwide.

E-zine—A part-promotional, part-informational newsletter or magazine distributed on the Internet.

FAQ (frequently asked questions)—A commonly used abbreviation for "Frequently Asked Questions." Most Internet sites will have a FAQ page or section to explain what is in the area and how to use its features.

Flame—1. An intentionally crude or abusive e-mail message or usenet post. Rule: Don't do it. Ever. Not only is it bad netiquette, but you leave a trail. 2. A complaint message from a spam recipient, sent over the Internet to the advertiser.

Forms—The pages in most browsers that accept information in text-entry fields. They can be customized to receive company sales data and orders, expense reports, or other information. They can also be used to communicate.

Frames—The use of multiple, independent sections to create a single Web page. Each frame is built as a separate html file but with one "master" file to identify each section. When a user requests a page with frames, several pages will be displayed as panes. Sites using frames may report one page request with several panes as multiple page requests. Most audit firms count only the master html page request and therefore can accurately report the page requests.

GIF (graphic interchange format)—GIF (pronounced "gift") is a graphics format that can be displayed on almost all Web browsers. It is a common compression format used for transferring graphics files between different computers. Most of the "pictures" you see online are GIF files. They display in 256 colors and have built-in compression. GIF images are the most common form of banner creative.

Hit—The sending of a single file, whether text, graphic, audio, or other type of file. When a page request is made, all elements or files that comprise the page are recorded as hits on a server's log file. While there is no accurate formula for determining the number of visitors to a page or site based on the number of hits—one visitor could go back and forth twenty times, or twenty people could visit a single time each—a hit at least indicates somebody was there. Thus, hits can be far more valuable than the tracking devices in any other media.

Home page—The page designated as the main point of entry of a website (or main page) or the starting point when a browser first connects to the Internet. Typically, it welcomes you and introduces the purpose of the site, or the organization sponsoring it, and then provides links to the lower-level pages. In business terms, it's the grabber. If your home page downloads too slowly, or it's unclear or uninteresting, you will probably lose a customer.

HTML (hypertext markup language)—A coding language used to make hypertext documents for use on the Web. HTML resembles old-fashioned typesetting code, where a block of text is surrounded by codes that indicate how it should appear. HTML allows text to be "linked" to another file on the Internet.

HTTP (hyper-text transfer protocol)—A standard method of publishing information as hypertext in html format on the Internet, http is the format of the World Wide Web. When a browser sees "http" at the beginning of an address, it knows that it is viewing a WWW page.

HTTPS—HTTP with SSL (secure socket layer) encryption for security purposes.

Hyperlink—This is the clickable link in text or graphics on a Web page that takes you to another place on the same page, another page, or a whole other site. It is the single most powerful and important function of online communications. Hyperlinks are revolutionizing the way the world gets its information.

Hypertext—Any text that that can be chosen by a reader and which causes another document to be retrieved and displayed.

Internet—1. A collection of approximately 60,000 independent, interconnected networks that use the TCP/IP protocols and that evolved from ARPANet of the late 1960s and early 1970s. The Net is a worldwide system of computer networks providing reliable and redundant connectivity between disparate computers and systems by using common transport and data protocols. 2. Generally any network made up of two or more interconnected local or wide area networks.

Internet Domain Name—The unique name that identifies an Internet entity.

Interstitial—1. "Something in between" and is a page that is inserted in the normal flow of content between a user and a site. An interstitial ad is an "intrusive" ad unit that is spontaneously delivered without specifically being requested by a user. Blocking the site behind it, interstitial ads are designed to grab consumers' attention for the few nanoseconds it takes them to close the window. Interstitials can be full pages or small daughter windows. Also referred to as "pop-ups." 2. A banner appearing in a location other than a home page or near the masthead of an e-zine.

Intranet—Private networks, usually maintained by corporations for internal communications, which use Internet—usually Web—protocols, software, and servers. They are relatively cheap, fast, and reliable networking and information warehouse systems that link offices around the world. They make it is easy for corporate users to communicate with one another and to access the information resources of the Internet.

IP address (Internet Protocol address)—Every system connected to the Internet has a unique IP address, which consists of a number in the format A.B.C.D where each of the four sections is a decimal number from 0 to 255. Most people use domain names instead, and the resolution between domain names and IP addresses is handled by the network and the domain name servers. With virtual hosting, a single machine can act like multiple machines (with multiple domain names and IP addresses).

ISP (Internet service provider)—1. A business that provides access to the Internet. Its services are available to either individuals or companies and include a dial-in interface with the Internet, software supply, and often website and intranet design. There are currently more than 3,000 ISPs in the United States alone. It's a growth business, and as a result pricing is highly competitive, so shop around. 2. A company that, for a fee, provides businesses and consumers with access to the Internet.

Java—An object-oriented programming language created by Sun Microsystems that supports enhanced features such as animation, or real-time updating of information. If you are using a Web browser that supports Java, an applet (Java program) embedded in the Web page will automatically run.

JPEG (joint photographic experts group)—JPEG (pronounced "jay peg") is a graphics format newer than GIF which displays photographs and graphic images with millions of colors; it also compresses well and is easy to download. Unfortunately, not many browsers currently support it, so don't use it for your logo.

Link—An electronic connection between two websites (also called "hot link"). When an item on one Web page is clicked on, the user is transferred to another Web page or another area on the same Web page.

Listserver—A program that automatically sends e-mail to a list of subscribers. It is the mechanism that is used to keep newsgroups informed.

Load—Usually used with upload or download, it means to transfer files or software—to "load"—from one computer or server to another computer or server. In other words, it's the movement of information online.

Meta Tags—Used to identify the creator of a Web page, what html specs the page follows, the keywords, and description of the page.

MIME (multipurpose Internet mail extensions)—A method of encoding a file for delivery over the Internet.

Newsgroup—A discussion group on Usenet devoted to talking about a specific topic. Currently, there are more than 15,000 newsgroups. Also called usenets, newsgroups consist of messages posted on electronic bulletin boards. Each board has a theme, and there are tens of thousands of newsgroups concerning every imaginable topic. Many of them cover professional subjects and societies and are rich sources of business information; others are junk and contain little but mindless drivel.

Opt-in—To agree to receive promotional e-mails when registering on a particular website from the site owner and other companies to whom she may rent your e-mail address.

Opt-out—To request that an e-list owner take your name off the list or at least makes sure you are not sent any promotional e-mails.

Page—All websites are a collection of electronic "pages." Each Web page is a document formatted in html that contains text, images, or media objects such as RealAudio player files, QuickTime videos, or Java applets. The "home page" is typically a visitor's first point of entry and features a site index. Pages can be static or dynamically generated. All frames and frame parent documents are counted as pages.

PDF (portable document format)—Adobe's translation format used primarily for distributing files across a network, or on a website. Files with a .pdf extension have been created in another application and then translated into .pdf files so they can be viewed by anyone—regardless of platform.

Portal—A website or service that offers a broad array of resources and services, such as e-mail, forums, search engines, and online shopping malls. The first Web portals were online services, such as AOL, that provided access to the Web, but by now most of the traditional search engines have transformed themselves into Web portals to attract and keep a larger audience.

Push—The delivery ("pushing") of information that is initiated by the server rather than being requested ("pulled") by a user. Pointcast is the most well known push service that pushes information based on the user's profile.

RealAudio—A commercial software program that plays audio on demand, without waiting for long file transfers. For instance, you can listen to National Public Radio's entire broadcast of "All Things Considered" and "Morning Edition" on the Internet.

Registration—A process for site visitors to enter information about themselves. Sites use registration data to enable or enhance targeting of ads. Some sites require registration in order to access their content. Some sites use voluntary registration. Fee-based sites conduct registration in the form of a transaction (take a credit card to pay for the content). A registered user is a user who visits a website and elects, or is required, to provide certain information. Nonregistered users may be denied access to a site requiring registration.

Rich media—Interactive multimedia presentations in Internet direct mail, banner ads, and Web pages.

Search engine—A program that searches documents for specified keywords and returns a list of the documents where the keywords were found. Although search engine is really a general class of programs, the term is often used to specifically describe systems like AltaVista and Excite that enable users to search for documents on the World Wide Web and Usenet newsgroups.

Server—Servers are the backbone of the Internet, the computers that are linked by communication lines and "serve up" information in the form of text, graphics, and multimedia to online computers that request data—that's you. (When a server "goes down" it loses its online link and the information it holds cannot be accessed.)

Shockwave—A plug-in that allows for multimedia movies to play through a browser.

Signature File—A personal footer that can be automatically attached to e-mail.

Spam—The use of mailing lists to blanket usenets or private e-mail boxes with indiscriminate, unsolicited messages of a promotional nature. Very bad netiquette. Even worse, it's bad business. The future of marketing online is about customizing products and information for individual users. Anyone who tries to use old mass market techniques in the new media environment is bound to fail.

Spider—A term used to describe search engines such as Yahoo! and Alta Vista, because of the way they cruise all over the World Wide

Web to find information. It is a software program that combs the Web for new sites and updated information on old ones, like a spider looking for a fly.

Splash page—A bridge page between a banner advertisement and an advertiser's website that provides product information and hot links. Splash pages are replacing many home pages—particularly on sites more involved with news and publishing—as gateways into Web content. They start with a bigger "splash," more graphics and timely information, and change often—like the cover of a magazine.

Stickiness—A measure used to gauge the effectiveness of a site in retaining individual users. The term is typically used in promotional material when traffic numbers are too low to be effective in lauding a site's performance. Never mind the quantity, feel the stick. Sticky refers to a website people want to stay on and frequently revisit.

URL (uniform resource locator)—An http address used by the World Wide Web to specify a certain site. This is the unique identifier, or address, of a web page on the Internet. URL can be pronounced "you-are-ell" or "earl." It is how web pages, ftp's, gophers, newsgroups, and even some e-mail boxes are located.

Usenet—Internet message boards, also known as newsgroups. Each board has a theme, and there are tens of thousands of usenets concerning every imaginable topic. Many of them cover professional subjects and societies and are rich sources of business information; others are junk and contain little more than mindless drivel.

Viral Marketing—Any advertising that propagates itself. When Hotmail users send e-mail, they unwittingly infect the recipient with the tagline at the bottom of the message.

Web page—An html document on the Web, usually one of many together that make up a website.

Website—A collection of files that are arranged on the World Wide Web under a common address and allow retrieval via a browser.

World Wide Web (WWW or Web)—Allows computer users to access information across systems around the world using URLs to identify files and systems and hypertext links to move between files on the same or different systems. The Web is a client/server information system that supports the retrieval of data in the form of text, graphics, and multimedia in a uniform html format. Allowing hypertext links and interactivity on an unprecedented level, its introduction transformed a sleepy, academic communications system into a powerful marketing tool linking businesses and customers around the world.

Bibliography

Books on Internet Marketing

Anderson, Daniel, Bret Benjamin, and Bill Paradese-Holt. *Connections: A Guide to Online Writing*. Boston: Allyn and Bacon, 1997.

Anderson Allen, Moira. *Writing.com*. New York City: Allworth Press, 1999.

Baynes, Kim. *The Internet Marketing Plan*. New York City: John Wiley & Sons, 1999.

Bonime, Andrew, and Ken C. Pohlman. *Writing for New Media*. New York: John Wiley & Sons, 1997.

Canter, Laurence A., and Martha S. Siegel. *How to Make a Fortune on the Information Superhighway*. New York City: HarperCollins, 1995.

Flynn, Nancy and Tom. *Writing Effective E-Mail*. Menlo Park, CA: Crisp Publications, 1998.

Glossbrenner, Alfred and Emily. *Making Money on the Internet*. New York City: McGraw-Hill, 1996.

Godin, Seth. *Permission Marketing*. New York City: Simon & Schuster, 1999.

Hartman, Diane B., and Karen Nantz. *The 3Rs of E-Mail*. Menlo Park, CA: Crisp Publications, 1996.

303

Hurley, Brian, and Peter Birkwood. *A Small Business Guide to Doing Business on the Internet.* Bellingham, WA: Self Counsel, 1996.

Janal, Dan. *Online Marketing Handbook.* New York City: John Wiley & Sons, 1998.

Kasavana, Michael L. *Untangling the Web.* Orlando, FL: Educational Institute, 1995.

Kent, Peter, and Tara Calishain. *Poor Richard's Internet Marketing and Promotions.* Denver: Top Floor Publishing, 1999.

Krcma, Marianne. *Web Site Wizardry.* Scottsdale, AZ: Coriolis Group Books, 1996.

Lant, Dr. Jeffrey. *Web Wealth.* Cambridge, MA: JLA Publications, 1997.

Lewis, Herschell Gordon, and Jamie Murphy. *Cybertalk That Sells.* Lincolnwood, IL: Contemporary Books, 1998.

Parker, Roger C. *Guide to Web Content and Design.* New York City: MIS Press, 1997.

Peppers, Don, Martha Rogers, and Bob Dorf. *The One-to-One Fieldbook.* New York City: Bantam Books, 1999.

Perillo, Chris. *Poor Richard's E-Mail Publishing.* Denver: Top Floor Publishing, 1999.

Strauss, Judy, and Raymond Frost. *Marketing on the Internet.* Upper Saddle River, NJ: Prentice Hall, 1999.

Silverstein, Barry. *Business-to-Business Internet Marketing.* Gulf Breeze, FL: Maximum Press, 2001.

Van Skiver, Joy. *Simple Steps to E-Mail Writing Success.* Chatham, NJ: The Writing Exchange, 1999.

Vitale, Joe. *Cyberwriting.* New York City: Amacom, 1996.

Yudkin, Marcia. *Marketing Online, Second Edition.* New York City: Morris Publishing, 1995.

Zeff, Robin, and Brad Aronson. *Advertising on the Internet.* New York City: John Wiley & Sons, 1997.

Books on Writing and Marketing

Blake, Gary, and Robert W. Bly. *The Elements of Business Writing.* New York City: Macmillan, 1991.

Bly, Robert W. *The Copywriter's Handbook*. New York City: Henry Holt & Company, 1990.

Flesch, Rudolf. *The Art of Readable Writing*. New York City: Harper & Row, 1949.

Hampe, Barry. *Video Scriptwriting*. New York City: New American Library, 1993.

Helmering, Doris Wild. *The 7th Sense*. New York City: William Morrow and Company, 1999.

Marsh, Winston. *The Rules of the New Millennium*. Melbourne, Australia: Business Growth Centre, 1998.

Parker, Roger C. *One-Minute Designer*. New York City: MIS Press, 1997.

Thomas, Francis-Noel, and Mark Turner. *Clear and Simple as the Truth: Writing Classic Prose*. Princeton, NJ: Princeton University Press, 1994.

Wunderman, Lester. *Being Direct*. New York City: Random House, 1996.

Index

About the Author

BOB BLY IS an independent copywriter and consultant specializing in business-to-business and direct-response marketing.

Bob writes sales letters, direct mail packages, ads, websites, Internet direct mail, white papers, and PR materials for more than one hundred clients nationwide. These include IBM, AT&T, The BOC Group, EBI Medical Systems, Associated Global Systems, CoreStates Financial Corp., PSE&G, Alloy Technology, M&T Chemicals, ITT, Takeda Chemicals, UniSys, Fala Direct Marketing, Citrix Systems, Machine Technologies, and Grumman Corp.

Bob is the author of fifty books including *The Copywriter's Handbook* (Henry Holt), *The Advertising Manager's Handbook* (Prentice Hall), *Public Relations Kit for Dummies* (IDG), and *Internet Direct Mail* (NTC Business Books). His articles have appeared in *Direct, Business Marketing, Computer Decisions, Chemical Engineering, Direct Marketing, Writer's Digest, Amtrak Express, Cosmopolitan, New Jersey Monthly, City Paper,* and many other publications.

Mr. Bly's work has won numerous awards including the Direct Marketing Association's Gold Echo Award and the Web Marketing Association's Standard of Excellence Award. He taught copywriting at New York University, and has presented workshops on copywriting and Internet marketing to numerous organizations including IBM, Foxboro Company, Arco Chemical, Thoroughbred Software Leaders Conference, Appliance Parts Distributors Association, Dow Chemical, and the Direct Marketing Association.

Bob holds a B.S. in engineering from the University of Rochester. He is a member of the Business Marketing Association and the Newsletters and Electronic Publishers Association.

Questions and comments on *The Online Copywriter's Handbook* may be sent to:

Bob Bly
22 E. Quackenbush Avenue
Dumont, NJ 07628
Phone: 201-385-1220
Fax: 201-385-1138
E-mail rwbly@bly.com
bly.com